AF564631

Modern Techniques in Teaching

Modern Techniques in Teaching

Edited by

Dr. S.K. PANNER SELVAM

Assistant Professor, Department of Education

Bharathidasan University, T.N

and

Dr. R. SUMATHI

Principal,

Cheran College of Education,

Karur, Tamil Nadu.

RANDOM PUBLICATIONS

NEW DELHI (INDIA)

Modern Techniques in Teaching

ISBN 978-93-5111-891-6

Published in 2016 in India by

RANDOM PUBLICATIONS

4376-A/4B, Gali Murari Lal, Ansari Road
New Delhi-110 002
Phone : +9111-43580356, 011-43142548, 011-23289044
e-mail : sales@randompublications.com
info@randompublications.com
randomexports@gmail.com

Reprinted 2023

Type Setting by : Shah Computer Graphics, Delhi-110094
Digitally Printed at: Replika Press Pvt. Ltd.

Contents

1. Consciousness of Online Learning

Chapter - I

INTRODUCTION

Education in its general sense is a form of learning in which knowledge, skills, and habits of a group of people are transferred from one generation to the next through teaching, training, research, or simply through autodidacticism. Generally, it occurs through any experience that has a formative effect on the way one thinks, feels, or acts.

A curriculum is prescriptive, and is based on a more general syllabus which merely specifies what topics must be understood and to what level to achieve a particular grade or standard. An academic discipline is a branch of knowledge which is formally taught, either at the university–or via some other such method. Each discipline usually has several sub-disciplines or branches, and distinguishing lines are often both arbitrary and ambiguous. Examples of broad areas of academic disciplines include the natural sciences, mathematics, computer science, social sciences, humanities and applied sciences.

The emergence of secondary education in the United States did not happen until 1910, caused by the rise in big businesses and technological advances in factories (for instance, the emergence of electrification), that required skilled workers. In order to meet this new job demand, high schools were created, with a curriculum focused on practical job skills that would better prepare students for white collar or skilled blue collar work.

Under the Education for All programs driven by UNESCO, most countries have committed to achieving universal enrollment in primary education by 2015, and in many countries, it is compulsory for children to receive primary education. The division between primary and secondary education is somewhat arbitrary, but it generally occurs at about eleven or twelve years of age. Some education systems have separate middle schools, with the transition to the final stage of secondary education taking place at around the age of fourteen. Schools that provide primary education are mostly referred to as primary schools.

Primary schools in these countries are often subdivided into infant and school. Years, out of which children receive elementary education for 8 years. Elementary schooling consists of five years of primary schooling and 3 years of upper primary schooling. Various states in the republic of India provide 12 years of compulsory school education based on national curriculum framework designed by the National Council of Educational Research and Training.

Instructors in post- secondary institutions might be called teachers, instructors, or professors, depending on the type of institution; and they primarily teach only their specific discipline. Studies from the United States suggest that the quality of teachers is the single most important factor affecting student performance, and that countries which score highly on international tests have multiple policies in place to ensure that the teachers they employ are as effective as possible.

With the passing of NCLB in the United States (No Child Left Behind), teachers must be highly qualified. A popular way to gauge teaching performance is to use student evaluations of teachers (SETS), but these evaluations have been criticized for being counterproductive to learning and inaccurate due to student bias.

EDUCATION TECHNOLOGY

One of the most substantial uses in education is the use of technology. Also technology is an increasingly influential factor in education. Computers and mobile phones are used in developed countries both to complement established education practices and develop new ways of learning such as online education (a type of distance education). This gives students the opportunity to choose what they are interested in learning. The proliferation of computers also means the increase of programming and blogging.

Technology offers powerful learning tools that demand new skills and understandings of students, including Multimedia, and provides new ways to engage students, such as Virtual learning environments. One such tool are virtual manipulative, which are an "interactive, Web-based visual representation of a dynamic object that presents opportunities for constructing mathematical knowledge" (Moyer, Bolyard, & Spikell, 2002).

In short, virtual manipulative are dynamic visual/pictorial replicas of physical mathematical manipulative, which have long been used to demonstrate and teach various mathematical concepts. Virtual manipulative can be easily accessed on the Internet as stand-alone applets, allowing for easy access and use in a variety of educational settings.

Emerging research into the effectiveness of virtual manipulative as a teaching tool have yielded promising results, suggesting comparable, and in many cases superior overall concept-teaching effectiveness compared to standard teaching methods. Technology is being used more not only in administrative duties in education but also in the instruction of students.

The Open University of the United Kingdom (UKOU), established in 1969 as the first educational institution in the world wholly dedicated to open and distance learning, still relies heavily on print-based materials supplemented by radio, television and, in recent years, online programming. Similarly, the Indira Gandhi National Open University in India combines the use of print, recorded audio and video, broadcast radio and television, and audio conferencing technologies.

The term "computer-assisted learning" (CAL) has been increasingly used to describe the use of technology in teaching. Classrooms of the 21st century contain interactive white boards, tablets,mp3 players, laptops, etc. Wiki sites are another tool teachers can implement into

CAL curricula for students to understand communication and collaboration efforts of group work through electronic means. Teachers are encouraged to embed these technological devices and services in the curriculum in order to enhance students learning and meet the needs of various types of learners.

Use of the Internal itself may bring on disordered behavior more readily. Without doubt, the Internet is the fastest growing communication technology today. The Internet revolution has brought effective changes to the area of education. Especially in the last 25 years, emerging "new technologies" such as computer and the Internet have attracted many people to practice focused on improving education with technology.

An important reason that many people think computers are integral to a school's in the 21st century systems from the current e-culture. New Internet technologies have progressed more rapidly than most people imagined to transform banking, commerce, travel, communications, and other sectors of everyday life.

As a result, many people believe that computers must be in schools, no other than to prepare students for their e-future. These keep schools up to date with the technologies. According to internet world Statistics, the use of communication technology is also growing rapidly in college and universities. The assumption about the Internet is that it benefits the college students tremendously and learning appears to be a rich field that is just beginning to be discovered. Lack of information creates a negative impact on our live, particularly on the educated segment of the society.

The Internet is one of the most important mass media in the world as it has changed the world in many ways. students are the most important group in society because they are envisaged to build society in the future, especially the female students who have a tremendous affect both on society and home.

Internet users which are socially engaged and have greater social awareness, will tend to know more about the privacy debate, privacy policies, privacy risks associated with Internet, legal implications of privacy invasions and identity the thefts. Thus, these users would have would have formed a stronger awareness about privacy and the importance of privacy in social life. The greater the citizenship engagement and social awareness of an individual, the greater importance that individual would place on privacy as a societal value.

CONCEPT OF TEACHING

Integrating the Internet into classroom activities

When introduced to the Internet, teachers were overwhelmed and excited by the tremendous educational potential of the Web.

Once they moved beyond the initial intimidation of navigating the Web, they focused on their specific teaching needs and were concerned with customizing the Web to answer the learning needs of their students. Teachers chose fundamental concepts or proven problem learning areas as a basis for exploration and experimentation with the Internet.

Oliva (1992) defines an instructional strategy as “methods, procedures, and techniques the teacher uses to present the subject matter to students and to bring about effective outcomes” (p. 403). Teachers chose instructional strategies that were best suited to the Internet. They were focused on the needs of their students, the school and state mandated curriculum and instructional problems associated with some fundamental concepts. In addition to these traditional techniques, however, they focused on the educational opportunities of the Internet to rethink their instructional strategies. Teachers focused on the following characteristics of the Internet in creating their lesson plans:

1. Electronic information source with access to worldwide databases of information.
2. Interactive and easy to use information exchange medium.
3. Source for meaningful learning experiences through application of real world problems and data.
4. An avenue to electronic portfolios of their teaching activities.
5. As a means of communication and collaboration with colleagues beyond the walls of their individual classroom.

Teachers re-evaluated their roles as content providers and gravitated toward becoming facilitators in these electronic environments.

They viewed the Internet as a dynamic teaching and learning medium with which to facilitate learning, enhance comprehension and provide rich contextual learning environments for their students. Teachers immediately recognized that students are more familiar and adept with these technologies than they themselves are and sought to take advantage of these student skills to rethink teaching as a collaborative journey.

Teachers started to think of themselves as directors of student learning, providing guidelines and pathways for students to attempt. Students were now expected to take an active part in exploring these pathways, venturing on new ones and taking responsibility for their learning. The constructivist philosophies of the teachers took precedence over the more traditional approaches when integrating the Internet.

Teachers with more essentialist philosophies used this medium quite differently than those with interdisciplinary and student-centered approaches. Those teachers with constructivist or student-centered philosophies adapt easily to the Internet and are able to immediately identify enriching learning opportunities. Those with more traditional approaches found it more difficult to create lessons and adapt to this new hyperlinked environment.

Interdisciplinary Learning Approaches

Teachers in the OWL ink project, whose lessons are discussed in this section, collaborated with their colleagues to teach across distances, subject areas and grade levels. This experimental tele-distance project, which has as a primary goal to cause rethinking traditional teaching and learning approaches, has produced some interesting interdisciplinary projects and change processes.

The Golden Ratio is a model example of information exchange and collaborative learning across the Internet. Students accessed teacher-researched Internet sites that were linked to online lesson plans to research the Golden Ratio. Students from three different schools then calculated their body measurements; exchanged cumulative data from each site and compared the school means to the golden ratio. Interesting discoveries were made which led to discussion and dialogue among the students at the different sites. The golden ratio concept was explored across the disciplines of architecture, mathematics and science.

Students from the different age levels were able to learn, explore and investigate the application of the concept simultaneously.

Golden Rabbit Stew with Honey, Flowers, and Music takes advantage of the mathematical resources on the web. The teacher asks students to explore the interdisciplinary relationships of the Fibonacci numbers, traditionally taught in mathematics, to not only geometry but nature, art, and music as well. The teacher asks the students to explore the concept across the disciplines by linking relevant sites and then apply the knowledge gained by creating personal examples based on these concepts.

Mandalas: Geometric Link between Medicine and History is a lesson plan that asks students in high school geometry courses to relate the mathematical concept of symmetry and to ancient cultures and modern medicine. The teacher creatively links together resources on the Internet to allow high school students and younger students to explore the properties of mandalas across disciplines. Students use paint programs to create their own mandalas, use the internet to access mandala resources, learn about symmetry and the ancient Aztec cultures.

This lesson serves as a good example of intellectual broadening of the concept in the students' minds, allowing learners to make connections among subject areas and actively leading the learner to form these connections through guided exploration.

Problem Based Learning Approaches

Problem-based learning approaches emphasize connections between school content and its application to life outside of school. They provide the learner with opportunities to explore concepts and study examples of the concept available in the world around us. The internet provides a wealth of information for teachers and students to use in this way. Teachers and students can access data to explore a concept in real life, download data, modify and process it for different contexts.

Following are a few examples of lesson plans that use the problem -based approach in mathematics. These have been further subdivided into three curricular perspectives outlined by McNeil.

The Instructional Systems Approach

This traditional approach where the teacher is in control and is responsible for student learning uses objective driven instruction. The teacher is the knowledge giver and the students are the recipients.

This traditional approach requires less creativity on the part of the teacher in using the web. However this approach lends itself less to rethinking teaching on the part of the teacher. Using Standard Deviation asks the students to download weather data to explore the concepts of Standard Deviation.

A connects students to sites that host computer history. The students answer questions as directed by the teacher. This lesson plan can be expanded to encompass a broader educational objective by including activities that require the learner to interact with the information. Those Uses databases on animals to have students explore mathematical equations.

INFORMATION AND COMMUNICATION TECHNOLOGY

Information and Communications Technology or (ICT), is often used as an extended synonym for information technology (IT), but is a more specific term that stresses the role of unified communications and the integration of telecommunications (telephone lines and wireless signals), computers as well as necessary enterprise software, middleware, storage, and audio-visual systems, which enable users to access, store, transmit, and manipulate information.

The phrase ICT had been used by academic researchers since the 1980s, but it became popular after it was used in a report to the UK government by Dennis Stevenson in 1997 and in the revised National Curriculum for England, Wales and Northern Ireland in 2000.

The term ICT is now also used to refer to the convergence of audio-visual and telephone networks with computer networks through a single cabling or link system. There are large economic incentives (huge cost savings due to elimination of the telephone network) to merge the audio-visual, building management and telephone network with the computer network system using a single unified system of cabling, signal distribution and management.

The term Info communications is used in some cases as a shorter form of information and communication(s) technology. In fact Info communications is the expansion of telecommunications with information processing and content handling functions on a common digital technology base.

Information and Communication Technologies for Development (ICT4D)

Refers to the use of Information and Communication Technologies (ICTs) in the fields of socioeconomic development, international development and human rights. The theory behind this is that more and better information and communication furthers the development of a society.

Aside from its reliance on technology, ICT4D also requires an understanding of community development, poverty, agriculture, healthcare, and basic education. Richard Heeks suggests that the I in ICT4D is related with "library and information sciences", the C is associated with "communication studies", the T is linked with "information systems", and the D for "development studies". It is aimed at bridging the digital divide and aid economic development by fostering equitable access to modern communications technologies. It is a powerful tool for economic and social development. Other terms can also be used for "ICT4D" or "ICT4Dev" ("ICT for development") like ICTD ("ICT and development", which is used in a broader sense) and development informatics.

ICT4D can mean as dealing with disadvantaged populations anywhere in the world, but it is more seen with applications in developing countries. It concerns with directly applying information technology approaches to poverty reduction. ICTs can be applied directly, wherein its use directly benefits the disadvantaged population, or indirectly, wherein it can assist aid organizations or non-governmental organizations or governments or businesses to improve socio-economic conditions.

The field is an interdisciplinary research area through the growing number of conferences, workshops and publications. This is partly due to the need for scientifically validated benchmarks and results that can measure the effectiveness of current projects. This field has also produced an informal community of technical and social science researchers which rose out of the annual ICT4D conferences.

The ICT4D discussion falls into a broader school of thought that proposes to use technology for development. The theoretical foundation can be found in the Schumpeterian notion of socio-economic evolution, which consists of an incessant process of creative destruction that modernizes the modus operandi of society as a whole, including its economic, social, cultural, and political organization.

The motor of this incessant force of creative destruction is technological change. While the key carrier technology of the first Industrial Revolution (1770–1850) was based on water-powered mechanization, the second Kondratiev (1850–1900) was enabled by steam-powered technology, the third (1900–1940) was characterized by the electrification of social and productive organization, the fourth by motorization and the automated mobilization of society (1940–1970), and the most recent one by the digitization of social systems.

Each one of those so-called long waves has been characterized by a sustained period of social modernization, most notably by sustained periods of increasing economic productivity. According to Carlota Perez: "this quantum jump in productivity can be seen as a technological revolution, which is made possible by the appearance in the general cost structure of a particular input that we could call the 'key factor', fulfilling the following conditions:

(1) Clearly perceived low-and descending-relative cost

(2) Unlimited supply for all practical purposes

(3) Potential all-pervasiveness

(4) A capacity to reduce the costs of capital, labour and products as well as to change them qualitatively.

Digital Information and Communication Technologies fulfill those requirements and therefore represent a general purpose technology that can transform an entire economy, leading to a modern, and more developed form of socio-economic and political organization often referred to as the post-industrial society, the fifth Kondratiev, Information society, digital age, and network society, among others.

The declared goal of ICT-for-development is to make use of this ongoing transformation by actively using the enabling technology to improve the living conditions of societies and segments of society. As in previous social transformations of this kind (industrial revolution, etc.), the resulting dynamic is an interplay between an enabling technology, normative guiding policies and strategies, and the resulting social transformation.

In the case of ICT4D, this three-dimensional interplay has been depicted as a cube. In line with the Schumpeterian school of thought, the first enabling factor for the associated socio-economic transformations is the existence technological infrastructure: hardware infrastructure and generic software services. Additionally, capacity and knowledge are the human requirements to make use of these technologies. These foundations are the basis for the digitization of information flows and communication mechanisms in different sectors of society.

ICT for Education

ICT for Education (ICT4E) is a subset of the ICT4D thrust. Globalization and technological change are one of the main goals of ICT. One of its main sectors that should be changed and modified is education. ICTs greatly facilitate the acquisition and absorption of knowledge; offering developing countries unprecedented opportunities to enhance educational systems, improve policy formulation and execution, and widen the range of opportunities for business and the poor.

One of the greatest hardships endured by the poor, and by many others, who live in the poorest countries, is their sense of isolation. The new communications technologies promise to reduce that sense of isolation, and open access to knowledge in ways unimaginable not long ago.

Education is seen as a vital input to addressing issues of poverty, gender equality and health in the MDGs. This has led to an expansion of demand for education at all levels. Given limited education budgets, the opposing demand for increased investment in education against widespread scarcity of resources puts intolerable pressure on many countries' educational systems.

Meeting these opposing demands through the traditional expansion of education systems, such as building schools, hiring teachers and equipping schools with adequate educational resources will be impossible in a conventional system of education. ICTs offer alternate solutions for providing access and equity, and for collaborative practices to optimize costs and effectively use resources.

CONCEPT OF ONLINE

The Internet is a network of computer networks. It makes it possible for any computer connected to it to send and receive data from any other computer connected to it.

America Online, Comcast, Earthlink, etc. are examples of Internet service providers. They make it physically possible for you to send and access data from the Internet. They allow you to send and receive data to and from their computers or routers which are connected to the Internet.

World Wide Web is an example of an information protocol/ service that can be used to send and receive information over the Internet. It supports:

1. Multimedia Information (text, movies, pictures, sound, programs
2. Hypertext Information (information that contains links to other information resources).
3. Graphic User Interface (so users can point and click to request information instead of typing in text commands).

The World Wide Web is an example of an information protocol/ service that works using a Client/Server software design. A service that uses Client/Server design requires two pieces of software to work: Client software which you use to request information, and Server software which an Information Provider uses to answer requests and provide their information. Most Internet information protocol/services are designed this way.

The Client/Server relationship is similar to the relationship between the TV in your house and the TV stations you can select. Your TV acts as a client by tuning in (requesting information) from a TV station which acts as a server by broadcasting (serving) the information.

This means that if you encounter an error while using your Web browser, this may be due to a problem with the Web server you are contacting for information. It does not necessarily mean that your browser isn't working, or that you installed something improperly. Just like in the case of the TV and the TV station, sometimes problems are due to a bad TV, and other times they are caused by a problem at the TV station.

The server software for the World Wide Web is called an HTTP server (or informally a Web server). Examples are Apache and IIS. The client software for World Wide Web is called a Web browser. Examples are: Netscape, Internet Explorer, Safari, Firefox, and Mozilla. These examples are particular "brands" of software that have a similar function, just like Lotus 123 and Excel are both spreadsheet software packages. There are many different information protocols/services besides HTTP (Hyper Text Transfer Protocol).

1. E-mail (SMTP) - for sending electronic mail messages.
2. Usenet News (NNTP) - for having electronic group discussions.
3. File Transfer Protocol (FTP) - for transferring files between computers.
4. Telnet - for running programs on remote computers.
5. Various Others . . .

Each of these works in a client/server manner by having a "language" defined that allows the client and server to communicate with each other in order to give users the information they request. These different languages have different purposes, capabilities, and advantages.

One of the nicest things about the World Wide Web is that it provides "one-stop shopping" for getting information over the Internet. In the past, you would have needed to learn how to use many different software applications in order to use all these services. Now you can use E-mail, News, FTP, Telnet, WAIS, Gopher, and HTTP services all through your favorite Web browser.

REQUIREMENT FOR ONLINE HARDWARE AND SOFTWARE

The software resources to be present on a computer. These prerequisites are known as (computer) system requirements and are often used as a guideline as opposed to an absolute rule. Most software defines two sets of system requirements: minimum and recommended. With increasing demand for higher processing power and resources in newer versions of software, system requirements tend to increase over time. Industry analysts suggest that this trend plays a bigger part in driving upgrades to existing computer systems than technological advancements.

Hardware requirement

The most common set of requirements defined by any operating system or software application is the physical computer resources, also known as hardware, A hardware requirements list is often accompanied by a hardware compatibility list (HCL), especially in case of operating systems.

An HCL lists tested, compatible, and sometimes incompatible hardware devices for a particular operating system or application. The following sub-sections discuss the various aspects of hardware requirements.

Architecture all computer operating systems are designed for a particular computer architecture. Most software applications are limited to particular operating systems running on particular architectures. Although architecture-independent operating systems and applications exist, most need to be recompiled to run on a new architecture. See also a list of common operating systems and their supporting architectures.

Processing power The power of the central processing unit (CPU) is a fundamental system requirement for any software. Most software running on x 86 architecture define processing power as the model and the clock of the CPU. Many other features of a CPU that influence its speed and power, like bus speed, cache, and MIPS are often ignored. This definition of power is often erroneous, as AMD and Intel Pentium CPUs at similar clock speed often have different throughput speeds. Intel Pentium CPUs have enjoyed a considerable degree of popularity, and are often mentioned in this category.

Memory All software, when run, resides in the random access memory (RAM) of a computer. Memory requirements are defined after considering demands of the application, operating system, supporting software and files, and other running processes. Optimal performance of other unrelated software running on a multi-tasking computer system is also considered when defining this requirement.

Secondary storage Hard-disk requirements vary, depending on the size of software installation, temporary files created and maintained while installing or running the software, and possible use of swap space (if RAM is insufficient).

Display adapter Software requiring a better than average computer graphics display, like graphics editors and high-end games, often define high-end display adapters in the system requirements.

Peripherals Some software applications need to make extensive and/ or special use of some peripherals, demanding the higher performance or functionality of such peripherals. Such peripherals include CD-ROM drives, keyboards, pointing devices, network devices, etc.

Software requirement Software requirements deal with defining software resource requirements and prerequisites that need to be installed on a computer to provide optimal functioning of an application. These requirements or prerequisites are generally not included in the software installation package and need to be installed separately before the software is installed.

Platform In computing, a platform describes some sort of framework, either in hardware or software, which allows software to run. Typical platforms include a computer's architecture, operating system, or programming and their runtime libraries.

Operating system is one of the first requirements mentioned when defining system requirements (software). Software may not be compatible with different versions of same line of operating systems, although some measure of backward compatibility is often maintained. For example, most software designed for Microsoft Windows XP does not run on Microsoft Windows 98, although the converse is not always true.

APIs and drivers Software making extensive use of special hardware devices, like high-end display adapters, needs special API or newer device drivers. A good example is DirectX, which is a collection of APIs for handling tasks related to multimedia, especially game programming, on Microsoft platforms.

HTML

Web browser most web applications and software depending heavily on Internet technologies make use of the default browser installed on system. Microsoft Internet Explorer is a frequent choice HyperText Markup Language (HTML) is the main markup language for creating web pages and other information that can be displayed in a web browser.

HTML is written in the form of HTML elements consisting of tags enclosed in angle brackets (like <html>), within the web page content. HTML tags most commonly come in pairs like <h1> and </h1>, although some tags, known as empty elements, are unpaired, for example <img>.

The first tag in a pair is the start tag, the second tag is the end tag (they are also called opening tags and closing tags). In between these tags web designers can add text, tags, comments and other types of text-based content.

The purpose of a web browser is to read HTML documents and compose them into visible or audible web pages. The browser does not display the HTML tags, but uses the tags to interpret the content of the page.HTML elements form the building blocks of all websites. HTML allows images and objects to be embedded and can be used to create interactive forms.

It provides a means to create structured documents by denoting structural semantics for text such as headings, paragraphs, lists, links, quotes and other items. It can embed scripts written in languages such as JavaScript which affect the behavior of HTML web pages.

Web browsers can also refer to Cascading Style Sheets (CSS) to define the appearance and layout of text and other material. The W3C, maintainer of both the HTML and the CSS standards, encourages the use of CSS over explicit presentational HTML markup.

Data types

HTML defines several data types for element content, such as script data and style sheet data, and a plethora of types for attribute values, including IDs, names, URIs, numbers, units of length, languages, media descriptors, colors, character encodings, dates and times, and so on. All of these data types are specializations of character data.

Document type declaration

HTML documents are required to start with a Document Type Declaration (informally, a "doc type"). In browsers, the doc type helps to define the rendering mode - particularly whether to use quirks mode of software running on Microsoft Windows, which makes use of ActiveX controls, despite their vulnerabilities.

Telephone Modem

A telephone modem is a device that converts the signals from your computer into a series of sounds and transmits them across the phone line. A telephone modem on the other side of the connection converts these sounds back to a signal the computer can understand, allowing the computers to communicate.

Dial-up connections are still widely in use despite faster connections being available to 89 percent of the U.S. population. Referred to as narrowband connections, these connections are slower and usually do not stay connected at all times.

Network Interface Card

Broadband connections provide much faster access to the Internet then narrowband connections. There are multiple types of broadband connections, including DSL, satellite, and cable access. Each of these types of access involves connecting to an access point using either a wired Ethernet connection or a wireless connection.

A Network interface card (NIC) allows you to connect an Ethernet cable to your computer from an access point. Communication to the access point travels through this cable. Connections using a wired NIC require that an Ethernet cable be connected from the computer to the access point at all times during Internet use. Network interface cards can be built in to the computer or purchased as an external device that you plug in to the computer.

Wired Access Points

Computers using a NIC and Ethernet cable connect through an access point. Access points are generally routers, cable modems, or

DSL modems that provide a link between the Internet service provider and your physical computer. NIC-based connections are widely used in local area networks, such as groups of computers in businesses. They can be used in homes, but many users prefer to use wireless connections for the added mobility.

Wireless Access Points

A wireless access point allows you to connect to an access point without using a physical connection. Wireless access can be configured in your home using a wireless router and a computer with a wireless interface. Wireless interfaces can be installed within the computer or purchased separately as a USB or PCI device that can be plugged in when needed. Many businesses, such as hotels and coffee shops, provide free wireless access in their buildings for the use of their customers.

ONLINE SERVICES

Technologies

Access technologies generally use a modem, which converts digital data to analog for transmission over analog networks such as the telephone and cable networks.

Local Area Networks

Dial-up access: Dial-up access uses a modem and a phone call placed over the public switched telephone network (PSTN) to connect to a pool of modems operated by an ISP. The modem converts a computer's digital signal into an analog signal that travels over a phone line's local loop until it reaches a telephone company's switching facilities or central office (CO) where it is switched to another phone line that connects to another modem at the remote end of the connection.

Operating on a single channel, a dial-up connection monopolizes the phone line and is one of the slowest methods of accessing the Internet. Dial-up is often the only form of Internet access available in rural areas as it requires no new infrastructure beyond the already existing telephone network, to connect to the Internet.

Typically, dial-up connections do not exceed a speed of 56 kbit/s, as they are primarily made using modems that operate at a maximum data rate of 56 kbit/s downstream (towards the end user) and 34 or 48 kbit/s upstream (toward the global Internet).

Broadband access The term broadband includes a broad range of technologies, all of which provide higher data rate access to the Internet. These technologies use wires or fiber optic cables in contrast to wireless broadband described later.

Multilink dial-up Multilink dial-up provides increased bandwidth by bonding two or more dial-up connections together and treating them as a single data channel. It requires two or more modems, phone lines, and dial-up accounts, as well as an ISP that supports multilinking - and of course any line and data charges are also doubled. This inverse multiplexing option was briefly popular with some high-end users before ISDN, DSL and other technologies became available. Diamond and other vendors created special modems to support multilinking.

Integrated Services Digital Network (ISDN)

Integrated Services Digital Network (ISDN), a switched telephone service capable of transporting voice and digital data, is one of the oldest Internet access methods. ISDN has been used for voice, video conferencing, and broadband data applications. ISDN was very popular in Europe, but less common in North America. Its use peaked in the late 1990s before the availability of DSL and cable modem technologies.

Basic rate ISDN, known as ISDN-BRI, has two 64 kbit/s "bearer" or "B" channels. These channels can be used separately for voice or data calls or bonded together to provide a 128 kbit/s service.

Multiple ISDN-BRI lines can be bonded together to provide data rates above 128 kbit/s. Primary rate ISDN, known as ISDN-PRI, has 23 bearer channels (64 kbit/s each) for a combined data rate of 1.5 Mbit/s (US standard). An ISDN E1 (European standard) line has 30 bearer channels and a combined data rate of 1.9 Mbit/s.

Cable Online Access

Cable Internet or cable modem access provides Internet access via Hybrid Fiber Coaxial wiring originally developed to carry television signals. Either fiber-optic or coaxial copper cable may connect a node to a customer's location at a connection known as a cable drop. In a cable modem termination system, all nodes for cable subscribers in a neighborhood connect to a cable company's central office, known as the "head end." The cable company then connects to the Internet using a variety of means – usually fiber optic cable or digital satellite and microwave transmissions. Like DSL, broadband cable provides a continuous connection with an ISP.

Wireless broadband access

Wireless broadband is used to provide both fixed and mobile Internet access.

Wi-Fi

Wi-Fi is the popular name for a "wireless local area network" that uses one of the IEEE 802.11 standards. It is a trademark of the Wi-Fi Alliance. Individual homes and businesses often use Wi-Fi to connect laptops and smart phones to the Internet. Wi-Fi Hotspots may be found in coffee shops and various other public establishments. Wi-Fi is used to create campus-wide and city-wide wireless networks.

Wi-Fi networks are built using one or more wireless routers called Access Points. "Ad hoc" computer to computer Wi-Fi" networks are also possible. The Wi-Fi network is connected to the larger Internet using DSL, cable modem, and other Internet access technologies. Data rates range from 6 to 600 Mbit/s. Wi-Fi service ranges is fairly short, typically 20 to 250 meters or from 65 to 820 feet. Both data rate and range are quite variable depending on the Wi-Fi protocol, location, frequency, building construction, and interference from other devices. Using directional antennas and with careful engineering Wi-Fi can be extended to operate over distances of up to several kilometers, see Wireless ISP below.

Wireless ISP

Wireless ISPs typically employ low-cost 802.11 Wi-Fi radio systems to link up remote locations over great distances, but may use other higher-power radio communications systems as well.

Traditional 802.11b is an unlicensed omnidirectional service designed to span between 100 and 150 meters (300 to 500 ft). By focusing the radio signal using a directional antenna 802.11b can operate reliably over a distance of many kilometres (miles), although the technology's line-of-sight requirements hamper connectivity in areas with hilly or heavily foliated terrain. In addition, compared to hard-wired connectivity, there are security risks (unless robust security protocols are enabled); data rates are significantly slower (2 to 50 times slower); and the network can be less stable, due to interference from other wireless devices and networks, weather and line-of-sight problems.

Rural Wireless-ISP installations are typically not commercial in nature and are instead a patchwork of systems other tall objects are available. There are currently a number of companies that provide this service. Motorola Canopy and other proprietary technologies offer wireless access to rural and other markets that are hard to reach using Wi-Fi or WiMAX.

Satellite broadband

Satellites can provide fixed, portable, and mobile Internet access. It is among the most expensive forms of broadband Internet access, but may be the only choice available in remote areas. Data rates range from 2 kbit/s to 1 Gbit/s downstream and from 2 kbit/s to 10 Mbit/s upstream. Satellite communication typically requires a clear line of sight, will not work well through trees and other vegetation, is adversely affected by moisture, rain, and snow (known as rain fade), and may require a fairly large, carefully aimed, directional antenna.

Satellites in geostationary Earth orbit (GEO) operate in a fixed position 35,786 km (22,236 miles) above the earth's equator. Even at the speed of light (about 300,000 km/s or 186,000 miles per second), it takes a quarter of a second for a radio signal to travel from the earth to the satellite and back. TCP tuning and TCP acceleration techniques can mitigate some of these problems. GEO satellites do not cover the earth's Polar Regions. HughesNet and ViaSat are GEO systems.

Satellites in Low Earth orbit (LEO, below 2000 km or 1243 miles) and Medium earth orbit (MEO, between 2000 and 35,786 km or 1,243 and 22,236 miles) are less common, operate at lower altitudes, and are not fixed in their position above the earth. Lower altitudes allow lower latencies and make real-time interactive Internet applications feasible. LEO systems include Global star and Iridium. The O3b Satellite Constellation is a proposed MEO system with latency of 125 ms. COMM

Stellation™ is a LEO system, scheduled for launch in 2015, that is expected to have a latency of just 7 ms.

Mobile broadband

Mobile broadband is the marketing term for wireless Internet access delivered through mobile phone towers to computers, mobile phones (called "cell phones" in North America and South Africa), and other digital devices using portable modems. Some mobile services allow more than one device to be connected to the Internet using a single cellular connection using a process called tethering. The modem may be built into laptop computers, tablets, mobile phones, and other devices, added to some devices using PC cards, USB modems, and USB sticks or dongles, or separate wireless modems can be used.

Roughly every ten years new mobile phone technology and infrastructure involving a change in the fundamental nature of the service, non-backwards-compatible transmission technology, higher peak data rates, new frequency bands, and wider channel frequency bandwidth in Hertz becomes available. These transitions are referred to as generations. The first mobile data services became available during the second generation (2G).

Access providers

ISPs employ a range of technologies to enable consumers to connect to their network. If users and small businesses, traditional options include: dial-up, DSL (typically Asymmetric Digital Subscriber Line, ADSL), wireless, cable, fiber to the premises (FTTH), and Integrated Services Digital Network (ISDN) (typically basic rate interface).

For customers with more demanding requirements, such as medium-to-large businesses, or other ISPs, DSL (often Single-Pair High-speed Digital Subscriber Line or ADSL), Ethernet, Metropolitan Ethernet, Gigabit Ethernet, Frame Relay, and upload satellite Internet access. Sync-optical cabling (SONET) is more likely to be used.

Many access providers also provide hosting and email services

Mailbox providers

A mailbox provider is a department or organization that provides email mailbox hosting services. It provides email servers to send, receive, accept, and store email for other organizations and/rend, on their behalf and upon their explicit mandate.

Many mailbox providers are also access providers, while others aren't (e.g., Yahoo! Mail, Hotmail, Gmail, AOL Mail, Pobox). The definition given in RFC 6650 covers email hosting services, as well as the relevant department of companies, universities, organizations, groups, and individuals that manage their mail servers themselves.

The task is typically accomplished by implementing Simple (SMTP) and possibly providing access to messages through Internet Message Access Protocol (IMAP), the Post Office Protocol, Webmail, or a proprietary protocol.

Hosting ISP

Hosting ISPs routinely provide email, FTP, and web-hosting services. Other services include virtual machines, clouds, or entire physical servers where customers can run their own custom software.

Transit ISPs

Just as their customers pay them for Internet access, ISPs themselves pay upstream ISPs for Internet access. An upstream ISP usually has a larger network than the contracting ISP and/or is able to provide the contracting ISP with access to parts of the Internet the contracting ISP by itself has no access to.

In the simplest case, a single connection is established to an upstream ISP and is used to transmit data to or from areas of the Internet beyond the home network; this mode of interconnection is often cascaded multiple times until reaching a Tier 1 carrier. In reality, the situation is often more complex. ISPs with more than one point of presence (PoP) may have separate connections to an upstream ISP at multiple PoPs, or they may be customers of multiple upstream ISPs and may have connections to each one of them at one or more point of presence.

Virtual ISPs

Virtual ISP (VISP) is an operation which purchases services from another ISP (sometimes called a "wholesale ISP" in this context) which allows the VISP's customers to access the Internet using services and infrastructure owned and operated by the wholesale ISP.

Free ISPs

Free ISPs are Internet Service Providers (ISPs) which provide service free of charge. Many free ISPs display advertisements while the user is connected; like commercial television, in a sense they are selling the users' attention to the advertiser. Other free ISPs, often called free nets, are run on a nonprofit basis, usually with volunteer staff.

ISPs may engage in peering, where multiple ISPs interconnect at peering points or Internet exchange points (IXs), allowing routing of data between each network, without charging one another for the data transmitted—data that would otherwise have passed through a third upstream ISP, incurring charges from the upstream ISP.

Peering

ISPs requiring no upstream and having only customers (end customers and/or peer ISPs) are called Tier 1 ISPs.

Network hardware, software and specifications, as well as the expertise of network management personnel are important in ensuring that data follows the most efficient route, and upstream connections work reliably. A tradeoff between cost and efficiency is possible. In the early to mid-1980s, most Internet access was from personal computers and workstations directly connected to local area networks or from dial-up connections using modems and analog telephone lines. LANs typically operated at 10 Mbit/s and grew to support 100 and 1000 Mbit/s, while modem data rates grew from 1200 and 2400 bit/s in the 1980s, to 28 and 56 kbit/s by the mid to late 1990s. Initially dial-up connections were made from terminals or computers running terminal emulation software to terminal servers on LANs.

These dial-up connections did not support end-to-end use of the Internet protocols and only provided terminal to host connections. The introduction of network access servers (NASs) supporting the Serial Line Internet Protocol (SLIP) and later the Point-to-point protocol (PPP) extended the Internet protocols and made the full range of Internet services available to dial-up users, subject only to limitations imposed by the lower data rates available using dial-up.

Broadband Internet access, often shortened to just broadband and also known as high-speed Internet access are services that provide bit-rates considerably higher than that available using a 56 kbit/s modem. In the U.S. National Broadband Plan of 2009, the Federal Communications Commission (FCC) defined broadband access.

The term broadband was originally a reference to multi-frequency communication, as opposed to narrowband or baseband. Broadband is now a marketing term that telephone, cable, and other companies use to sell their more expensive higher data rate products.

Most broadband services provide a continuous "always on" connection; there is no dial-in process required, and it does not "hog" phone lines. Broadband provides improved access to Internet services such as:

1. Faster world wide web browsing
2. Faster downloading of documents, photographs, videos, and other large files
3. Telephony, radio, television, and videoconferencing
4. Virtual private networks and remote system administration
5. Online gaming, especially massively multiplayer online role-playing games which are interaction-intensive

Availability

In addition to access from home, school, and the workplace Internet access may be available from public places such as libraries and Internet cafes, where computers with Internet connections are available. Some libraries provide stations for connecting users' laptops to local area networks (LANs).

Wireless Internet access points are available in public places such as airport halls, in some cases just for brief use while standing. Some access points may also provide coin operated computers. Various terms are used, such as "public Internet kiosk", "public access terminal", and "Web payphone". Many hotels also have public terminals, usually fee based.

Coffee shops, shopping malls, and other venues increasingly offer wireless access to computer networks, referred to as hotspots, for users who bring their own wireless-enabled devices such as alaptop or PDA. These services may be free to all, free to customers only, or fee-based. A hotspot need not be limited to a confined location. A whole campus or park, or even an entire city can be enabled. Grassroots efforts have led to wireless community networks.

Additionally, Mobile broadband access allows smart phones and other digital devices to connect to the Internet from any location from which a mobile phone call can be made, subject to the capabilities of that mobile network.

BENEFITS OF ONLINE

There is so much that students can do with the Internet. Not only can they communicate with international students, they can gain from others' knowledge and experiences, participate in chatrooms, share ideas and solutions and learn about the many diverse cultures out there.

While the Internet does a lot for students, there are also benefits for parents and teachers. The interactive learning that the Internet provides can help students and parents with little or no English skills to learn English. Parents can become more involved in their children's education by connecting the school with homes, libraries or other access ports.

Teachers can adjust to the different learning styles and in the classroom. They can also set their own pace of teaching. Individual teaching techniques can become more available, which has been proven to be a factor in student achievement. Teachers have the chance to be able to teach at more than one place simultaneously. They may be in a small town but through the Internet, they can be linked to students in more populated areas. Also, the Internet enables administrators and teachers to spend less time on administration and recordkeeping. This would also give them more time to spend with their students.

ONLINE BASED LEARNING

E-learning refers to the use of various kinds of electronic media and information and communication technologies (ICT) in education. E-learning is an inclusive terminology for all forms of educational technology that electronically or technologically support learning and teaching, and may, depending on an emphasis on a particular aspect or component or delivery method, sometimes be termed technology-enhanced learning (TEL), computer-based training (CBT), internet-based training (IBT), web-based training (WBT), virtual education, or digital educational collaboration.

E-learning includes numerous types of media that deliver text, audio, images, animation, and streaming video, and includes technology applications and processes such as audio or video tape, satellite TV, CD-ROM, and computer-based learning, as well as local intranet/ extranet and web-based learning. Information and communication systems, whether free-standing or based on either local networks or the Internet in networked learning, underly many e-learning processes.

E-learning can occur in or out of the classroom. It can be self-paced, asynchronous learning or may be instructor-led, synchronous learning.

E-learning is suited to distance learning and flexible learning, but it can also be used in conjunction with face-to-face teaching, in which case the term blended learning is commonly used.It is commonly thought that new technologies make a big difference in education. Many proponents of e-learning believe that everyone must be equipped with basic knowledge of technology, as well as use it as a medium to reach a particular goal.

Computer-supported collaborative learning (CSCL) uses instructional methods designed to encourage or require students to work together on learning tasks. CSCL is similar in concept to the terminology, “e-learning 2.0”.

Collaborative learning is distinguished from the traditional approach in which the instructor is the principal source of knowledge and skills. For example, the neologism “e-learning 1.0” refers to the direct transfer method in computer-based learning and training systems (CBL). In contrast to the linear delivery of content, often directly from the instructor’s material, CSCL uses blogs, wikis, and cloud-based document portals (such as Google Docs and Dropbox). With technological Web 2.0 advances, sharing information between multiple people in a network has become much easier and use has increased. One of the main reasons for its usage states that it is "a breeding ground for creative and engaging educational endeavors."

Using Web 2.0 social tools in the classroom allows for students and teachers to work collaboratively, discuss ideas, and promote information. According to Sendall (2008), blogs, wikis, and social networking skills are found to be significantly useful in the classroom. After initial instruction on using the tools, students also reported an increase in knowledge and comfort level for using Web 2.0 tools. The collaborative tools additionally prepare students with technology skills necessary in today's workforce.

Locus of control remains an important consideration in successful engagement of e-learners. According to the work of Cassandra B. Whyte, the continuing attention to aspects of motivation and success in regard to e-learning should be kept in context and concert with other educational efforts. Information about motivational tendencies can help educators, psychologists, and technologists develop insights to help students perform better academically.

Computer-based learning or training (CBT)

Refers to self-paced learning activities delivered on a computer or handheld device. CBT often delivers content via CD-ROM, and typically presents content in a linear fashion, much like reading an online book or manual. For this reason, CBT is often used to teach static processes, such as using software or completing mathematical equations. Computer-based training is conceptually similar to web-based training (WBT), the primary difference being that WBTs are delivered via Internet using a web browser.

Assessing learning in a CBT is often by assessments that can be easily scored by a computer such as multiple choice questions, drag-and-drop, radio button, simulation or other interactive means. Assessments are easily scored and recorded via online software, providing immediate end-user feedback and completion status. Users are often able to print completion records in the form of certificates.

CBTs provide learning stimulus beyond traditional learning methodology from textbook, manual, or classroom-based instruction. For example, CBTs offer user-friendly solutions for satisfying continuing education requirements. Instead of limiting students to attending courses or reading printed manuals, students are able to acquire knowledge and skills through methods that are much more conducive to individual learning preferences.

CBTs offer visual learning benefits through animation or video, not typically offered by any other means. CBTs can be a good alternative to printed learning materials since rich media, including videos or animations, can easily be embedded to enhance the learning.

However, CBTs pose some learning challenges as well. Typically the creation of effective CBTs requires enormous resources. The software for developing CBTs (such as Flash or Adobe Director) is often more complex than a subject matter expert or teacher is able to use. In addition, the lack of human interaction can limit both the type of content that can be presented as well as the type of assessment that can be performed. Many learning organizations are beginning to use smaller CBT/WBT activities as part of a broader online learning program which may include online discussion or other interactive elements.

CONCEPT OF ONLINE TECHNOLOGY

Audio

The radio has been around for a long time and has been used in educational classrooms. Recent technologies have allowed classroom teachers to stream audio over the internet. There are also webcasts and podcasts available over the internet for students and teachers to download. For example, iTunes has various podcasts available on a variety of subjects that can be downloaded for free.

Video

Videos may allow teachers to reach students who are visual learners and tend to learn best by seeing the material rather than hearing or reading about it. Teachers can access video clips through the internet instead of relying on DVDs or VHS tapes. Websites like YouTube are used by many teachers.

Teachers can use Skype or webcams to interact with guest speakers and other experts. Interactive video games are being integrated in the curriculum at both K-12 and higher education institutions.

Computers, Laptops and Tablets

Having a computer or laptop in the classroom allows students and teachers access to websites and other programs, for example, Microsoft Word, PowerPoint, PDF files, and images.

Blogging

Blogs allow students and teachers to post their thoughts, ideas, and comments on a website. Blogging allows students and instructors to share their thoughts and comments on the thoughts of others which could create an interactive learning environment.

Mobile Devices

Mobile devices, for example, Smartphones operate similar to personal computers.

Learning Management Systems

Learning management systems, for example, BlackBoard or Moodle, are online based applications that institutions used to reach their students. It allows educators to create and deliver course material using the internet. Educators can post announcements, grade assignments, check on course activity, and participate in class discussions. Students can submit their work, read and respond to discussion questions, and take quizzes.

Whiteboards

Interactive whiteboards allow teachers and students to write on the touch screen, so learning becomes interactive and engaging.

Educational Technology

Along with the terms learning technology, instructional technology, the term Educational Technology is generally used to refer to the use of technology in learning in a much broader sense than the computer-based training or Computer Aided Instruction of the 1980s. It is also broader than the terms Online Learning or Online Education which generally refer to purely web-based learning. In cases where mobile technologies are used, the term M-learning has become more common. E-learning, however, also has implications beyond just the technology and refers to the actual learning that takes place using these systems.

In higher education especially, the increasing tendency is to create a Virtual Learning Environment (VLE) (which is sometimes combined with a Management Information System (MIS) to create a Managed) in which all aspects of a course are handled through a consistent user interface standard throughout the institution.

A growing number of physical universities, as well as newer online-only colleges, have begun to offer a select set of academic degree and certificate programs via the Internet at a wide range of levels and in a wide range of disciplines. While some programs require students to attend some campus classes or orientations, many are delivered completely online. In addition, several universities offer online student support services, such as online advising and registration, e-counseling, online textbook purchase, student governments and student newspapers.

Communication Technologies

Communication technologies are generally categorized as asynchronous or synchronous. Asynchronous activities use technologies such as blogs, wikis, and discussion boards. The idea here is that participants may engage in the exchange of ideas or information without the dependency of other participant's involvement at the same time. Electronic mail (Email) is also asynchronous in that mail can be sent or received without having both the participants' involvement at the same time.

Asynchronous learning also gives students the ability to work at their own pace. This is particularly beneficial for students who have health problems or have child care responsibilities and regularly leaving the home to attend lectures is difficult. They have the opportunity to complete their work in a low stress environment and within a more flexible timeframe.

Synchronous activities involve the exchange of ideas and information with one or more participants during the same period of time. A face-to-face discussion is an example of synchronous communications. In an "E" learning environment, an example of synchronous communications would be a Skype conversation or a chat room where everyone is online and working collaboratively at the same time. Synchronous activities occur with all participants joining in at once, as with an online chat session or a virtual classroom or meeting.

Advantages and Disadvantages of eLearning

There are many advantages to online and computer-based learning when compared to traditional face-to-face courses and lectures. There are a few disadvantages as well.

Advantages of Online or Computer-based Learning

1. Class work can be scheduled around work and family
2. Reduces travel time and travel costs for off-campus students
3. Students may have the option to select learning materials that meets their level of knowledge and interest
4. Students can study anywhere they have access to a computer and Internet connection
5. Self-paced learning modules allow students to work at their own pace
6. Flexibility to join discussions in the bulletin board threaded discussion areas at any hour, or visit with classmates and instructors remotely in chat rooms
7. Instructors and students both report eLearning fosters more interaction among students and instructors than in large lecture courses
8. eLearning can accommodate different learning styles and facilitate learning through a variety of activities
9. Develops knowledge of the Internet and computers skills that will help learners throughout their lives and careers
10. Successfully completing online or computer-based courses builds self-knowledge and self-confidence and encourages students to take responsibility for their learning
11. Learners can test out of or skim over materials already mastered and concentrate efforts in mastering areas containing new information and/or skills

Disadvantages of Online or Computer-based Learning

1. Learners with low motivation or bad study habits may fall behind
2. Without the routine structures of a traditional class, students may get lost or confused about course activities and deadlines
3. Students may feel isolated from the instructor and classmates
4. Instructor may not always be available when students are studying or need help
5. Slow Internet connections or older computers may make accessing course materials frustrating
6. Managing computer files and online learning software can sometimes seem complex for students with beginner-level computer skills
7. Hands-on or lab work is difficult to simulate in a virtual classroom.

NEED AND SIGNIFICANCE OF THE STUDY

The study wills more light into the advancement using among the online teaching and learning in education and made bond among the higher secondary school students. The investigation here made is *"A Study on the Awareness of Online Learning among Higher Secondary Students"*. The outcome of the study is therefore expected to stimulate and to improve online usage among the higher secondary school students. The variables which have been found to have using of internet to use in Educational and in other field.

SCOPE OF THE STUDY

This study that focus on the using online usage in the education field among the higher secondary school students. Due to the varying characteristics, supports and individual internet educational using program of students with abilities, the studies may always be appropriate for creating using of "Online usage among the higher secondary school students". And Studies that use an online to determine technology include studies impacting development in educational and life process.

STATEMENT OF THE PROBLEM

The important on the online using, particularly students of a Nation can be over emphasized. However, we cannot lose sight of the fact that using internet in any teaching – learning situation of the students, the teachers, the curriculum and the learning environments. These are the four pivots. It is on the basis of this that the study constructed and tested as to find *"A Study on the Awareness of Online Learning among Higher Secondary Students"*. This providing an explanation of higher secondary school students on using the internet.

ONLINE

The Online is a network of computer networks. It makes it possible for any computer connected to it to send and receive data from any other computer connected to it. The concept of data communication– transmitting data between two different places, connected via some kind of electromagnetic medium, such as radio or an electrical wire – predates the introduction of the first computers. Such communication systems were typically limited to point to point communication between two end devices. Telegraph systems and telex machines can be considered early precursors of this kind of communication.

BROWSING

A web browser (commonly referred to as a browser) is a software application for retrieving, presenting and traversing information resources on the World Wide Web. An information resource is identified by a Uniform Resource Identifier (URI) and may be a web page, image, video or other piece of content.

Hyperlinks present in resources enable users easily to navigate their browsers to related resources. A web browser can also be defined as an application software or program designed to enable users to access, retrieve and view documents and other resources on the Internet.

Education is the systematic development and cultivation of the natural powers. Education includes all the processes that develop human ability and behaviors. It is an organized and sustained instruction designed to communicate a combination of knowledge, Skills and understanding valuable for all the activities of life.

Online Awarness: have progressed more rapidly than most people imagined to transform information, communications, obtaining knowledge and other sectors of everyday life. As a result, many people believe that computers must be in schools for teaching purpose.

OBJECTIVES OF THE STUDY

1. To identify utilization of online learning among the higher secondary school students. To find out the extent of possible using online students at higher secondary level.
2. To find out the difference between the mean scores awareness of online learning among the Higher secondary school students on the basis of their Locality.
3. To find out the significant difference if any between the different group of demographic variables such as Sex, Students residential place, Type of school, Type of subject in online learning among the higher secondary level.

HYPOTHESES OF THE STUDY

1. There is Significant mean difference in the mean scores of Awareness of Online learning among the higher secondary school (Male and Female)students in terms of their Gender.
2. There is Significant mean difference in the mean scores of Awareness of Online learning among the higher secondary school (XI and XII)students in terms of their standard doing.
3. There is Significant mean difference in the mean scores of Awareness of Online learning among the higher secondary school (Rural and Urban) students in terms of their Locality.
4. There is Significant mean difference in the mean scores of Awareness of Online learning among the higher secondary school (Government and Private) students in terms of their Type of School.
5. There is Significant mean difference in the mean scores of Awareness of Online learning among the higher secondary school (Private and Aided) students in terms of their Type of School.

6. There is Significant mean difference in the mean scores of Awareness of Online learning among the higher secondary school (Aided and Government) students in terms of their Type of School.
7. There is Significant mean difference in the mean scores of Awareness of Online learning among the higher secondary school (Mathematics and Computer Science) students in terms of their Type of Subject.
8. There is Significant mean difference in the mean scores of Awareness of Online learning among the higher secondary school (Computer Science and Vocational) students in terms of their Type of Subject .
9. There is Significant mean difference in the mean scores of Awareness of Online learning among the higher secondary school (Vocational and Mathematics) students in terms of their Type of Subject.

LIMITATIONS OF THE STUDY

1. The following are some of the limitations of the present Study.
2. The Study is continued to the area of in and around Pudukkottai.
3. Only Four schools are petered for the present study.
4. The total number of samples is collected only 250 from students.
5. The samples were collected only from Government Aided School, Government School, Private Schools located in around Pudukkottai area.
6. In this study is the investigator considered only few usage internet faced by secondary school students.

CONCLUSION

Being Awareness of Online Learning among the students must have good skills. Definitely those skills in Technology should be developed through internet. In order to achieve success in current trend school must have knowledge about internet usage. The present study will helpful in understanding the importance of Awareness of Online Learning among the school students.

Chapter - II

Review of Realated Literature

INTRODUCTION

Literature reviews that focus on research outcomes are perhaps the most common. A review of the literature on contract instructors from federal training agencies and other literature sources. The chapter highlights recurring themes and recommended practices that evolve from this literature review.

The review of related studies is essential for several reasons. It helps in identifying the unanswered questions in the concerned field on the one hand and it locating the specific issues which require immediate and pointed attach by the investigator on the other. It is highly essential for a researcher to make a comprehensive survey of what has already been done in the related areas.

A literature review is an evaluative report of studies found in the literature related to your selected area. The review should describe, summarize, evaluate and clarify this literature. It should give a theoretical basis for the research and help you determine the nature of your own research. Select a limited number of works that are central to your area rather than trying to collect a large number of works that are not as closely connected to your topic area.

David N. Boote and Penny Beile argues that the literature review is the fundamental task of dissertation and research preparation. They claim that research students receive minimal formal training and little guidance from faculty or published sources, in how to analyze an synthesize research literature.

As a result, they argue, most dissertation literature reviews are poorly conceptualized and written and research students may not be learning what it means to make and justify educational claims. They conclude that "Literature reviewing should be a central focus of pre dissertation coursework, integrated throughout the program".

THE PURPOSE OF THE REVIEW OF LITERATURE

The Purpose of the Review of Literature is to build up the context and background of research as well as to provide a basis for formulation of the hypothesis. Since a good research is based upon everything that is known in the area of research.

The review of research provide to this effect. The authors clearly hold a foundation list conception of the place and function of literature reviews in research. The repeatedly refer to the literature review as the "foundation" or "precondition" of research, and to its "centrality" in the research process and assert that the ability to analyze and synthesize research should be the focal, integrative activity of pre dissertation.

This foundational metaphor may be part of the motivation for their view of the dissertation literature review as necessarily broad, thorough and topic-focused. Conducting a literature review is a means of demonstrating an author's knowledge about a particular field of study, including vocabulary, theories, key variables and phenomena and its methods and history.

Conducting a literature review also informs the student of the influential researchers and research groups in the field. Finally, with some modification, the literature review is a "legitimate and publishable scholarly document".

Apart from the above reasons for writing a review i.e., proof of knowledge, a publishable document, and the identification of a research family, the scientific reasons for conducting a literature review are many.

Gall, Borg, and Gall (1996) argue that the literature review plays a role in:

1. Delimiting the research problem,
2. Seeking new lines of inquiry,
3. Avoiding fruitless approaches,
4. Gaining methodological insights,
5. Identifying recommendations for further research and
6. Seeking support for grounded theory.

Better Hart (1998) contributes additional reasons for reviewing the literature including:

1. Distinguishing what has been done from what needs to be done,
2. Discovering important variables relevant to the topic,
3. Synthesizing and gaining a new perspective,
4. Identifying relationships between ideas and practices,
5. Establishing the context of the topic or problem,
6. Rationalizing the significance of the problem,
7. Enhancing and acquiring the subject vocabulary,
8. Understanding the structure of the subject,
9. Relating ideas and theory to applications,
10. Identifying the main methodologies and research techniques that have been used and
11. Placing the research in a historical context to show familiarly with state-of-the-art developments.

According to good, Barr and Scates "The competent physician must keep abreast of the latest discoveries in the field of medicine... Obviously the careful student of education, the research worker and investigator should become familiar with location and use of sources of educational information".

Charter V. Good "The keys to the vast storehouse of published literature may open doors to sources of significant problems and explanatory hypotheses and provide helpful orientation for definition of the problem, background for selection of procedure and comparative data for interpretation of results. In order to be creative and original, one must read extensively and critically as a stimulus to thinking".

A goal of many reviews is to integrate or synthesize research outcomes. Thus, a common metric or measure must be identified into which all of the research outcomes can be translated. In a quantities synthesis, for example, the common metric might be the difference in proportions between control and treatment groups.

STUDIES CONDUCTED IN INDIA

Niranjan (1998) compared the experiences of graduate students' awareness in Web learning to complete preparation, procedures, contrasting those who used more basic online training with those who used an enhanced interface that incorporated a context-sensitive set of features, including integrated tutorials, expert systems and content delivered in visual, aural and textual forms. Nruyen found that this combination of enhancements had a positive effect among the college students.

Mohan-Martin (1998) The vulnerability of school students College students among the most at-risk populations in terms of demographics. Suggests two lines of reasoning for increased use among school students, including access and expectation of computer and Online use. The majority of school students own or have ready access to a computer. Current incoming students have been raised with modern Internet technology and computers were not perceived as negatively as they use to be, particularly among males. In terms of their daily lives, college student schedules provide them with a lot of flexibility and free time resulting in the flexibility to spend long epochs on various Internet applications. Moreover, college students have easy access through direct Internet connections in dorms, libraries and computer labs.

Becker (2001) Using the online for instructional purposes especially stirred the public's imagination and thus in the 2000's, there was a rush to wire virtually on colleges. The sheer amount of technology in schools in the United States has greatly increased.

Dede in the year of (2003) investigated whether the inclusion of awareness improved student learning through Online. The study used a randomized, controlled, crossover trial, in which each collegiate student took four modules, two with the awareness on Online and two without. The order of modules was randomly assigned. Collegiate student performance was statistically higher on tests taken immediately after completion of modules that included awareness in self-assessment. After completion of those without such cause an effect that the authors attributed to the stimulation of reflection. This effect, on which all the collegiate students performed having awareness on Online usage.

According to Bhuvanesh in the year (2006) has pointed awareness on Online and the World Wide Web made inroads into North East India undergraduates quite late but once the ball was set rolling there was no stopping it. There was almost a deluge of websites, both personal and corporate emerging from this part of India. College going students preparing most of the educational websites, individuals and academic institutions too realizing the enormous potential of the web awareness. Information on almost all aspects of the North East Indian collegiate was available on the web. Whether it is well presented on another matter of course. A more important concern about the awareness of this information. And awareness about web resources among the students were brought about by the following means:

1. Through verbal communication,
2. Through print sources,
3. Through the radio and television,
4. Through search engine.

The concern of this awareness about and use of Online search engines amongst the Higher secondary students in North East India.

Suryani in the year (2007) has stated eagerness in the Online Usage among Undergraduates increase School level learning and educational development thus they would encourage others pupil to take advantage of the usage of online.

Fazil and Moghan in the year (2008) pointed educational internet awareness among the higher secondary students in developing countries growing rapidly, especially among women. Women who use the Online tend to be more open-minded than those who do not use the Online.

Ambrose (2009) in Learner diversity technologies can support students without learning difficulties by providing a platform for training and rehearsal and by making learning available in new ways. Interactive, media-rich web sites provide a forum for practice, feedback, clear progression structures, visualization and explorative environments.

Citizens Online and National Centers for Social Research 2008 proceeds awareness on Online learning sites such as BBC bite size were identified as key contact points for undergraduate student in education, employment or training.

According to Karl in the year (2010) has pointed awareness on internet usage among Undergraduates and remote control devices enhance the control of the viewing environment, which leads to increased entertainment and informational gratification. He studied people's use of the mass media like internet to meet specific needs and presented a five-fold classification of needs, which they say all internet users essentially have these needs;

1. Cognitive needs: needs related to strengthening of information, knowledge and understanding of our environment.
2. Affective needs: needs related to strengthening aesthetic, pleasurable and emotional experiences.
3. Personal integrative needs: needs to strengthening credibility, confidence, stability and status of individuals.
4. Social integrative needs: needs related to strengthening contact with family, friends and the world.
5. Escapist needs: needs related to escape, release tension and the desire for diversion.

Online learning-for students and for teachers-is one of the fastest growing trends in educational uses off technology. The National Center for Education Statistics (2008) estimated that the number of college students enrolling in a technology-based distance education course grew by 86 percent in the two years from 2008 to 2010. On the basis of a more recent district survey, Picciano and Seaman (2009) estimated that more than a million students took online courses in school year 2010-11.

Riyazkahn (2011) reached conclusions similar to those of Honey Ryan hypothesized that exposure to internet awareness would affect student performance. He compared a group of under graduate students to treatment, which engaged in online learning that included interaction with web resource and peers using online collaboration, which have access to instruction in the use of internet.

Baskarlal, (2012) states Teacher technological competence should be viewed as a critical teacher skill for addressing and meeting student's educational need results in the development of new cognitive abilities that translate into the key skills for our transformed world.

STUDIES CONDUCTED ABROAD

Hepburn (1995) previous research had linked educational awareness using increases the undergraduate individual attitudes and cognitive development. An individual with high internet awareness would tend to understood how a democracy works and exhibit interest in educational system raised.

According to Hunter in the year (1996) carried out a theoretical research on the uses and gratification of the Web , the World Wide Web can gratify the major needs through the popular uses of browsing the Web.

That seeking the information and entertaining. Hunter suggested that the gratification users receive from browsing can be seen as an extension of their affective and cognitive needs. Information seeking mostly satisfies cognitive needs and entertainment satisfies aesthetic and escapist needs. The two most important tools are the WWW and the e-mail according to studies done on uses and gratification derived from the Online. They seem to gratify most of the needs which arise out of using the Internet that could used by the undergraduates.

Scherer (1997) At the very least, these terminals were used for email when the student is not engaged in academic work. Additionally, colleges were increased relying on the Online as a method of disseminating information. Students increase to use the Internet as a means of distributing assignments, readings, grades and course syllabi.

Some programs now require students to purchase a computer, often a laptop, as part of the admissions and educational process. With increasingly more students receiving instruction on Internet use by the time they reach college, they were proficient users. Even students who did not use the online at young ages were fast becoming "experts" on online use. The basics of the Internet are easy to learn and exploring the Internet can be a highly positive experience.

Upon moving away from home, college students often encounter intimidating circumstances as they try to fit in. The online makes it easy to procrastinate from studying, especially when students are undergoing elevated stress levels from their course work. Online users have a high degree of control over their computer and Internet environments which can be seductive. Especially college students whose social relationships may be faltering.

Use of the Online was highly individualized activity. It anonymous endeavor that does not require coordination with friends or anyone else, nor does it require any planning ahead.

Greenfield (1999) argued that awareness on Online use makes the most sense in term of Online use employed for this study in recognition that intensive Online use lead to problems but not necessarily severe pathology as implied by many of the other terms currently in use which lack sufficient empirical evidence and theoretical support.

Voorbij (2000) conducted a nationwide survey among students and academics to explore the use and perceived importance of the Online for study or work related purposes. More specifically, the study focused on searching information resources on the World Wide Web. The user survey consisted of two parts. First, a rather detailed questionnaire was sent to justify the academic community. Second, three focus group interviews were held with experience Internet users.

Among other findings the study revealed that searching the World Wide Web was not without difficulty. The web has used primarily to search general factual, ephemeral or very specific information. At the moment, full test resources play only a minor role in the academic research process. The Online may have conquered a place for itself, but it has not pushed aside traditional printed and other information sources among the students.

Shen, Lee (2002) found a combination of awareness in Online learning effects for self-regulation and opportunities to learn through realistic problems. They compared the performance of under graduate students who receive instruction in online increase the self-regulation.

Learning strategies such as managing study time, goal setting and self-evaluation. The group that received instruction in self-regulated learning performed better in their online learning.

San Diego State University (2002) The Web model encourages college students to create for their new activities and adapt successful ones to take advantage of the Web's power. A higher- level application of this model has students develop their own web activities to support the subject matter they were studying and share the Web with their peers.

Kelley et al. in the year (2003) founded that several important and justifiable reasons to investigate and understand the factors affecting under graduates individuals Internet privacy concerns:

1. Internet was increased becomes a part of the life of every undergraduate individual,
2. Such understanding would help to promote and encourage further and more extensive voluntary usage that includes more extensive and frequent engagement in e-learning and
3. It would also help in understanding the ways to narrow the gap between the need for personal information and updates to supply. Such achieved more cohesion and digital inclusion of more diverse educational groups to benefit from the Internet use.

Thus it focuses on exploring certain factors which we believe are salient to Internet privacy concerns, namely Internet technical literacy awareness. The contribution of this research in the attempt to explore psychological antecedents to privacy concerns that could direct towards strategies of broadening.

Internet web sites and applications, thus opening more opportunities for growth and competitive advantage.

Mittermeyer (2004) in his study the incoming first-year undergraduate students found that many reported that they use the online extensively for seeking course-related information.

Kerins et al. in the year (2005) has carried out a study on online aware among the undergraduate students and found that the majority reported that the Internet was the first source of information they would use for their resources collection and updates on education.

Sim et al, (2006) stated online awareness in classroom setting could not fail to meet its potential because of over structuring of tasks and curriculum constraints. Learning from interactive internet was necessarily correlated with fun, informative or usability.

Rodrigues (2007) Factors that influence engagement with interactive internet create awareness that include levels of distraction and vividness of the information. The logic and instructions presented and relevant prior knowledge possessed by the undergraduates and rich rather than superficial interaction was essential for engagement.

Osbourne(2008) evidence that online learning has a greater impact on undergraduate students who were eligible for source learners and those for whom was a second language learner. The Internet may be 'in' but it is not totally foolproof, a fact substantiated by thirteen respondents who complain that while it does provide "something" to meet their needs, "but not as much as needed". Three respondents felt that it provides "enough" information.

One brave soul told it as it was Online provides more information than is needed. Despite their difference of opinion, the respondents were unanimous in their agreement on the fact that the Internet does have its uses.

Bastani and Fazel-Zaraland in the year (2009) has investigated the influence of the online on social connections among online users in India. They found that far from alienating people from their richer relations. The Internet has not changed the relationships significantly for most respondents and for a noticeable portion in the study has increased their social contacts with different groups. The principal component analysis was applied to the dataset to unearth the common patterns of user behavior.

An increase in social contacts as evident among women. This despite the fact that there was a significant gender gap in online use in India. This finding suggests that as maintaining relationship was important for the offline world, it also important for then when they are online. Another interesting finding is that although ethnicity plays a major role in having access to the Online, it does not have a significant impact on social contacts.

Griffiths and Donald (2009) the Online was accessed about 7.5 billion times to seek education related information 11% of all important Online uses. The Online was used more for educational purposes by undergraduates 25% than by school students 15%. Other educational information needs were related to information about colleges, education requirements, financial aid, counseling etc. The services on the Online that were accessed consisted of search engines such as Google or Yahoo, viewing or downloading e-books, viewing or downloading articles, viewing websites, using e-mail and chat mail.

Vernadakis et al (2010) evidences that a multimedia format could lead to higher attainment than a traditional format. Research in this area limited and inconclusive. There also evidence that recognized benefits of multimedia use with students do not always hold true and that increased media richness could lead to greater cognitive overhead and learning.

DongningBai, John Dacey, Ori Ashman, Larry Ludlow and faculty who participated Computer Industry Almanac Inc., 2002. Since the mid-1990s, the awareness on Online has experienced unprecedented growth in both its size and number of users. Approximately 160 million people in the United States have access to the Online, representing a 24% share of the world's Online user population and this number continues to increase.

Among the Online-using population, the fastest growing group was the category of graduate students. While individuals ranging from 18-24 years of age represent the "most active online users". Additionally, it was estimated that by 2004, almost 91% of this age group will be online. College students in particular represent a substantial part of this growth.

The Online affects individuals on varying levels of occupational, academic, interpersonal, financial and physical health. The increasingly reliant on computer applications, especially the Internet and related products and services. For example, new technological

Acknowledgements. The author was grateful to the following for their contributions to the project.

Abbot in the year(2011) has carried a study namely awareness of internet Technologies and online resources can help to overcome learning difficulties of the graduates in three specific ways

1. By providing a platform for training or rehearsal
2. Through the use of assistive technologies; and

By using technologies to make learning possible where it was not possible before.

Kay and Knaack (2012) subjected impact of the use of online learning among the higher secondary students. There was little real evidence in the comparative effects of using internet and traditional learning methods (possibly because of the difficulty and ethical issues associated with setting up studies of the nature). These discuss a meta-review of evidence for the impact of learning of specific concepts by enhancing amplifying and guiding the cognitive processes of learners". They conclude that a number of problems with many of the existing evaluations of learning object in that the focus on technology before learning.

They focus on impressions rather than specific features, concentrate on either formative or summative evaluation were carried out on small sample populations.

CONCLUSION

From an overview of the literature shows that the Awareness of Online learning Among Higher Secondary School Students. But, very few studies have been reported on the association of awareness Online Learning among the higher secondary school students the next chapter deals with methodology and research procedures as follows.

Chapter-III

Methodology

INTRODUCTION

The research methods must be appropriate to the objective of the study. If you perform a case study of one commit in order to investigate users' perceptions of the efficiency of public transport in Bangkok, your method is obviously unsuited to your objectives.

The methodology should also discuss the problems that were anticipated and explain the steps taken to prevent them from occurring, and the problems that did occur and the ways their impact was minimized. In some cases, it is useful for other researchers to adapt or replicate your methodology, so often sufficient information is given to allow others to use the work. This is particularly the case when a new method had been developed, or an innovative adaptation used.

Methodology can be the analysis of the principles of method, rules, and postulates employed by a discipline.

Methodology may refer to nothing more than a simple set of methods or procedures, or it may refer to the rationale and the philosophical assumptions that underline a particular study relative to the scientific method. For example, scholarly literature often includes a section on the methodology of the researchers.

RESEARCH DESIGN

This chapter presents details regarding the following:

1. Selection of Dependent variables and categorical variables.
2. Construction of tools to measure the Awareness of Online Learning among Higher Secondary students.
3. Methods of establishing the reliability, validity of the tools constructed.
4. Sampling procedure adopted in this study.
5. Scheduling the survey and collecting the data.

METHOD AND ITS PROCEDURE

1. Selecting a problem.
2. Identification of the variables.
3. The learning outcome.
4. Selection and development of tools.
5. Selection of sample from higher secondary school students.
6. Administration of tools.
7. Collection of data.
8. Data analysis.
9. Testing the Hypotheses.
10. Findings and conclusion.
11. Implications.

STATEMENT OF THE PROBLEM

The important on the internet using, particularly students of a Nation can be over emphasized. However, we cannot lose sight of the fact that using Online in any teaching- learning situation of the students, the teachers, the curriculum and the learning environments. These are the four pivots.

It is on the basis of this that the study constructed and tested as to find the *"A Study on the Awareness of Online Learning among Higher Secondary Students"*.

This providing an explanation of higher secondary school students on using the Online.

OBJECTIVE OF THE STUDY

1. To identify awareness of online learning among the higher secondary school students.
2. To find out the extent of possible using online students at higher secondary level.
3. To find out the difference between the mean scores awareness of online learning among the Higher secondary school students on the basis of their Locality.
4. To find out the significant difference if any between the different group of demographic variables such as Standard Doing, Sex, Type of school, Type of major in awareness of online learning among the higher secondary level.

HYPOTHESES OF THE STUDY

1. There is Significant mean difference in the mean scores of Awareness of Online Learning Among Higher Secondary School (Male and Female)students in terms of their Gender.
2. There is Significant mean difference in the mean scores of Awareness of Online Learning Among Higher Secondary School (XI and XII)students in terms of their standard doing.
3. There is Significant mean difference in the mean scores of Awareness of Online Learning Among Higher Secondary School (Rural and Urban) students in terms of their Locality.
4. There is Significant mean difference in the mean scores of Awareness of Online Learning Among Higher Secondary School (Government and Private) students in terms of their Type of School.
5. There is Significant mean difference in the mean scores of Awareness of Online Learning among Higher Secondary School (Private and Aided) students in terms of their Type of School.

6. There is Significant mean difference in the mean scores of Awareness of Online Learning Among Higher Secondary School (Aided and Government) students in terms of their Type of School.
7. There is Significant mean difference in the mean scores of Awareness of Online Learning Among Higher Secondary School (Mathematics and Computer Science) students in terms of their Type of Subject.
8. There is Significant mean difference in the mean scores of Awareness of Online Learning Among Higher Secondary School (Computer Science and Vocational) students in terms of their Type of Subject.
9. There is Significant mean difference in the mean scores of Awareness of Online Learning Among Higher Secondary School (Vocational and Mathematics) students in terms of their Type of Subject.

LIMITATIONS OF THE STUDY

The following are some of the limitations of the present Study.

1. The Study is contained to the area in and around Pudukkottai Educational District.
2. Only Four schools are used for present study.
3. The total numbers of samples 250were collected from the higher secondary school students in around Pudukkottai Educational District.
4. The samples were collected only from government Aided School, Government School, Private Schools located in around Pudukkottai Educational District.
5. The study was conducted in the year 2014-2015.

RESEARCH METHOD

The investigator preferred survey method for the present study. In this study, the investigator used stratified sampling method to collect data and to study the awareness of online learning among the higher secondary school students.

RESEARCH TOOLS

The world 'tool' is defined a means to collect evidence. A research tool plays a major role in any worthwhile research is the role factor in determining the around data and in arriving at perfect conclusion about the problem or study on hand, which ultimately, helps in providing suitable remedial measures to the problem concerned.

CONSTRUCTION OF RESEARCH TOOLS

The research tool on *"A Study on the Awareness of Online Learning Among Higher Secondary Students"* was constructed by the investigator in the present study. All the question items are closed type.

The responded who respondent the correct answers were given two scores, moderate response has one score and no response has zero score, these score were considered for data analysis. The selection and use of tools can be done in two ways. The first one is to construct a tool independently by the researcher for this own study.

i. Personal Data Sheet developed by the Investigator.

ii. Awareness of online learning among the higher secondary school students as questionnaire.

SAMPLE OF THE STUDY

After finalizing the variables of present study, consideration was given to whether the entire population is to be made the subject for data collection or a particular group is to be selected as representation of the whole population.

The 250 population here refers to awareness of online learning among the higher secondary school students.

TABLE 1: SAMPLING FRAME FOR THE PRESENT STUDY

		Sample Collected		
S.NO	Name and Place of the School	Male	Female	Total
1.	Govt. Higher Secondary School, ADW Mullangurichi	41	43	84
2.	St. Joseph Higher Secondary School Venkatakulam	42	41	83

3.	Govt. Boys Higher Secondary School, Alangudi	41	-	41
4.	Govt. Girls Higher Secondary School, Alangudi	-	42	42
	TOTAL	124	126	250

DESCRIPTION OF RESEARCH TOOL AND SCORING PROCEDURE

The response sheets of the subject were scored according to the guidelines given by the constructor of the tool. It is a three point of likerts types of tool.

PILOT STUDY

The investigator collected only 50 samples from the above two school. On the basis of the responses of the respondents the frequencies user offered by the investigator. The investigator conducted pilot study in ADW Higher Secondary School,. Govt. Boys Higher Secondary School located near to investigator's place. Before administering the research tool the investigator gave some instructions regarding how to answer for all questions. Then the investigator allowed them to give their response for the each and every item of the questionnaire.

VALIDITY OF THE TOOL

In validation process, the investigator used two measures in order to establish validation of tools. The investigator established content validity. To find out to validity of research tool, the investigator discussed each and every item of the questionnaire with the experts in the relevant field to identify the *"A Study on the Awareness of Online Learning among Higher Secondary Students"*.

RELIABILITY OF THE TOOL

After collecting data the investigator attempted to find out the reliability for the questioner usage initialization of internet faced by students in calculation. The reliability of the tool refers to the internet consistency observed in measurement in the different set of equivalent item.

In this study Pearson product moment formula and spearman brown formula used to identify the reliability value the reliability value is 0.98

$$r=\frac{2r}{r+1}$$

$$=\frac{2(0.99)}{0.99+1}$$

$$=\frac{1.98}{1.99}$$

$$\mathbf{r = 0.99}$$

The reliability value for the present tool is 0.99.Such that the tool is highly reliable.

SAMPLING METHOD

The Sampling procedure is used to collect the data is Stratified Random sampling. The investigator collected samples from secondary schools located in around Pudukkottai area. Before going to administer the research tool, the investigator revealed the purpose of the present studies to the Higher Secondary School students and the asked them to given their responses for each and every item that are given in the questionnaire. The responses of the Higher Secondary School were recorded.

COLLECTION OF DATA

The investigator himself visited the secondary school teachers located in and around Pudukkottai by getting permission from the headmasters of various schools. Before administering the research tool the investigator explain the aim and purpose of the study and then administered the research tool for secondary school Student's. Then the investigator asked the entire student to respond for each and every item that is given in the questionnaire.

The responses were recorded and the demographic particulars were collected from the student. The collected data were used for data analysis. After collection data, the investigator gave frequencies for all the question item and then entered in master table (and these frequencies were converted into score).

ANALYSIS OF DATA

The term analysis refers to the compilation of certain measures along with searching for pattern among groups. For the present study the investigator collected the data from Higher Secondary School students using the tool developed to find out questioner of sample to identify the awareness of online learning among the higher secondary school students. This involves computing measures of central tendency like Mean and the measures of variability like Standard deviation and t-test.

STATISTICAL TECHNIQUES USED

Statistical Techniques serves the fundamental purpose of the description and inferential analysis. It is concerned with numerical description of a particular group observed. Any similarity to those outside the group cannot be taken for granted. The data describe one group only. Simple educational research involves descriptive statistics and provides valuable information about the nature of a particular group or class. Data collection from tests have little meaning or significance until they have been classified or rearrange in a systematic way.

1. Mean (M)
2. Standard Deviation(S.D)
3. 't' – test for determine the significance of difference between means of sub-group.

ARITHMETIC MEAN FROM A FREQUENCY DISTRIBUTION

Sometimes it is more convenient to desire mean form a frequency Distribution. An additional column may be opened to record the products of frequency distribution. The total of this frequency distribution will be divided by total of 'F' (i.e.) N to get mean. Where,

A -Assumed mean value

CI -Class Interval

N -Total number of scores

THE STANDARD DEVIATION:

Standard Deviation most widely used measure of dispersion of a series and is commonly denoted by the symbol ó(sigma) standard deviation is defined as the square root of the average of squares of deviation when such deviations for the values of individual items in a series are obtained from the arithmetic average.

't' –TEST

The test of significance of the difference between two mean is known as 't' – test. It involves the computation of the ratio between experimental variance (observed difference between two sample means) and error variance (the sampling error factor).

When small samples are involved the t-table is used to determine statistical significance, rather that the normality, probability table. This concept of small sample size was developed around 1915 by William Sealy Grossest, consulting tacticians for Guinness Breweries of bubluin, Ireland, Gusset critical values, carefully calculated for small samples area reproduced in the t- distribution table.

The t- critical values necessary for rejection of a null hypothesis are higher for the samples of a given level of significances. Each t – critical value for rejection is based upon the appropriate number of degrees of freedom.

M1= Mean of First Group

M2= Mean of Second Group

S1 = SD of the First Group

S2 = SD of the Second Group

N1 = No. of Students in First Group

N2 = No. of Students in Second Group.

CONCLUSION

The research procedure adopted in this study was discussed in this chapter. The data were collected for a sample of 250 students studying in higher secondary school students. The data were analysis with suitable statistical techniques and interpreter in the next chapter.

Chapter -IV

Data Analysis and Interpretation

INTRODUCTION

In the general process of analysis of research data, statistical method has contributed a great deal. It finds a place in almost any research study dealing with large or even small group of individuals. Complex statistical computations from the basis of many types of research.

Statistics is the body of mathematical techniques or processes for gathering, describing, organizing and interpreting numerical data. It is a basic tool of measurement and research. It is concerned with more than the manipulation of data. It goes back to fundamental purposes of analysis.

In order to achieve results from facts gathered through the methods, several techniques are utilized. Analysis is one of them. In order to arrive at result from the collected data, it is necessary to classify it. Analysis is the reduction of data into categories.

ANALYSIS OF DATA

The term analysis refers to the compilation of certain measures along with searching for pattern among groups. For the present study the investigator collected the data from Higher Secondary School students using the tool developed to find out questionnaire of sample to identify the awareness of online learning among the higher secondary school students. This involves computing measures of central tendency like Mean and the measures of variability like Standard deviation and t-test.

To Identify the Level of Awareness of Online Learning among the Higher Secondary School Students

Table 1

Distribution of overall percentages of male and female higher secondary school student's overall and Usage of Online

Sl. No.	Gender	N	Overall Percentages
1.	Male	126	77.74%
2.	Female	124	78.46%

The above table reveals the overall mean percentage of male and female student's and Usage of Online.

If the overall percentages are compared, female student's higher level than male student's in using online.

Finding

Female student's overall using Online is higher than the male student's in higher secondary level.

Table 2

Distribution of percentages of XI and XII higher secondary school student's overall and Usage of Online.

Sl. No.	Qualification	N	Overall Percentages
1.	XI	150	79.05%
2.	XII	100	76.65%

The above table reveals the overall mean percentage of XI and XII student's and Usage of online.

If the overall percentages are compared, XI student's higher level than XII student's in using online.

Finding

XI student's overall using online is higher than the XII student's in higher secondary level.

Table 3

Distribution of percentages of Rural and Urban secondary school student's Overall and Usage of Online

Sl. No.	Locality	N	Overall Percentages
1.	Rural	92	74.71%
2.	Urban	158	80.06%

The above table reveals the overall mean percentage of Rural and Urban student's and Usage of online.

If the overall percentages are compared, urban student's higher than rural student's in using online.

Finding

Urban student's overall using Online is higher than the rural student's in higher secondary level.

Table 4

Distribution of percentages of Government, Private and Aided Higher secondary school student's overall and Usage of online.

Sl. No.	Type of college	N	Overall Percentages
1.	Government	84	74.51%
2.	Private	83	83.32%
3.	Aided	83	76.48%

The above table reveals the overall mean percentage of Government, Private and Aided.

If the overall percentages are compared, Private student's higher than Government and Aided student's in using online.

Finding

Private student's overall using online is higher than the Government and Aided student's in higher secondary level.

Table 5

Distribution of percentages of Mathematics, Computer science and vocational higher secondary school student's overall and Usage of online

Sl. No.	Type of class	N	Overall Percentages
1.	Mathematics	81	80.28%
2.	Computer science	83	79.39%
3.	vocational	86	77.36%

The above table reveals the Overall mean percentage of Mathematics, Computer science and vocational.

If the overall percentages are compared Mathematics student's higher than Computer science, vocational student's in using online.

Finding

Mathematics student's overall using online is higher than the Computer science, Vocational student's in higher secondary level.

HYPOTHESIS OF THE DATA

HYPOTHESIS: 1

There is Significant mean difference in the mean scores of awareness of online learning among the higher secondary school (Male and Female)students in terms of their Gender

Table 6

The above table reveals the Mean, Standard Deviation and 't' value for the Gender groups of Male and Female.

Sl.No.	Group	Mean	S.D	N	't' value	Levelof Significance
1.	Male	50.46	8.49	123		Not
2.	Female	49.28	6.63	127	1.22	significant
	df=248					

INTERPRETATION:

Since the calculated 't' value 1.22 is smaller than the table value 1.96 at 0.05% level of significant with df=248.

There is significant difference between the male and female student's in using Online.

RESULT:

The null hypothesis is accepted.

HYPOTHESIS: 2

There is Significant mean difference in the mean scores of Awareness of Online learning among the higher secondary school (XI and XII)students in terms of their standard doing

Table 7

The above table reveals the Mean, Standard Deviation and 't' value for the standard groups of XI and XII.

Sl.No.	Group	Mean	S.D	N	't' value	Levelof Significance
1.	XI	50.33	7.56	151	1.20	Not
2.	XII	49.14	7.69	99		significant

df=248

INTERPRETATION

Since the calculated 't' value 1.20 is smaller than the table value 1.96 at 0.05% level of significant with df=248.

There is significant difference between XI and XII student's in using Online.

RESULT:

The null hypothesis is accepted.

HYPOTHESIS: 3

There is Significant mean difference in the mean scores of Awareness of Online learning among the higher secondary school (Rural and Urban) students in terms of their Locality

Table 8

The above table reveals the Mean, Standard Deviation and 't' value for the Locality groups of Rural and Urban.

Sl.No.	Group	Mean	S.D	N	't' value	Levelof Significance
1.	Rural	48.33	6.94	92		
2.	Urban	50.82	7.38	158	2.62	significant

df=248

INTERPRETATION

Since the calculate 't' value 2.62 is greater than the table value 1.96 at 0.05% level of significant with df=248.

There is no significant difference between Rural and Urban student's in using Online.

RESULT:

The null hypothesis is rejected.

HYPOTHESIS: 4

There is significant mean difference in the mean scores of Awareness of Online learning among the higher secondary school (Government and Private) students in terms of their Type of School

Table 9

The above table reveals the Mean, Standard Deviation and 't' value for the Type of school groups of Government and Private.

Sl.No.	Group	Mean	S.D	N	't' value	Levelof Significance
1.	Government	47.17	5.5	84		
2.	Private	53.57	7.21	83	6.46	significant

df=165

INTERPRETATION

Since the calculated 't' value 6.46 is greater than the table value 1.96 at 0.05% level of significant with df=165.

There is no significant difference between Government and Private student's in using Online.

RESULT

The null hypothesis is rejected.

HYPOTHESIS: 5

There is Significant mean difference in the mean scores of Awareness of Online learning among the higher secondary school (Private and Aided) students in terms of their Type of School

Table 10

The above table reveals the Mean, Standard Deviation and 't' value for the Type of school groups of Private and Aided.

Sl.No.	Group	Mean	S.D	N	't' value	Levelof Significance
1.	Private	53.57	7.21	83	4.25	Significant
2.	Aided	48.51	8.17	83		

df=164

INTERPRETATION

Since the calculated 't' value 4.25 is greater than the table value 1.96 at 0.05%level of significant with df=164.

There is no significant difference between Private and Aided Student's in using Online.

RESULT

The null hypothesis is rejected.

HYPOTHESIS: 6

There is Significant mean difference in the mean scores of Awareness of Online learning among the higher secondary school (Aided and Government) students in terms of their Type of School

Table 11

The above table reveals the Mean, Standard Deviation and 't' value for the Type of school groups of Aided and Government.

Sl.No.	Group	Mean	S.D	N	't' value	Levelof Significance
1.	Aided	48.51	8.17	83		
2.	Government	47.17	5.5	84	1.24	NotSignificant
	df=165					

INTERPRETATION

Since the calculated 't' value 1.24 is smaller than the table value 1.96 at 0.05% level of significant with df=165.

There is significant difference between Aided and Government student's in using Online.

RESULT

The null hypothesis is accepted.

HYPOTHESIS: 7

There is Significant mean difference in the mean scores of Awareness of Online learning among the higher secondary school (Mathematics and Computer Science) students in terms of their Type of Subject

Table 12

The above table reveals the Mean, Standard Deviation and 't' value for the Type of Subject groups of Mathematics and Computer Science

Sl.No.	Group	Mean	S.D	N	't' value	Levelof Significance
1.	Mathematics	50.07	7.85	81	0.61	Not Significant
2.	Computer science	49.36	7.05	83		

df=162

INTERPRETATION

Since the calculated 't' value 0.61 is smaller than the table value 1.96 at 0.05% level of significant with df=162.

There is significant difference between Mathematics and Computer Science student's in using Online.

RESULT:

The null hypothesis is accepted.

HYPOTHESIS: 8

There is Significant mean difference in the mean scores of Awareness of Online learning among the higher secondary school (Computer Science and Vocational) students in terms of their Type of Subject

Table 13

The above table reveals the Mean, Standard Deviation and 't' value for the Type of Subject groups of Computer Science and Vocational.

Sl.No.	Group	Mean	S.D	N	't' value	Levelof Significance
1.	vocational	49.92	7.71	86	0.13	Not significant
2.	Mathematics	50.07	7.81	81		

df=165

INTERPRETATION

Since the calculated 't' value 0.13 is smaller than the table value 1.96 at 0.05% level of significant with df=165.

There is significant difference between Vocational and Mathematics student's in using Online.

RESULT

The null hypothesis is accepted.

CONCLUSION

Thus the scores obtained higher secondary school students were put into differential analysis to determined and interpret the type of stay. The findings, recommendations and suggestions that are brought by the study are enlisted in a detailed manner in the upcoming chapter.

Chapter-V

Summary of Findings and Conclution

INRODUCTION

Cook et al. (2005), investigated whether the inclusion of improved student learning through Online. The study used a randomized, controlled, crossover trial, in which each collegiate student took four modules, two with the awareness of Online and two without. The order of modules was randomly assigned. School student performance was statistically higher on tests taken immediately after completion of modules that included awareness in self-assessment. After completion of those without such cause an effect that the authors attributed to the stimulation of reflection. This effect, on which all the School students performed having awareness of online learning.

According to Internet World Statistics, the use of communication technology is also growing rapidly in School and universities. The assumptions about the Internet are that it benefits the School students tremendously and learning appears to be a rich field that is just beginning to be discovered. Lack of information creates a negative impact on our lives, particularly on the educated segment of the society.

The Online is one of the most important mass media in the world as it has changed the world in many ways. Students are the most important group in society because they are envisaged to build society in the future, especially the female student who has a tremendous effect both on society and home.

Online users which are socially engaged and have greater social awareness, will tend to know more about the privacy debate, privacy policies, privacy risks associated with Internet, legal implications of privacy invasions and identity thefts.

Thus, these users would have formed a stronger awareness about privacy and the importance of privacy in social life. The greater the citizenship engagement and social awareness of an individual, the greater importance that individual would place on privacy as a societal value. Therefore, we would expect that the individual's privacy concerns would be higher as well.

As technology has created change in all aspects of society, it is also changing our expectations of what students must learn in order to function in the new world. Students will have to learn to navigate through large amounts of information to analyze and make decisions and to master new knowledge domains in an increasingly technology society. They will need to be lifelong learners, collaborating with others in accomplishing complex tasks and effectively using different systems for representing and communicating knowledge to others. A shift from teacher-centered instruction to learner-centered instruction is needed to enable students to acquire the new 21st century knowledge and skills.

NEED AND SIGNIFICANCE OF THE STUDY

The study wills more light into the advancement using among the Online teaching and learning in education an among the Higher secondary school students. The investigation here made is *"A Study On The Awareness Of Online Learning Among Higher Secondary Students"*. The outcome of the study is therefore expected to stimulate and to improve online learning among the higher secondary school students. The variables which have been found to have using of online to use in Educational and in other field.

STATEMENT OF THE PROBLEM

The important on the internet using, particularly students of a Nation can be over emphasized. However, we cannot lose sight of the fact that using internet in any teaching situation of the students, the teachers, the curriculum and the learning environments. These are the four pivots. It is on the basis of this that the study constructed and tested as to find the *"A Study on the Awareness of Online Learning among Higher Secondary Students"*. This providing an explanation of higher secondary school students on using the online.

OBJECTIVES OF THE STUDY

1. To identify Awareness of online learning among the higher secondary school students.
2. To find out the extent of possible using online students at higher secondary level.
3. To find out the difference between the mean scores Awareness of online learning among the Higher secondary school students on the basis of their Locality.
4. To find out the significant difference if any between the different group of demographic variables such as Standard Doing, Sex, Type of school, Type of subject in Awareness of online learning among the higher secondary level.

FINDINGS OF THE STUDY

1. There is Significant mean difference in the mean scores of Awareness of Online learning among the higher secondary school (Male and Female)students in terms of their Gender.
2. There is Significant mean difference in the mean scores of Awareness of Online learning among the higher secondary school (XI and XII)students in terms of their standard doing.
3. There is no Significant mean difference in the mean scores of Awareness of Online learning among the higher secondary school (Rural and Urban) students in terms of their Locality.
4. There is no Significant mean difference in the mean scores of Awareness of Online learning among the higher secondary school (Government and Private) students in terms of their Type of School.

5. There is no Significant mean difference in the mean scores of Awareness of Online learning among the higher secondary school (Private and Aided) students in terms of their Type of School.
6. There is Significant mean difference in the mean scores of Awareness of Online learning among the higher secondary school (Aided and Government) students in terms of their Type of School.
7. There is Significant mean difference in the mean scores of Awareness of Online learning among the higher secondary school (Mathematics and Computer Science) students in terms of their Type of Subject.
8. There is Significant mean difference in the mean scores of Awareness of Online learning among the higher secondary school (Computer Science and Vocational) students in terms of their Type of Subject.
9. There is Significant mean difference in the mean scores of Awareness of Online learning among the higher secondary school (Vocational and Mathematics) students in terms of their Type of Subject.

SUGGESTIONS FOR FURTHER RESEARCH

1. Research studies may be conducted to identify usage of Online experienced by the students studying in usage Higher Education, Post Graduate levels.
2. Studies may be conducted on usage of Online Higher secondary students.
3. Comparative studies may be taken up between the Under Graduate and post Graduate School College students in more than are district.
4. Studies may be conducted in school to identify the awareness of online on school Teachers at primary, secondary, higher secondary levels of education.
5. Research studies may be conducted to improve the awareness of online on Student studying B.Ed. colleges located.

6. Comparative studies may be taken up between Colleges and Higher Secondary School level.

RECOMMENDATION OF THE STUDY

1. Teacher must use other method such as demonstration activity based method of teaching.
2. Teacher should always conduct the class test often and often to identify the comprehensive level of the students.
3. Teacher should always prefer simple and effective illustration to discuss about the concept that is present in computer science.
4. Teacher should conduct computer lab, Symposium for the students to discuss about the concept in improving the computer science knowledge and skill.

CONCLUSION

The present investigation has yield a lot of interesting finding. These findings are results are not the end of the problem but just a beginning of the search for innovation the present study has investigated the *"A Study on the Awareness of Online Learning among Higher Secondary Students"*. It is found that the higher secondary student have favorable awareness of online by applying these result the quality of awareness of online learning improvement.

REFERENCE

1. Aaron, s. & Bartlett, J. (2003).Using action research to determine technology effectiveness in secondary and postsecondary setting. In proceedings of society for Information Technology and Teacher Education, 2003(1),661-666.
2. Anderson, C. L. & Petch-Hogan, B. (2000). The impact of technology use in special education field experience on pre-service teachers perceived technology expertise. Journal of special Education Technology.
3. Clark, A. (1997). Being There: Putting Brain, Body, and World Together Again. Cambridge, MA: MIT Press.
4. Cuban, L. (2001). Oversold and underused: Computers in the classroom. Cambridge, MA: Harvard University Press.

5. Ditzhazy, H. E. R., &Pool sup, S. (2002, spring). Successful integration of technology into the classroom. The Delta kappa Gamma Bulletin, 68(3), 10-14.

6. Fullan, M. (2001). The meaning of education change (3rded). New York: Teachers College Press.

7. Hannanfin, M. J., & Hill, J. R. (2002). Epistemology and the design of learning environments. In R. Reiser (Ed.), Trends and issues in instructional design and technology (pp. 70-82).Upper Saddle River, NJ: Merrill/Prentice-Hall.

8. Feng Wang and Thomas C. Reeves 63 Jonassen, D., Peck, K., & Wilson, B. (1999). Teaching with technology: A constructivist perspective. Upper saddle River, NJ: Prentice Hall.

9. Kelly, A. E. (2003). Design-based research: An emerging Paradigm for educational inquiry. Education Researcher, 32(1), 3-4.

10. Legemann, E, C. (2000). An elusive science: The troubling history of education: From blackboard to web. Thousand Oaks, CA: Corwin Press.

11. Landoni, M, & Diaz, P. (2003). E-education: Design and evaluation for teaching and learning. Journal of Digital information, 3(4). Available online at http://jodi.ecs. Soton.ac.uk/Articles/v03/i04/editorial.

12. Mandinach, E. B., & Cline, H. F. (2000). It won't happen soon: Practical, Curricular, and methodological problem in implementing technology-based constructivist approaches in classrooms. In S. P. Lajoie(Ed), Computers as cognitive tools. No more walls (pp. 377-395). Mahwah, NJ: Lawrence Erlbaum Associates. Means, B. (Ed.). (1994). Technology and education reform. San Francisco: Jossey-Bass.

13. Means, B., & Olsen, K. (1994).The link between technology and authentic learning. Educational Leadership, 51(7), 15-18.

14. National Center for Education Statistics. (2002) . Internet access in U.S. public School and classroom: 1994-2001. Washington, Dc: U.S. Department of Education.

15. Neal, E. (1998). Does using technology in instruction enhance learning Or The artless state of comparative research. The Technology Source. Available online at http:// ts.mivu.org

16. Office of Technology Assessment, U. S. Congress. (1995). Teachers and technology: Making the connection to aware. Washington, DC: U. S. Government Printing Office. Oswald, D. F. (2003).A conversation with Michael Molenda. Education Technology, 43(2), 59-63.

17. Papert, S. (1993). The Children's machine: Rethinking School in the age of the computer. New York: Basic Books.

18. Perlman, L. J. (1992). School's out: Hyper learning, the new technology York: William Morrow.

JOURNALS

19. Brown, J. S., Collins, A., & Duguid, P. (1989).Situated cognition and the culture of learning. Education Researcher, 18(1), 32-41.

20. Dede, C. (2000). Emerging influence of information technology on school curriculum Studies, 32(2), 281-303.

21. Dillon, A., & Gabbard, R. B. (1998). Hypermedia as an educational technology: A review of the empirical literature on learner comprehension, control and style. Review of Education Research, 68(3), 322-349.

22. Ertmer, P. A. (1999). Addressing first and second-order barriers to change: Strategies for technology integration. Education Technology Research and Development, 47(4), 47-61.

23. Hudgins, B. (2001). Leveraging handheld technology in the classroom. T.H.E. Journal, 29(5), 4

24. Nisan-Nelson, P. D. (2001). Technology integration: A case of professional development. Journal of Technology Awareness and teacher Education, 9(1), 83-103.

25. Noble, D. D. (1991).The Classroom arsenal: Military research, information technology and public education. New York: Falmer Press.

26. Noble, D. F. (2001). Digital diploma mills: The automation of higher education. New York: Monthly Review Press.

27. Norman, D. A. (1990).The design of everyday things. New York: Doubleday. Norum, K., Grabinger, R. S., & Duffield, J. A. (1999). Healing the universe is an inside job: Teachers views on integrating technology. Journal of Technology and Teacher Education, 7(3), 187-203.

DISSERTATIONS

28. Regunathan A G (1998), "Problems Based by the students in Awareness of Education Technology", M.Phil. Dissertation, Alagappa University.

29. Sundhara Pandian (2009), "A study on the Awareness of Technology education among the Degree holders", M.Phil., Dissertation, Bharathidasan University.

ENCYCLOPEDIA AND DICTIONARIES

30. Bausch, M. E., Mittler, J. E., Hasselbring, T. S. & Cross, D. P. (2005). "Encyclopedia of Education Technology", Anmol Publications Pvt. Ltd., New Delhi.

31. Crawford, C. M. & Martin, S. S. (2001). "Encyclopedia of Education Recent Technology". Anmol Publications Pvt. Ltd., New Delhi.

32. Destefano, L., Shriner, J. G., & Lloyd, C. A. (2010). "Dictionary of Education". Mohit Publication, New Delhi.

33. Meloy, L. L., Deville, C., &Frisbie, D. A. (2002). Encyclopedia of Technology Education

34. Norman J. M. & Collins, B. C. (2007). "Encyclopedia of Research methods in Education". Anmol Publications Pvt. Ltd., New Delhi.

35. Winn, W. (1989). Encyclopedic Dictionary of Education, Rajat publication, New Delhi.

2. Effect of Sound and Light Equipments in Eradicating Errors in Pronunciation

Chapter I

Introduction

Education began in the earliest prehistory, as adults trained the young in the knowledge and skills deemed necessary in their society. In pre-literate societies this was achieved orally and through imitation. Story-telling passed knowledge, values, and skills from one generation to the next. As cultures began to extend their knowledge beyond skills that could be readily learned through imitation, formal education developed. Schools existed in Egypt at the time of the Middle Kingdom. Matteo Ricci (left) and Xu Guangqi (right) in the Chinese edition of *Euclid's Elements* published in 1607Plato founded the Academy in Athens, the first institution of higher learning in Europe.[5] The city of Alexandria in Egypt, founded in 330 BCE, became the successor to Athens as the intellectual cradle of Ancient Greece. There, mathematician Euclid and anatomist Herophilus constructed the great Library of Alexandria and translated the Hebrew Bible into Greek. European civilizations suffered a collapse of literacy and organization following the fall of Rome in AD 476.

In China, Confucius (551-479 BCE), of the State of Lu, was the country's most influential ancient philosopher, whose educational outlook continues to influence the societies of China and neighbours like Korea, Japan and Vietnam. Confucius gathered disciples and searched in vain for a ruler who would adopt his ideals for good governance, but his Analects were written down by followers and have continued to influence education in East Asia into the modern era.

After the Fall of Rome, the Catholic Church became the sole preserver of literate scholarship in Western Europe. The church established cathedral schools in the Early Middle Ages as centers of advanced education. Some of these ultimately evolved into medieval universities and forebears of many of Europe's modern universities. During the High Middle Ages, Chartres Cathedral operated the famous and influential Chartres Cathedral School. The medieval universities of Western Christendom were well-integrated across all of Western Europe, encouraged freedom of inquiry, and produced a great variety of fine scholars and natural philosophers, including Thomas Aquinas of the University of Naples; Robert Grosseteste of the University of Oxford, an early expositor of a systematic method of scientific experimentation; and Saint Albert the Great, a pioneer of biological field research. The University of Bologne is considered the oldest continually operating university.

Mathematics flourished under the Islamic caliphate established across the Middle East, extending from the Iberian Peninsula in the west to the Indus in the east and to the Almoravid Dynasty and Mali Empire in the south.

The Renaissance in Europe ushered in a new age of scientific and intellectual inquiry and appreciation of ancient Greek and Roman civilizations. Around 1450, Johannes Gutenberg developed a printing press, which allowed works of literature to spread more quickly. The European Age of Empires saw European ideas of education in philosophy, religion, arts and sciences spread out across the globe. Missionaries and scholars also brought back new ideas from other civilizations- as with the Jesuit China missions who played a significant role in the transmission of knowledge, science, and culture between China and Europe, translating works from Europe like Euclid's Elements for Chinese scholars and the thoughts of Confucius for

European audiences. The Enlightenment saw the emergence of a more secular educational outlook in Europe.

In most countries today full-time education, whether at school or otherwise, is compulsory for all children up to a certain age. Due to this the proliferation of compulsory education, combined with population growth, UNESCO has calculated that in the next 30 years more people will receive formal education than in all of human history thus far.

Learning to pronounce written words means learning the intricate relations between a language's writing system and its speech sounds. When children learn to read and write in primary school they face such a learning task, as do students when mastering the writing system, the speech sounds, and the vocabulary of a language different from their mother tongue. Learning to pronounce words can also be modelled on Training. The latter, rather than simulating learning to pronounce written words in humans is the topic of the present study. In contrast with humans, machines can be modelled (i.e., realised, set up) in such specific ways that the pronunciation of written words is modelled on these machines. For instance, a machine can be set up to accommodate a data base of representations of word-pronunciation knowledge, without having learned any of those representations by itself: it is hardwired in memory by the system's designer. In fact, the hardwiring of word-pronunciation knowledge is common practice in the development of speech synthesizers (Allen, Hunnicutt, and Klatt 1987; Daelemans 1987). A major part of language-engineering work on word-pronunciation applications has been based on mainstream linguistic theories which consider only the modelling of word-pronunciation knowledge to be of scientific interest. The American linguist Noam Chomsky can be seen as the principal promoter of this tradition. His work on syntax (Chomsky, 1957), and later work on phonology (Chomsky and Halle, 1968) has influenced linguistics deeply and across the board from the 1950s onwards.

Despite the influential arguments of Chomskyan linguistics against the existence of a generic learning method capable of language learning, the possibility of the existence of such a method has been conjectured and investigated within the area of linguistic structuralism (Robins, 1997). The field of linguistic structuralism has appeared and reappeared under the names of descriptive, quantitative, statistical, or corpus-based linguistics from the 1930s onwards (Robins, 1997). Thus, two contrasting views exist on the learnability of word pronunciations by a generic learning method: the Chomskyan view on the one hand, and the linguistic-structuralist view on the other hand. To gain a better understanding of the gap between the two views to language learning, Section 1.2 introduces inductive language learning as our interpretation of the linguistic structuralist view, and sketches the historical line of research in linguistics both in favour of and against a generic method for language learning

Tamil is a vehicle for Mother Tongue communication. In order to meet the demands of modern society, Tamil teachers need to pay more attention to the development of learners' competence and focus on a more effective and successful method. However traditional approaches to Tamil language teaching still dominate Thai classrooms. Language teachers should not focus on reciting but should teach from their own understanding of language learning and help learners gain more competence with confidence. This study is a collaborative action research investigation to develop pronunciation training and communicative competence for Thai students studying Tamil in Thailand. This study investigated pronunciation training and language learning strategies, how they influenced the learning behaviour of Thai students studying Tamil and improved their speaking confidence. The purpose of the training was to improve students' pronunciation and spoken intelligibility. It drew upon data collected in pronunciation training in one school in Thailand using language learning strategies and evaluated improvement after being trained in developing speaking confidence. The project contained two cycles, the first of which was to train five teachers using pronunciation training and language learning strategies. We evaluated their improvement in correct speech and in developing speaking confidence. In the second cycle, these teachers in turn taught a group of four students each and similar improvements were observed. The action phases showed the implications of the importance of pronunciation training in the Thai context and the usefulness of dictionary usage to help learners to improve their competence and to have more confidence to speak Tamil. The project resulted in a change of policy by the school to include pronunciation teaching and to allocate Tamil classes to teachers who understood that process. The pronunciation learning strategies in this study and those of other researcher's xii were presented to formulate strategies as a contribution for teachers to include teaching pronunciation in their classroom instruction.

Need and Significance of the Study:

Tamil people and students are not able to pronounce their mother tongue in proper way. Therefore this study will help the Tamil students to identify and understand the proper pronunciation.

Scope of the Study

Extensive and intensive studies in Tamil pronunciation are highly effective for present situation of usage Tamil language. Therefore this study will help the students to understand the errors in pronunciation and rectify in by proper usage. Therefore this study has been taken by using the assistance of technology.

Statement of the problem

The Problem of the present research is as follows *"A Study on Effect of Sound and Light Equipments in Eradicating Errors in Pronunciation Among IXth Standard Students. "*.

Operational definition of Key Terms Cased

STUDY

Study skills or *study strategies* are approaches applied to learning. They are generally critical to success in school,[1] considered essential for acquiring good grades, and useful for learning throughout one's life. Respicius Rwehumbiza in his book "Understanding Examination Techniques and Effective study Strategies" in 2013 asserted that, most students fail in examinations simply because they lack study skills and/or examination taking techniques.

Study skills are an array of skills which tackle the process of organizing and taking in new information, retaining information, or dealing with assessments. They include mnemonics, which aid the retention of lists of information; effective reading; concentration techniques;[2] and efficient note taking.

While often left up to the student and their support network, study skills are increasingly taught in high school and at the university level. A number of books and websites are available, from works on specific techniques such as Tony Buzan's books on mind-mapping, to general guides to successful study such as those by Stella Cottrell and Understanding Examination Techniques and Effective study Strategies by Respicius Rwehumbiza.

More broadly, any skill which boosts a person's ability to study and pass exams can be termed a study skill, and this could include time management and motivational techniques.

Study skills are discrete techniques that can be learned, usually in a short time, and applied to all or most fields of study. They must therefore be distinguished from strategies that are specific to a particular field of study e.g. music or technology, and from abilities inherent in the student, such as aspects of intelligence or learning styles.

Sound Equipments

Listen and repeat

This will be the first and most common method of teaching sound specific pronunciation in Tamil. You say the target sound and have your students repeat it after you. If you are teaching a long word with multiple syllables, start with the final syllable of the word and have your class repeat it. Then add the penultimate syllable and say the two together having your class repeat after you. Work backwards in this manner until your students are able to pronounce the entire word correctly.

Isolation

When working on a specific sound, it may help your students to isolate that particular sound from any others. Instead of presenting a certain sound as part of a complete word in Tamil, you can simply pronounce the sound itself repeatedly. When you do, your students can say it along with you repeatedly, focusing on the small nuances in the correct pronunciation and also engraining the sound pattern into their minds. This is especially helpful when you have several students struggling with a specific sound delineation.

Minimal pairs

Minimal pairs are a great way to focus pronunciation on just one sound. If you are not familiar with linguistics, a minimal pair is two words that vary in only one sound. For example, *rat* and *rate* are minimal pairs because only the vowel sound differs between the two words. Additional minimal pairs are *pin* and *pen*, *dim* and *dime*, and *bat* and *pat*. You can use minimal pairs to help your students with their pronunciation by focusing on one particular sound. In addition to the pronunciation benefits, your students will also expand their vocabularies when you teach minimal pairs.

Record and replay

At times, your students may think they are using correct pronunciation when in fact they are saying something quite different. By using a device to record what your students are actually saying, you have empirical data to play back for each person. Encourage him to listen to what he actually said rather than what he thinks he said. You may also want him to compare a recording of a native speaker against his recording of himself. In this way, your students will have a more objective understanding of their true pronunciation and be able to take steps to correct it.

Use a mirror

Giving your students a chance to view their own physical movements while they are working on their pronunciation can be of great value. You can always encourage your students to look at your mouth and face as you pronounce certain sounds, but they will also benefit from seeing what movements *they* are making as they speak. Sometimes, becoming aware of the physical movements involved in pronunciation is all your students will need to correct pronunciation issues of which they are unaware.

Phonetics

When your students are facing a pronunciation challenge, it could be that **Tamil spelling** is adding to the mystery of the spoken word. Instead of spelling new vocabulary out on the white board, try using phonetic symbols to represent the sounds (rather than the alphabet to represent the spelling). If you were to use phonetic symbols, the word seat would be written /si:t/ and eat would be written /i:t/. You can find a list of the phonetic symbols on several websites or in introductory linguistics books. Once you teach your students the *International Phonetic Alphabet*, you can use those symbols any time you introduce new vocabulary to your students.

Show a vowel diagram

If you are using phonetic symbols to help you teach vowel pronunciation, a diagram of where each Tamil vowel sound is produced can be eye opening for your students. Print copies to distribute in class or show your students where they can find this diagram online. When students know which area of the mouth in which they should be making their sounds, they may have an easier time distinguishing between similar sounds because they are produced in different areas of the mouth.

Sing

Surprisingly enough, singing can be a good way for your ESL students to practice their vowel pronunciation. Because **singing** requires a person to maintain vowel sounds over more than just a moment, it can give your students a chance to focus in on the target sound and adjust what sound she is making.

Tongue twisters

Though tongue twisters are probably more popular for practicing consonant pronunciation, they are still a valuable resource for vowel practice. Not only are they a challenge to your students' pronunciation abilities, they add an element of fun to the classroom that can help your students relax and therefore free them to be more daring in their attempts at Tamil. See our 'Top 20 Tongue Twisters' classroom poster.

Target language specific sounds

Some pronunciation patterns are found consistently in students with the same native language. Being aware of these patterns is helpful in addressing problems your students may not even know they have. You can find practice exercises to target specific pronunciation patterns, or you can write your own to target the specific needs of your class. Either way, making students aware of pronunciation patterns of speakers of their native language can be the biggest help in eliminating the mispronunciations.

Light Equipments

Model the way you would like the words to be pronounced. When you teach your lesson do not fall into the trap of speaking colloquially. If you are teaching TAMIL is a mother tongue for instance, and you come from a part of your country that has a pronounced accent, the accent may detract from your students' ability to learn correct pronunciation. By using only standard pronunciation, your students will better learn to speak the target language correctly.

Project simple sounds and pronunciations on a screen with an overhead projector. Break up vocabulary words into syllables and have students view the syllables as they pronounce them. Ensure that syllables are pronounced according to the target language. Use visual representations of tongue and lip positions to practice a language's sounds. Transparencies for lessons are quite easily typed on a word processor then photocopied onto a plastic transparency for use with the overhead projector. Have basic pronunciations on the projector such as the ct, sh and ph sounds. The tendency of adult students is to pronounce words of a new language with the same pronunciation as their native language. Practice will overcome this tendency.

Teaching students the correct pronunciation of the vowels of the target language will help ensure they learn to speak the language like a native. Accents are largely governed by vowels. For instance, in Tamil a long a is pronounced "ay"; it is forward in the mouth and the bottom jaw closes a little with the tongue against the upper molars. In Italian, the pronounced "ah" with the tongue back and in the middle of the mouth; the lips don't move except for opening the mouth. Diagrams of the lip-mouth positions can be displayed on the projector.

Adorn the walls of the classroom with pictures. As each significant new word is learned students can make a small poster of it and place it with either a translation or a picture representation on the wall of the classroom. This visual aid has the advantage of always being there to refer to. In case a word is forgotten, a quick glance will bring it back to mind.

A proven way to teach pronunciation is to listen to songs in the target language. The teacher should provide a visual representation of each sound as it is being sung. At first the words will seem very fast but as the students learn them, they can sing along and learn the pronunciation effectively. The teacher can make a transparency of the lyrics of the song and display it prominently on the projector as students sing. A karaoke machine is ideal for this or the teacher can use a pointer on each word as it is sung.

Eradicating Errors in Pronunciation among IXth Standard Students Phonological Variety and Complexity of Indian Languages

In India, Tamil sounds are pronounced with a lot of influence of mother tongue one speaks. No two languages are the same. Each one is different from the other. The sound system, the structure and the vocabulary of Tamil do not have similarities in any of the various languages of India. Backgrounds of Rural Students.

The students from rural background have studied up to twelfth standard in Tamil medium schools. For them, Tamil is introduced only from class third onwards. For a child who is accustomed to the sounds of his mother tongue alone, the sounds of Tamil seem strange in the beginning. But, when he starts speaking, certain features of his mother tongue interfere in his Tamil speech. It continues up to his college level. Error Analysis Error analysis is a branch in applied linguistics. Scholars like S.P. Corder (1967:161) advocated the importance of error analysis in language learning process in Tamil language teaching.

Error Analysis

In language acquisition process stimulated major changes in teaching practice. The errors committed by second language learners help the teachers to frame a systematic way of teaching.

On Defining Error

Error is defined as a mistake or inaccuracy in speech, opinion or action. Kacher (1965:394) states, "it may contain deviations from the varieties of Tamil and those formations which are considered as mistakes or sub-standard formations". Slips and lapses are distinguished from errors. They are self-correlative. They are otherwise called 'mistakes'. They are unsystematic.

OBJECTIVES OF STUDY

The study has been designed with the following specific objectives:

1. To find out whether any significant is there difference in the attitude towards A Study on Effect of Sound and Light Equipments in Eradicating Errors in Pronunciation among IXth Standard Students between the Male and Female Students.
2. To find out whether any significant is there difference in the attitude towards Study on Effect of Sound and Light Equipments in Eradicating Errors in Pronunciation among IXth Standard Students between the Rural and Urban area Student.
3. To find out whether any significant is there difference in the attitude towards Study on Effect of Sound and Light Equipments in Eradicating Errors in Pronunciation among IXth Standard Students between Hosteller and Non- Hosteller Students.
4. To find out whether any significant is there in the attitude towards Study on Effect of Sound and Light Equipments in Eradicating Errors in Pronunciation Among IXth Standard Students between the Family types of Student.
5. To find out whether any significant in the attitude towards Study on Effect of Sound and Light Equipments in Eradicating Errors in Pronunciation Among IXth Standard Students between Parent Occupation types of students.
6. To find out whether any significant in the attitude towards Study on Effect of Sound and Light Equipments in Eradicating Errors in Pronunciation Among IXth Standard Students between Parent Yearly income.
7. To find out whether any significant in the gain ratio of IXth standard students, after the administration of the communicative approach with Pre- Test and Post- Test.

Hypotheses of the Study

The following hypothesis were formulated based on the variables related to the study

1. There is no significant difference in the attitude towards A Study

on the Effect of Sound and Light Equipments in Eradicating Errors in Pronunciation among IXth Standard Students between the Male and Female Students.

2. There is no significant difference in the attitude towards a Study on the Effect of Sound and Light Equipments in Eradicating Errors in Pronunciation among IXth Standard Students between the Rural and Urban area Student.
3. There is no significant difference in the attitude towards A Study on the Effect of Sound and Light Equipments in Eradicating Errors in Pronunciation among IXth Standard Students between Hosteller and Non- Hosteller Students.
4. There is no significant difference in the attitude towards A Study on the Effect of Sound and Light Equipments in Eradicating Errors in Pronunciation among IXth Standard Students between the Family types of Student.
5. There is no significant difference in the attitude towards A Study on the Effect of Sound and Light Equipments in Eradicating Errors in Pronunciation among IXth Standard Students between Parent Occupation types of students.
6. There is no significant difference in the attitude towards A Study on the Effect of Sound and Light Equipments in Eradicating Errors in Pronunciation among IXth Standard Students between Parent Yearly incomes.
7. There is significant difference in the gain ratio of IXth standard students, after the administration of the communicative approach with Pre- Test and Post- Test.

LIMITATIONS OF THE STUDY

The present study has the following limitations.

1. Data collection of this study is restricted to Sivagangai District only.
2. Sample size is confined to 40 Students Only.

3. Investigator conducted the study only related to the attitude Effect of Sound and Light Equipments in Eradicating Errors in Pronunciation among IXth Standard Students.
4. the study is confined only to the IXth Standard Students.

CONCLUSION

In this Chapter, we discuss about overview of the problem and its significance, its need and objectives of the study. The next chapter deals with the review of related literature.

Chapter II

Literature Review

Introduction

Empirical studies are essential to improving our understanding of the relationship between accent and pronunciation teaching. However, the study of pronunciation has been marginalized within the field of applied linguistics. As a result, teachers are often left to rely on their own intuitions with little direction. Although some instructors can successfully assist their students under these conditions, many others are reluctant to teach pronunciation.

In this article we call for more research to enhance our knowledge of the nature of foreign accents and their effects on communication. Research of this type has much to offer to teachers and students in terms of helping them to set learning goals, identifying appropriate pedagogical priorities for the classroom, and determining the most effective approaches to teaching. We discuss these possibilities within a framework in which mutual intelligibility is the primary consideration, although social ramifications of accent must also be taken into account.

We describe several problem areas and identify some misconceptions about pronunciation instruction. In addition, we make suggestions for future research that would address intelligibility, functional load, computer-assisted language learning, and the role of the listener. Finally, we recommend greater collaboration between researchers and practitioners, such that more classroom relevant research is undertaken.

DEFINITION:

According to Good, Barr and Scates, "The Competent physician must keep abreast of latest discoveries in the field of medicine. Obviously the careful student of education, the research worker and investigator should become familiar with location and use of sources of educational information".

According to W.R. Borg, "The literature in any field forms the foundation upon which all future work will be built. if we fail to build the foundation of knowledge provided by the review of literature our work is likely to be shallow and naive and will often duplicate work that has already been done better by someone else"

According to Charter V. Good, "The keys to the vast store house of published literature may open doors to sources of significant problems and explanatory hypotheses and provide helpful orientation for definition of the problem, background for selection of procedure, and comparative data for interpretation of results. In order to be creative and original, one must read extensively and critically as a stimulus to thinking."

Need of Review of Literature

The Review of literature is essential due to the following reasons.

1. One of the early steps in planning a research work is to review research done previously in the particular area of interest and relevant area quantitative and qualitative analysis of this research usually gives the worker an indication of the direction.
2. It is very essential for every investigator to be up-to-date in his information about the literature, related to his own problem already done by others. It is considered the most important prerequisite to actual planning and conduction the study.
3. It avoids the replication of the study of findings to take an advantage from similar or related literature as regards to

methodology, techniques of data collection, procedure adopted and conclusions drawn. He can justify his own endeavour in the field.

4. It provides as source of problem of study an analogy may be drawn for identifying and selecting his own problem of research. the researcher
5. Formulation his hypothesis on the basis of review of literature. It also provides the rationale for the study. The results and findings for the study can also be discussed at length.

The review of literature indicates the clear picture of the problem to be solved. The scholarship in the field can be developed by reviewing the literature of the field.

OBJECTIVES OF REVIEW OF LITERATURE

The review of literature serves the following purposes in conducting research work:

1. It provides theories, ideas, explanation or hypothesis which may prove useful in the formulation of a new problem.
2. It indicates whether the evidence already available solves the problem adequately without requiring further investigation. It avoids the replication.
3. It provides the sources for hypothesis. The researcher can formulate research hypothesis on the basis of available studies.
4. It suggests Method, Procedure, sources of data and statistical techniques appropriate to the solution of the problem.
5. It locates comparative data and findings useful in the interpretation and discussion of results. The conclusions drawn in the related studies may be used as the subject for the findings of the study.
6. It helps in developing experts and general scholarship of the investigator in the area investigated.
7. It contributes towards the accurate knowledge of the evidence or literature in one's area of activity is a good avenue towards making oneself. This knowledge is an assert ever after wards,

whether one is employed in an institution of higher learning or a research organization.

PURPOSE OF THE REVIEW OF LITERATURE

Review of the related literature besides, to allow the researcher to acquaint himself with current knowledge in the field or area in which he or she is going to conduct his or her research, serves the following specific purposes.

1. The review of related literature enables the researcher to define the limits of his field. It helps the researcher to delimit and define his problem. The knowledge of related literature brings the researcher up to data on the work which others have done and them to state the objectives clearly and concisely
2. By reviewing the related literature the researchers can avoid unfruitful and useless problem areas. He can select those areas in which positive findings are likely to result and his endeavours would be likely to add to the knowledge in a meaningful way
3. Through the review of related literature the researcher can avoid unintentional duplication of well established findings. It is no use of replicate a study when the stability and valididty of its result have been clearly established.
4. The review of related literature gives the researcher an understanding of research methodology which refers to the way the study is to be conducted. It help the researcher to know about the tools and instruments which proved to be useful and promising the previous studies. The advantage of the related literature is also to provide insight into statistical methods through which validity of results is to be established.
5. The final and important specific reason for reviewing the related literature i to know about the recommendations of previous researcher for farer research which they have listed in their studies.

STUDIES CONDUCTED IN INDIA

K.Valarmathi(2011) in their article “Language teaching in India” the position of Tamil in Tamilnadu gaining more and more impetus,

Because India themselves felt the need of Tamil language for variety of purpose such as education, business and administration hence the teaching in pronunciation nominally. But is order to teach a language more effectively, and towards the goal of proficient. It is necessary for prospective teachers to be conversant with the theories, approaches and methods of teaching i.e., What should be taught. The attitude that second and foreign language teachers had, towards teaching methods and classroom techniques varied, when the teacher centered lecturing approaches give way to the more of them.

V. Meenakshi(2010) in his article "Improve spoken Tamil Pronunciation" Good Tamil speaking skills are required in every aspect of our life. We all know that English the language that unities of the world, as it is the language known to maximum number of individuals around the globe. Today it we want a decent job, ir desure respect society; everything circles to your speaking skills.

V. Sekar(2009) in his article "Developing Spoken Tamil in Tamilnadu Students" Tamil Language is a window that open to the outside world. As a language teacher, have been working on many projects to develop the skills among the Tamil Students the skills among the students practice pronunciation in Tamil.

R. Rajaram,(2009) says that a group of speakers may share the same inter-language and that there would be mutual intelligibility among such speakers of the same inter-language. Selinker, (1972:214) goes on to say 'the set of utterances for most learners a second language is not identical to the hypothesized corresponding set of utterances which would have been produced by a native speaker of a target language had he attempted to express the same meaning as the learner.

K. Balamurali (2008)argue against Selinker's view that inter-language is a language somewhere between the first and the second language with structural features from both. They argue that inter-language is 'an intermediate system characterized by features resulting from language learning strategies'. They emphasise that inter-language is an unstable language.

V. Shankar(2007) argues that inter-language is the inter-nalised result of a learner's creative attempts to produce second language. It is evidence of a learner's cognitive strategies and hypotheses and it is variable. Larsen-Freeman and Long, (1991:60) argue that the learner's inter-language is systematic, that is, it is rule-governed and all learners pass through a stage of developing an inter-language.

STUDIES CONDUCTED IN ABROAD

Shapira, (1978) describes fossilisation as 'non-learning' while Selinker and Lamendella, (1979) describe it as 'stabilisation'. Selinker and Lamendella go on to say that it is a permanent cessation of LI learning before the learner has attained TL norms at all levels of linguistic structure and in all discourse domains in spite of the learner's positive ability, opportunity and motivation to learn and acculturate into target society (Selinker and Lamendella, 1978:187).

Selinker, (1986) also refers to fossilization as the process whereby the learner creates a cessation of inter-language learning, thus stopping the inter-language from developing, it is hypothesized, in a permanent way....The argument is that no adult can hope to ever speak a second language in such a way that she or he is indistinguishable from native speakers of that language (Selinker, 1996).

Furthermore, Lowther, (1983:127) says fossilization as presented in much of the literature, is understood to be the inability of a person to attain native-like ability in the target language. According to Ellis, (1985:48) fossilization structures can be realized as errors or as correct target language forms. If, by the fossilization it occurs that the learner has reached a stage of development in which feature 'x 'in his inter-language has assumed the same form as in the target language, then fossilization of the correct form will occur. He goes on to say, that if, however, the learner has reached a stage in which feature 'y', still does not have the same form as the target language, the fossilization will manifest an error.

Vigil and Oller, (1976: 282) say, "we will extend the notion of fossilization to any case where grammatical rules, construed in the broadest sense, become relatively permanently incorporated into a psychologically real grammar....". They go on to say that, it is not only the fossilization of so- called 'errors' that must be explained, but also the fossilization of correct forms that conform to the target language norms.

Hyltenstam, (1988:68) says fossilization ...according to observations ... is a process that may occur in the second language acquisition context as opposed to first language acquisition. He goes on to say that it covers features of the second language learners inter-language that deviate from the native speaker norm and are not developing any further, or deviant features which- although conditions. Thus the learner has stopped learning or has reverted to earlier.

Tarone, (1994:1715) says, a central characteristic of any inter-language is that it fossilizes—that is, it ceases to develop at some point short of full identity with the target language. Han, (1998: 50), says fossilisation involves those cognitive processes, or underlying mechanisms that produce permanently stabilized interlanguage (IL). He goes on to say that fossilisation involves those stabilized inter-language forms that remain in learner speech or writing over time, no matter what the input or what the learner does.

CONCLUSION

The review gave lot of insight to the investigator in selecting the research problem and suitable methodology. The research gap was also identified on the basis of the review. The methodology adopted by the researcher in this study in this study was discussed in the following Chapters.

Chapter III

Methodology

Introduction

Method is a style of conducting a research work which is determined by the value of the problem. Webster defined "Methodology" as "The Science of the method or arrangement". The research design is the plan, structure and strategy of answer to research questions and to control the variance. So in this context, this explains design of the study, population, size of the sample and how they are subjected as variables, the source and techniques of gathering data and statistical techniques and so on.

STATEMENT OF THE PROBLEM

To find out the *"A Study on Effect of Sound and Light Equipments in Eradicating Errors in Pronunciation Among IXth Standard Students "*.

OBJECTIVES OF STUDY

The study has been designed with the following specific objectives:

1. To find out whether any significant is there difference in the attitude towards A Study on Effect of Sound and Light

Equipments in Eradicating Errors in Pronunciation among IXth Standard Students between the Male and Female Students.

2. To find out whether any significant is there difference in the attitude towards Study on Effect of Sound and Light Equipments in Eradicating Errors in Pronunciation among IXth Standard Students between the Rural and Urban area Student.

3. To find out whether any significant is there difference in the attitude towards Study on Effect of Sound and Light Equipments in Eradicating Errors in Pronunciation among IXth Standard Students between Hosteller and Non- Hosteller Students.

4. To find out whether any significant is there in the attitude towards Study on Effect of Sound and Light Equipments in Eradicating Errors in Pronunciation Among IXth Standard Students between the Family types of Student.

5. To find out whether any significant in the attitude towards Study on Effect of Sound and Light Equipments in Eradicating Errors in Pronunciation Among IXth Standard Students between Parent Occupation types of students.

6. To find out whether any significant in the attitude towards Study on Effect of Sound and Light Equipments in Eradicating Errors in Pronunciation Among IXth Standard Students between Parent Yearly income.

7. To find out whether any significant in the gain ratio of IXth standard students, after the administration of the communicative approach with Pre- Test and Post- Test.

Hypotheses of the Study

The following hypotheses were formulated based on the variables related to the study

1. There is no significant difference in the attitude towards A Study on the Effect of Sound and Light Equipments in Eradicating Errors in Pronunciation among IXth Standard Students between the Male and Female Students.

2. There is no significant difference in the attitude towards a Study

on the Effect of Sound and Light Equipments in Eradicating Errors in Pronunciation among IXth Standard Students between the Rural and Urban area Student.

3. There is no significant difference in the attitude towards A Study on the Effect of Sound and Light Equipments in Eradicating Errors in Pronunciation among IXth Standard Students between Hosteller and Non- Hosteller Students.
4. There is no significant difference in the attitude towards A Study on the Effect of Sound and Light Equipments in Eradicating Errors in Pronunciation among IXth Standard Students between the Family types of Student.
5. There is no significant difference in the attitude towards A Study on the Effect of Sound and Light Equipments in Eradicating Errors in Pronunciation among IXth Standard Students between Parent Occupation types of students.
6. There is no significant difference in the attitude towards A Study on the Effect of Sound and Light Equipments in Eradicating Errors in Pronunciation among IXth Standard Students between Parent Yearly incomes.
7. There is significant difference in the gain ratio of IXth standard students, after the administration of the communicative approach with Pre- Test and Post- Test.

LIMITATIONS OF THE STUDY

The present study has the following limitations.

5. Data collection of this study is restricted to Sivagangai District only.
6. Sample size is confined to 40 Students Only.
7. Investigator conducted the study only related to the attitude Effect of Sound and Light Equipments in Eradicating Errors in Pronunciation among IXth Standard Students.
8. the study is confined only to the IXth Standard Students.

PLAN AND PROCEDURE

The method of this study is experimental research. The investigator has taken the IXth standard students for the experiment by using Sound and Light Equipment. The data is taken and analyzed quantitatively to find the effectiveness of teaching methods.

DEVELOPMENT OF TOOL

A writing package was developed to conduct the experiment. It was organized on the techniques of communicative approach to develop certain Tamil Pronunciation grammar among IX Standard School Students. It consisted of communicative exercise relegated to identity the Sentence, Tamil Sounds and Speech which part is working to promote communicative approach in Tamil pronunciation. The Sound and Light Equipment model in the writing package was based on the 8 steps Viz., Introduction, presentation, practice, production and evaluation. The Instructional material in the writing package was taught to the students of class IX for four weeks.

With the preparation of the writing package the objective, to design a training programme and to develop a strategy to improve communicative approach in developing certain Tamil Pronunciation among IX standard students has been realized.

STAGES OF DEVELOPMENT

The investigator has followed the four stages mentioned below.

1. Preparation
2. Approaches to show Sound and Light Equipment Practical Exercise.
3. Preliminary try outs
4. Testing

Preparation

The preparation stage goes through the following five steps.

I. Selection of the topic

1. Give training to the Student in Tamil pronunciation skill.

2. Developing specific out lines of conten to be communication
3. Writing Objectives in behavioral terms
4. Preparing a criterion test.

Step 1:

Selection of the topic:

As the investigator is a specialist in Tamil Pronunciation teaching and possessing a post graduate degree in Tamil language he has selected topic of Tamil Pronunciation Language Teaching.

The research has selected the topic Tamil Pronunciation from the IX standard Tamil text books prescribed b the Tamilnadu text book society.

The length of the topic is neither too long nor too short, but could be completed within time limit assigned for this purpose.

Step 2:

The Investigator has selected the student learning in IXth standard with age group 14 years.

The investigator had chosen the students from different localities both from rural and urban areas.

The investigator has planned to know about the abilities skills interest, Knowledge and achievement of the learners through evaluation of students cumulative records and test papers. An interview was conducted with a group of school teachers handling IX standard classes to know more about them.

Step 3:

The topic Tamil Pronunciation is analyzed and the various concepts presented in the text book were again referred. The investigator referred many books and the content material is Further classified into concepts and teaching points.

Step 4:

Writing objectives in Behavioral terms:

After fixing the extent of the content material and preparation of teaching points for the topic Tamil Pronunciation. The investigator had developed the objectives of the lesson in behavioral term.

Step 5:

Preparation of Criterion Test:

There criterion test was developed with the view to be used as pretest as well as post test. This Test converged whole of the portion covered in the communicative approach and many type questions alone were used. All the test items were written in such away as to reflect the terminal behavior of the learner. The items were properly worded and content. The replication of the Text book test items was avoided. The main purpose of this criterion test is to measure the instructional and the first prepared question paper consisted to 50 items.

VALIDATION OF THE DEVELOPMENT TOOLS

CONTENT VALIDITY

The prepared question paper is presented to two educational experts in the field of Tamil Pronunciation Skill tested for appropriateness of vocabulary and accuracy of content user. Modification was done based on their comments.

Try-Out

The question with the following items:

Paper with 50 marks identify the sentence, fill in the blanks, Answer the following question, Fill in the blanks, Match the following Text, Optional types questions,

Descriptive question, True or False Question, Short answer questions in Tamil pronunciation question. The investigator purpose full selected 40 IX standard candidates from St. Mary's Higher Secondary School Rajakembiram, Manamadurai, Sivagnagai District. There criterion test question paper was administered to 40 students after giving the necessary ascending order on the basis of total score. High and Low groups wer formed by converting the top most student respectively. The difficulty index and discriminative index were calculated for each and every item included in the question paper.

Difficulty Leve is $\frac{RU+RC}{T}$ x 100

Discriminative Index $= \frac{RU-RC}{1/2T}$ x 100

RU- Number of students responded the items correctly in upper groups.

RL- Number of students responded the items correctly in Lower Groups

T- Total Number of Student included in the terms analysis.

The questions with the difficulty level 40-60 with discrimination index above 0.2 were selected for the final question papers.

Reliability

The scores of odd and even items were computed independent for each respondent the spearson's product moment correlation coefficient (r) was computer, and it was the reliability co - efficient for half of the criterion test question paper.

The reliability co-efficient for the whole question paper was obtained by using spearman Brown formula,

$$R = \frac{2r}{1+r}$$

Hence the reliability co-efficient for the Whole question paper,

$$R = \frac{2x(0.73)}{1+0.73} = 0.84$$

From the 'r' value it is clear that the prepared criterion test question paper was a reliable one.

TESTING

A method to determine a student's ability to complete certain tasks or demonstrate mastery of a skill or knowledge of content. Some types would be multiple choice tests, or a weekly spelling test. While it is commonly used interchangeably with assessment, or even evaluation, it can be distinguished by the fact that a test is one form of an assessment.

Assessment: The process of gathering information to monitor progress and make educational decisions if necessary. As noted in my definition of test, an assessment may include a test, but also includes methods such as observations, interviews, behavior monitoring, etc.

Evaluation: Procedures used to determine whether the subject (i.e. student) meets preset criteria, such as qualifying for special education services. This uses assessment (remember that an assessment may be a test) to make a determination of qualification in accordance with a predetermined criteria.

Measurement, beyond its general definition, refers to the set of procedures and the principles for how to use the procedures in educational tests and assessments. Some of the basic principles of measurement in educational evaluations would be raw scores, percentile ranks, derived scores, standard scores, etc.

TREATMENT

Learning through communicative language teaching:

After the administration of the pre - test the learners was made seated comfortable. Then she was introduced to the complete the sentence of Tamil Pronunciation fifty main teaching questins method was involved in treatment the questino will be presented to the learner till be achieves mastery in a question Method, he is presented with the next teaching main question method. But incase, he gives wrong response, the remedial question-1 will be presented to the learner.

When the response of the learner is correct, in remedial question-1 a new teaching Method is presented with feedback. If the response is wrong, the second remedial question is presented again and again till the learner gets the correct response with an appropriate feedback.

Administration of Post-Test

After completion of the question method, 5 minutes interval was given. After the post test was administered to them. The pre - test and post - test question papers are the same. The response of the students was again collected. The test is a self - paced one in which each pupil tool his own time to complete the test. the other calculation comparison of their performance in pre-test and post test were done properly.

Statistical Techniques Used

In this study statistical techniques are used in Gain ratio and percentage analysis.

$$\text{Gain ratio} \quad \frac{\text{Post-test Mark - Pre-Test Mark}}{\text{Maximum Mark - Pre- Test Mark}} \text{X100}$$

Gain Means acquire as profiles as the result of changed conditions(oxford 1990's) Ration Means the quantitative relations between two similar magnitudes determined by the number of times one conditions the other integrally(or) fractionally oxford 1990's.

SCORING PROCEDURE

The answer scripts for the conducted achievements tests were collected and scored. Based on the scoring it was decided to give one mark as weight age for each correct answer. Thus a maximum 50 marks could be given to learner who responded all the eight items correctly.

DATA GATHERING DEVICES

The pre test and post test scores on the communicative approach based achievement test and Tamil Language inventory were the data gathering devices for both the experimental groups in the experimental study. At the end of the training programme, a post test was administered to measure the competencies of the students in this written Tamil for both the experimental groups. The responses of IX standard students were manipulated by providing variations in adopting the process of leaving. A logical association between Training strategy an observed respondent effects was attempted.

SCORING OF DATA

The score obtained by the students in the Tamil pronunciation based achievement test was taken as the pronunciation based achievement score of the student in written Tamil. The responses given by the students in the Tamil languages usage inventory were converted into numerical scored. The total score obtained by the student was considered as the ability to use Pronunciation based achievement test score and the score on the Tamil language usage inventory was taken as the performance of the students in written Tamil.

Analysis of Data

The difference between pre- test and post-test of both the groups of students were analysed. The analysis revealed that there was improvement between the pre-test and the post-test scores of both the groups. But comparatively a larger difference was found in all the pronunciation approach between pre-test and post-test scores of the students who were exposed to the treatment under communicative approach. The differences were tested by applying Gain ration Level.

Conclusion

The Methodology of the study is given in third chapter. The Chapter IV deals with analysis and interpretation of data.

Chapter-IV

Analysis and Interpretation of Data

INTRODUCATION:

Analysis of data means studying the tabulated material in order to determine inherent factor or meaning. It involved breaking down existing complex factor into simpler parts and putting the parts together in new arrangement for purpose of interpretation. The analyzed data is given below in the table form and interpretation is also given.

DATA ANALYSIS:

Research Hypothesis - I

There is effectiveness in every individual after the administration of the Error eradicating Tamil pronunciation.

Hypothesis-I

There is no significance difference between the pre-test and post - test of the IX Standard who have learnt Error eradicating Tamil Pronunciation.

Table 1: Mastery Level Of Over All Population

Mastery Level	No. of. Student	Percentage(%)
M1(90-100)%	1	2.5
MII(80-89)%	2	17.5
MIII(70-79)%	23	57.5
MIV(60-69)%	12	30
MV(50-59)%	2	5

1. Among the whole population

   1 student have scored above 90% Mastery level1

   2 student have gained above 80% Mastery Level 2

   23 student have gained above 80% Mastery Level 3

   12 student have gained above 80% Mastery Level 4

   2 student have gained above 80% Mastery Level 5
2. Hence the research hypothesis there is effectiveness is accepted
3. The hypothesis there is no difference between the pretest and post-test of the IX standard students who have learnt Tamil Pronunciation in developing certain Tamil language is rejected.

Hypothesis-2

There is no difference between the IXth standard rural and Urban students in their gain ratio after learning through communicative approaches in certain Tamil Pronunciation.

Table 2 Gain Ratio of Individual Learners(Rural)

No	Pre-Test Score	Post- Test Score	Gain Score	Gain Ratio
1	35	40	5	33
2	32	43	11	61
3	32	43	11	61
4	36	39	3	21
5	38	40	2	16
6	35	40	5	33
7	36	45	9	64
8	32	42	10	55
9	35	37	2	13
10	33	39	6	35
11	36	43	7	50
12	37	45	8	61
13	27	40	13	56
14	34	42	8	50
15	29	32	3	14
16	33	46	13	76

Table 3: Gain Ratio of Individual Learners- Urban

No.	Pre-TestScore	Post-TestScore	Gain Score	Gain Ratio
1	35	44	9	60
2	34	43	9	56
3	33	39	6	35
4	36	38	2	14
5	35	41	6	40
6	29	43	14	66
7	36	44	8	57
8	34	40	6	37
9	31	41	10	52
10	37	42	5	38
11	38	40	2	16
12	39	40	1	9
13	39	43	4	36
14	39	41	2	18
15	40	44	4	40
16	35	39	4	26
17	35	41	6	40
18	35	44	9	60
19	32	43	11	61
20	32	43	11	61
21	36	42	6	42
22	46	48	2	50
23	41	44	3	33
24	37	43	5	38

Table 4: Mastery Level of IXth standard based on Locality

Mastery Level	Rural Frequency	Urban Percentage	Frequency	Percentage
MI(70-79)	1	2.5	0	0
MII(60-69)%	4	10	5	12.5
MIII(50-59)%	4	10	4	10
MIV(40-49)%	0	0	4	10
MV(30-39)%	3	7.5	6	15
MVI(20-29)	1	2.5	1	2.5
MVII(10-19)	3	7.5	3	4.5
MVIII(0-9)	0	0	1	2.5

From the table it is clear the 4(10) % rural students and 4(10) % urban students have attained master level III. There is a no difference in percentage of urban students when compared to rural students. Hence it was inferred that the urban have attained high Master level when compared to rural students.

At the Mastery Level II, four rural (10) % Student and five urban students (12.5) % have gain scored (60-69) % there is a difference in percentage of Urban students when compared to rural students. Hence It was inferred that, the urban have attained high Mastery level when compared to rural students.

Two rural students (10)% and one urban student(2.5)% have attained the Mastery Level VIII. There is a difference percentage of urban students when compared to rural students. Hence it was inferred that, the rural students have attained high mastery level when compared to urban students.

At mastery Level VII, three rural students (7.5) % and three urban students (4.5)% have attained gain scored (10-19)%. There is a difference in percentage of rural students when compared to urban students. Hence it was inferred that, the rural students have attained high Mastery level when compared to urban students.

Since there is difference in the percentage at four Mastery levels. The hypothesis there is no difference between the IXth standard Students with rural and urban in their gain ratio after learning through the Tamil pronunciation approach in developing pronunciation skill in Tamil is rejected.

CALCULATION OF GAIN RATIO OF THE LEARNERS OF GOVERNMENT AND PRIVATE EMPLOYED PARENTS

Hypothesis-3

There is no difference between the IXth standard students with Government and private employed parents in their gain ratio after learning through the Tamil pronunciation in developing certain Tamil Grammar.

Table 5. Gain Ratio of Learners (Government Employed Parents)

No	Pre-Test Score	Post- Test Score	Gain Score	Gain Ratio
1	35	40	5	33
2	35	44	9	60
3	34	43	9	56
4	32	43	11	61
5	33	39	6	35
6	32	43	11	61

7	29	32	3	14
8	37	43	5	38
9	41	44	3	33
10	33	46	13	76
11	46	48	2	50
12	36	42	6	42

Table 6. Gain Ratio of Individual Learners - Private Employed Parents

No	Pre-Test Score	Post- Test Score	Gain Score	Gain Ratio
1	40	44	5	50
2	35	39	9	60
3	35	37	9	60
4	33	39	11	64
5	36	43	6	42
6	35	41	11	73
7	35	44	3	20
8	32	43	5	27
9	37	45	3	23
10	27	40	13	56
11	32	43	2	11
12	34	42	6	37
13	39	41	2	18
14	39	43	4	36
15	39	40	1	9
16	38	40	2	16
17	37	42	5	38
18	31	41	10	52
19	34	40	6	37
20	32	42	10	55
21	36	44	8	57
22	36	45	9	64
23	29	43	14	66
24	35	40	5	33
25	35	41	6	40
26	38	40	2	16
27	36	38	2	14
28	36	39	1	7

Mastery Level of IXth Standard Students with Parents Occupation

Mastery Level	Government Employed Parents		Private Employed Parents	
	Frequency	Percentage	Frequency	Percentage
MI(70-79)%	1	2.5	1	2.5
MII(60-69)%	3	7.5	5	12.5
MIII(50-59)%	2	5	5	12.5

MIV(40-49)%	1	2.5	2	5
MV(30-39)%	4	10	5	12.5
MVI(20-29)%	0	0	3	7.5
MVII(10-19)	1	2.5	4	10
MVIII(1-9)	0	0	2	5

From table it is clear that 1(2.5%) government employee and 1 (2.5 %) Private employed parents have achieved equal Mastery level 1. There is a no difference in percentage of private employed parents when compared to government employed parents. Hence it was inferred that, Private and government parents have attained equal mastery level.

At the mastery level II, 3(5%) government employee and 5 (12.5 %) Private employed parents have achieved more than 75% Mastery level 2. There is a difference in percentage of private employed parents when compared to government employed parents. Hence it was inferred that, Private employed parents have attained high mastery level than the government employed parents.

At the mastery level III, 2(7.5%) government employee and 5 (12.5 %) Private employed parents have achieved more than 50% Mastery level 3. There is a difference in percentage of private employed parents when compared to government employed parents. Hence it was inferred that, Private employed parents have attained high mastery level than the government employed parents.

At the mastery level IV, 1(2.5%) government employee and 2(5 %) Private employed parents have achieved more than 50% Mastery level 4. There is a difference in percentage of private employed parents when compared to government employed parents. Hence it was inferred that, Private employed parents have attained high mastery level than the government employed parents.

At the mastery level V, 4(10%) government employee and 5 (12.5 %) Private employed parents have achieved more than 25% Mastery level5. There is a difference in percentage of private employed parents when compared to government employed parents. Hence it was inferred that, Private employed parents have attained high mastery level than the government employed parents.

At the mastery level VI, 0(0%) government employee and 3 (7.5 %) Private employed parents have achieved more than 50% Mastery level 6. There is a difference in percentage of private employed parents when compared to government employed parents. Hence it was inferred that, Private employed parents have attained high mastery level than the government employed parents.

At the mastery level VII, 1(2.5%) government employee and 4 (10 %) Private employed parents have achieved more than 75% Mastery level 2. There is a difference in percentage of private employed parents when compared to government employed parents. Hence it was inferred that, Private employed parents have attained high mastery level than the government employed parents.

At the mastery level VIII, 0(0%) government employee and 2 (5 %) Private employed parents have achieved more than 50% Mastery level 2. There is a difference in percentage of private employed parents when compared to government employed parents. Hence it was inferred that, Private employed parents have attained high mastery level than the government employed parents.

Calculation of Gain Ratio of Parents Annual Income

Hypothesis -4

There is no difference in the gain ratio of IXth standard students after learning through the Tamil pronunciation approach in developing certain Tamil grammar terms of Parent Annual income.

Table 8: Gain Ratio of Individual Learners below 50000 annual income of Parents

No	Pre-Test Score	Post- Test Score	Gain Score	Gain Ratio
1	35	40	5	33
2	35	44	9	60
3	34	43	9	56
4	32	43	11	61
5	33	39	6	35
6	32	43	11	61
7	29	32	3	14
8	37	43	5	38
9	41	44	3	33
10	33	46	13	76
11	46	48	2	50
12	36	42	6	42
13	38	40	2	16
14	36	38	2	14
15	36	39	1	7

Table 9: Gain Ratio of Individual Learners Above 50000 annual income of Parents

No	Pre-Test Score	Post- Test Score	Gain Score	Gain Ratio
1	40	44	5	50
2	35	39	9	60
3	35	37	9	60
4	33	39	11	64
5	36	43	6	42
6	35	41	11	73
7	35	44	3	20
8	32	43	5	27
9	37	45	3	23
10	27	40	13	56
11	32	43	2	11
12	34	42	6	37
13	39	41	2	18
14	39	43	4	36
15	39	40	1	9
16	38	40	2	16
17	37	42	5	38
18	31	41	10	52
19	34	40	6	37
20	32	42	10	55
21	36	44	8	57
22	36	45	9	64
23	29	43	14	66
24	35	40	5	33
25	35	41	6	40

Table 10. Mastery Level of IXth Standard students with Parent Annual Income

MasteryLevel	Below 50000		Above 50000	
	Frequency	Percentage	Frequency	Percentage
MI(70-79)%	1	2.5	1	2.5
MII(60-69)%	3	7.5	5	12.5
MIII(50-59)%	2	5	4	10
MIV(40-49)%	1	2.5	2	5
MV(30-39)%	4	10	5	12.5
MVI(20-29)%	2	5	3	7.5
MVII(10-19)	1	2.5	3	7.5
MVIII(1-9)	0	0	2	5

From table it is clear that 1(2.5%) annual income below 50000 and 1 (2.5 %) annual income above 50000 have achieved equal Mastery level 1. there is a no difference in percentage of 50000 above parents when compared to below 5000 parents. Hence it was inferred that, annual income parents have attained equal mastery level.

At the mastery level II, 3(5%) annual income below 50000 and 5 (12.5 %) annual income above 50000 have achieved more than 75% Mastery level 2. there is a difference in percentage of Above 50000 when compared to below 50000 parents. Hence it was inferred that, above 50000 attained high mastery level than annual income.

At the mastery level III, 2(7.5 annual income below 50000 and 5 (12.5 %) annual income above 50000 have achieved more than 50% Mastery level 3. there is a difference in percentage of Above 50000 when compared to below 50000 parents. Hence it was inferred that, above 50000 attained high mastery level than annual income

At the mastery level IV, 1(2.5%) annual income below 50000 and 2(5 %) annual income above 50000 have achieved more than 50% Mastery level 4. there is a difference in percentage of Above 50000 when compared to below 50000 parents. Hence it was inferred that, above 50000 attained high mastery level than annual income

At the mastery level V, 4(10%) annual income below 50000 and 5 (12.5 %) annual income above 50000 have achieved more than 25% Mastery level5. there is a difference in percentage of Above 50000 when compared to below 50000 parents. Hence it was inferred that, above 50000 attained high mastery level than annual income

At the mastery level VI, 0 (0%) annual incomes below 50000 and 3 (7.5 %) annual income above 50000 have achieved more than 50% Mastery level 6. there is a difference in percentage of Above 50000 when compared to below 50000 parents. Hence it was inferred that, above 50000 attained high mastery level than annual income.

At the mastery level VII,1(2.5%) annual income below 50000 and 4 (10 %) annual income above 50000 have achieved more than 75% Mastery level 2. there is a difference in percentage of Above 50000 when compared to below 50000 parents. Hence it was inferred that above 50000 attained high mastery level than annual income.

At the mastery level VIII, 0 (0%) annual incomes below 50000 and 2 (5 %) annual income above 50000 have achieved more than 50% Mastery level 2. there is a difference in percentage of Above 50000 when compared to below 50000 parents. Hence it was inferred that, above 50000 attained high mastery level than annual income.

Calculation of Gain Ratio on Student Family Types

Hypothesis -5

There is no difference in the gain ratio of IXth standard students after learning through the Tamil pronunciation approach in developing certain Tamil grammar terms of Student Family types.

Table 11: Gain Ration of Individual Learners Single Parent Family

No	Pre-Test Score	Post- Test Score	Gain Score	Gain Ratio
1	35	40	5	33
2	35	44	9	60
3	34	43	9	56
4	32	43	11	61
5	33	39	6	35
6	32	43	11	61
7	29	32	3	14
8	37	43	5	38
9	41	44	3	33
10	33	46	13	76
11	46	48	2	50
12	36	42	6	42
13	38	40	2	16

Table 12: Gain Ration of Individual Learners Joint Family

No	Pre-Test Score	Post- Test Score	Gain Score	Gain Ratio
1	40	44	5	50
2	35	39	9	60
3	35	37	9	60
4	33	39	11	64
5	36	43	6	42
6	35	41	11	73
7	35	44	3	20
8	32	43	5	27
9	37	45	3	23
10	27	40	13	56
11	32	43	2	11
12	34	42	6	37
13	39	41	2	18
14	39	43	4	36
15	39	40	1	9

16	38	40	2	16
17	37	42	5	38
18	31	41	10	52
19	34	40	6	37
20	32	42	10	55
21	36	44	8	57
22	36	45	9	64
23	29	43	14	66
24	35	40	5	33
25	35	41	6	40
26	36	38	2	14
27	36	39	1	7

From table it is clear that 1(2.5%) Single Parent family and 1 (2.5 %) Joint family has achieved equal Mastery level 1. There is a no difference in percentage of Joint family when compared to Single parent family. Hence it was inferred that, both family have attained equal mastery level.

At the mastery level II, 3(5%) Single Parent family and 5 (12.5 %) Joint Family has achieved more than 75% Mastery level 2. There is a difference in percentage of Joint Family when compared to Single Parent Family. Hence it was inferred that, Single Parent have attained high mastery level than the Joint Family.

At the mastery level III, 2(7.5%) government employee and 5 (12.5 %) Single Parent Family has achieved more than 50% Mastery level 3. There is a difference in percentage of Joint Family when compared to Single Parent Family. Hence it was inferred that Single Parent has attained high mastery level than the Joint Family.

At the mastery level IV, 1(2.5%) government employee and 2(5%) Single Parent Family has achieved more than 50% Mastery level 4. There is a difference in percentage of Joint Family when compared to Single Parent Family. Hence it was inferred that, Single Parent have attained high mastery level than the Joint Family.

At the mastery level V, 4(10%) government employee and 5 (12.5 %) Single Parent Family has achieved more than 25% Mastery level5. There is a difference in percentage of Joint Family when compared to Single Parent Family. Hence it was inferred that, Single Parent have attained high mastery level than the Joint Family.

At the mastery level VI, 0(0%) government employee and 3 (7.5%) Single Parent Family achieved more than 50% Mastery level 6. There is a difference in percentage of Joint Family when compared to Single Parent Family. Hence it was inferred that, Single Parent have attained high mastery level than the Joint Family.

At the mastery level VII,1(2.5%) government employee and 4 (10 %) Single Parent Family has achieved more than 75% Mastery level 2. There is a difference in percentage of Joint Family when compared to Single Parent Family. Hence it was inferred that, Single Parent have attained high mastery level than the Joint Family.

At the mastery level VIII, 0(0%) government employee and 2 (5 %) Single Parent Family has achieved more than 50% Mastery level 2. There is a difference in percentage Joint Family when compared to Single Parent Family. Hence it was inferred that, Single Parent have attained high mastery level than the Joint Family.

Calculation of Gain Ratio On Hosteller and Non- Hosteller

Hypothesis -6

There is no difference in the gain ratio of IXth standard students after learning through the Tamil pronunciation approach in developing certain Tamil grammar terms of Hosteller and Non-Hosteller.

Table 13: Gain Ration of Individual Learners Hosteller

No	Pre-Test Score	Post- Test Score	Gain Score	Gain Ratio
1	35	40	5	33
2	35	44	9	60
3	34	43	9	56
4	32	43	11	61
5	33	39	6	35
6	32	43	11	61
7	29	32	3	14
8	37	43	5	38
9	41	44	3	33
10	33	46	13	76
11	46	48	2	50
12	36	42	6	42
13	38	40	2	16
14	35	40	5	33
15	35	41	6	40
16	36	38	2	14
17	36	39	1	7

Table 14: Gain Ration of Individual Learners Non-Hosteller

No	Pre-Test Score	Post- Test Score	Gain Score	Gain Ratio
1	40	44	5	50
2	35	39	9	60
3	35	37	9	60
4	33	39	11	64
5	36	43	6	42
6	35	41	11	73
7	35	44	3	20
8	32	43	5	27
9	37	45	3	23
10	27	40	13	56
11	32	43	2	11
12	34	42	6	37
13	39	41	2	18
14	39	43	4	36
15	39	40	1	9
16	38	40	2	16
17	37	42	5	38
18	31	41	10	52
19	34	40	6	37
20	32	42	10	55
21	36	44	8	57
22	36	45	9	64
23	29	43	14	66

From table it is clear that 1(2.5%) Hosteller and 1 (2.5 %) Non Hosteller has achieved equal Mastery level 1. There is a no difference in percentage of Hosteller when compared to non hosteller. Hence it was inferred that both have attained equal mastery level.

At the mastery level II, 3(5%) hosteller and 5 (12.5 %) non hosteller have achieved more than 75% Mastery level 2. there is a difference in percentage of non hosteller when compared to hosteller. Hence it was inferred that, non hosteller have attained high mastery level than the hostel students.

At the mastery level III, 2(7.5%) hosteller and 5 (12.5 %) Non Hosteller has achieved more than 50% Mastery level 3. There is a difference in percentage of non hosteller when compared to hosteller. Hence it was inferred that, Private employed parents have attained high mastery level than the government employed parents.

At the mastery level IV, 1(2.5%) hosteller and 2(5 %) Non Hosteller has achieved more than 50% Mastery level 4. There is a difference in percentage of non hosteller when compared to hosteller. Hence it was inferred that, Private employed parents have attained high mastery level than the government employed parents.

At the mastery level V, 4(10%) hosteller and 5 (12.5 %) Non Hosteller has achieved more than 25% Mastery level5. There is a difference in percentage of non hosteller when compared to hosteller. Hence it was inferred that, Private employed parents have attained high mastery level than the government employed parents.

At the mastery level VI, 0(0%) hosteller and 3 (7.5 %) Non Hosteller has achieved more than 50% Mastery level 6. There is a difference in percentage of non hosteller when compared to hosteller. Hence it was inferred that, Private employed parents have attained high mastery level than the government employed parents.

At the mastery level VII, 1(2.5%) hosteller and 4 (10 %) Non Hosteller has achieved more than 75% Mastery level 2. There is a difference in percentage of non hosteller when compared to hosteller. Hence it was inferred that, Private employed parents have attained high mastery level than the government employed parents.

At the mastery level VIII, 0(0%) hosteller and 2 (5 %) Non Hosteller has achieved more than 50% Mastery level 2. There is a difference in percentage of non hosteller when compared to hosteller. Hence it was inferred that, Private employed parents have attained high mastery level than the government employed parents.

Calculation of Gain Ration for Female and Male Learners

Hypothesis -7

There is no difference in the gain ratio of IXth standard students after learning through the Tamil pronunciation approach in developing certain Tamil grammar terms of Female and Male Learners.

Table 15: Gain Ration of Individual Learners Female

No	Pre-Test Score	Post- Test Score	Gain Score	Gain Ratio
1	35	40	5	33
2	35	44	9	60
3	34	43	9	56
4	32	43	11	61

5	33	39	6	35
6	32	43	11	61
7	29	32	3	14
8	37	43	5	38
9	41	44	3	33
10	33	46	13	76
11	46	48	2	50
12	36	42	6	42
13	38	40	2	16
14	35	40	5	33
15	35	41	6	40
16	36	38	2	14
17	36	39	1	7
18	29	43	14	66

Table 16: Gain Ration of Individual Learners Male

No	Pre-Test Score	Post- Test Score	Gain Score	Gain Ratio
1	40	44	5	50
2	35	39	9	60
3	35	37	9	60
4	33	39	11	64
5	36	43	6	42
6	35	41	11	73
7	35	44	3	20
8	32	43	5	27
9	37	45	3	23
10	27	40	13	56
11	32	43	2	11
12	34	42	6	37
13	39	41	2	18
14	39	43	4	36
15	39	40	1	9
16	38	40	2	16
17	37	42	5	38
18	31	41	10	52
19	34	40	6	37
20	32	42	10	55
21	36	44	8	57
22	36	45	9	64

Table 17. Mastery Level of IXth Standard students Female and Male Learners

Mastery Level	Male		Female	
	Frequency	Percentage	Frequency	Percentage
MI(70-79)%	1	2.5	1	2.5

MII(60-69)%	3	7.5	5	12.5
MIII(50-59)%	2	5	5	12.5
MIV(40-49)%	1	2.5	2	5
MV(30-39)%	4	10	5	12.5
MVI(20-29)%	0	0	3	7.5
MVII(10-19)	1	2.5	4	10
MVIII(1-9)	0	0	2	5

From table it is clear that 1(2.5%) Male student and 1 (2.5 %) Female students have achieved equal Mastery level 1. There is a no difference in percentage of male student when compared to female. Hence it was inferred that, both have attained equal mastery level.

At the mastery level II, 3(5%) Male student and 5 (12.5 %) Female students have achieved more than 75% Mastery level 2. There is a difference in percentage of male students when compared to female students. Hence it was inferred that, female students have attained high mastery level than the male students.

At the mastery level III, 2(7.5%) Male student and 5 (12.5 %) Female students have achieved more than 50% Mastery level 3. There is a difference in percentage of male students when compared to female students. Hence it was inferred that, female students have attained high mastery level than the male students.

At the mastery level IV, 1(2.5%) Male student and 2(5 %) Female students have achieved more than 50% Mastery level 4. There is a difference in percentage of male students when compared to female students. Hence it was inferred that, female students have attained high mastery level than the male students.

At the mastery level V, 4(10%) Male student and 5 (12.5 %) Female students have achieved more than 25% Mastery level5. There is a difference in percentage of male students when compared to female students. Hence it was inferred that, female students have attained high mastery level than the male students.

At the mastery level VI, 0(0%) Male student and 3 (7.5 %) Female students have achieved more than 50% Mastery level 6. There is a difference in percentage of male students when compared to female students. Hence it was inferred that, female students have attained high mastery level than the male students.

At the mastery level VII,1(2.5%) Male student and 4 (10 %) Female students have achieved more than 75% Mastery level 2. There is a difference in percentage of male students when compared to female students. Hence it was inferred that, female students have attained high mastery level than the male students.

At the mastery level VIII, 0(0%) Male student and 2 (5 %) Female students have achieved more than 50% Mastery level 2. There is a difference in percentage of male students when compared to female students. Hence it was inferred that, female students have attained high mastery level than the male students.

CONCLUSION

In this chapter various data collected from IX standard students have been analyzed and interpretations. The next chapter deals with summary of the findings and conclusion.

Chapter-V

Finding, Conclusions and Suggestions

INTRODUCTION:

After finalizing the calculation the investigator now moves on to the summarization of the research work undertaken. Summery is the most used part of research report because it guides not only research scholars but also educationists and people who are interested in that particular problem. The important finding of the present study is summarized below.

Problem Restated

To prepare A Study on Effect of Sound and Light Equipments in Eradicating Errors in Pronunciation in developing certain Tamil grammar for IX standard students and to test the effectiveness o f pronunciation approach methods. The pronunciation method has been prepared by following principles and steps in the development of pronunciation in Tamil. After the development of Pronunciation skill methods the individual tryout and small group tryout are completed in the schools of Rajakembiram and necessary modifications were done. This modified pronunciation methods were subjected to mass tryout.

The present investigation was basically designed as an experimental study with the view to ascertain the effectiveness of sound and light equipment using aides for pronunciation developing skill which included under the unit light for IX standard students under Tamilnadu State Board syllabus by the investigator.

Effectives of Tamil pronunciation was measured as gain score in terms of four mastery levels of students performance in the population variables such as nativity, Parents Occupation, Parent educational Qualification gender suitable hypotheses were formulated and verified for drawing the following inferences.

Need for the Study

Tamil people and students are not able to pronounce their mother tongue in proper way. Therefore this study will help the Tamil students to identify and understand the proper pronunciation.

Statement of the problem

The Problem of the present research is as follows *"A Study on Effect of Sound and Light Equipments in Eradicating Errors in Pronunciation Among IXth Standard Students. "*.

OBJECTIVES OF STUDY

The study has been designed with the following specific objectives:

1. To find out whether any significant is there difference in the attitude towards A Study on Effect of Sound and Light Equipments in Eradicating Errors in Pronunciation among IXth Standard Students between the Male and Female Students.
2. To find out whether any significant is there difference in the attitude towards Study on Effect of Sound and Light Equipments in Eradicating Errors in Pronunciation among IXth Standard Students between the Rural and Urban area Student.
3. To find out whether any significant is there difference in the attitude towards Study on Effect of Sound and Light Equipments in Eradicating Errors in Pronunciation among IXth Standard Students between Hosteller and Non- Hosteller Students.

4. To find out whether any significant is there in the attitude towards Study on Effect of Sound and Light Equipments in Eradicating Errors in Pronunciation Among IXth Standard Students between the Family types of Student.
5. To find out whether any significant in the attitude towards Study on Effect of Sound and Light Equipments in Eradicating Errors in Pronunciation Among IXth Standard Students between Parent Occupation types of students.
6. To find out whether any significant in the attitude towards Study on Effect of Sound and Light Equipments in Eradicating Errors in Pronunciation Among IXth Standard Students between Parent Yearly income.
7. To find out whether any significant in the gain ratio of IXth standard students, after the administration of the communicative approach with Pre- Test and Post- Test.

FINDING

The major finding of the present study is listed below.

1. Each and every individual has gained the mastery level (from 1% to 100%) after learning the Tamil Grammar. Hence the Tamil pronunciation approach by the investigator is effective and reliable one for the IX standard students for learning Tamil grammar.
2. The Tamil Pronunciation approach was effective in developing Tamil grammar, among the rural and urban pupils rending mastery I level achievement to the urban pupils.
3. The attainment of master level I performance through Tamil pronunciation approach found positively influenced by the adequacy of parent's occupation while the mastery at other levels, Viz II,III and VIII is found independent of parent occupation
4. The student who have Tamil pronunciation in their parents are found in an advantages position as compared to their methods in attaining 80% gain performance.
5. There is a difference improvement in communicative, which is an important aspect in Tamil grammar among IX standard

students who were taught through Tamil Pronunciation approach.

6. The students who were taught through Tamil pronunciation performed well in their ability to use Tamil grammar

Suggestions for Further Research

Following are a few areas of research related to the present investigation which deserve further exploration.

1. Development of Tamil grammar in pronunciation skill approach with the view to fulfill the demands of heterogeneous population of learners within a standard.
2. Survey of knowledge of school teachers regarding Tamil pronunciation approach and its preparation and availability of basic skills in educational institutions at various levels.
3. Assessment of Tamil pronunciation among the Tamil teachers at various educational levels.
4. Development of Tamil pronunciation approach prepared for the various levels such as primary, secondary and higher secondary.
5. Development of Tamil grammar pronunciation approach prepared for the various subjects in high schools and higher secondary schools.
6. Development of Tamil grammar approach prepared for different topics in Tamil language.
7. To develop learners Tamil grammar approach in spoken Tamil in social contexts.
8. To find out the difference between the traditional method and Tamil pronunciation teaching approach in developing Tamil grammar in Spoken Tamil.

Recommendation of the study

The following implication has been made by the investigator saved on the finding:

1. The fact that a minimum of 90% pupils have attained a minimum of 60% gain performance in learning the unit indicates that

learning through Tamil grammar pronunciation approach very effective and its can be encouraged among all the learners.

2. Attention should be given in Tamil grammar pronunciation language teaching of methods by giving illustrations from rural events.

3. The study has revealed the fact that spelling of learner's Tamil grammar needs and then providing instructions to the learners can help the learners maintain and increase their interest in learning Tamil grammar.

4 Expoourc tu the real language helps the students to be accurate, appropriate and pronunciation competent.

5. the study makes crystal clear that the Tamil pronunciation is more effective in developing the communicative language teaching in Tamil grammar among IX standard students.

6. To develop self instructional methods to improve students' performance in pronunciation skill.

7. To study suggests that the pre-service and in service teachers should be oriented towards the techniques of Tamil pronunciation approach.

8. The teacher should give more exercises and comprehension in learning Tamil grammar.

9. the teacher can use any media that supports the teaching of Tamil grammar pronunciation approach to increase their ability, understanding and motivating in learning grammar text not only from text book but also from any sources for example internet and magazines etc.

10. The teacher should be attractive and entertainment in Teaching Tamil grammar in order to make students not bored.

CONCLUSION

A Tamil pronunciation approach in certain Tamil grammar was developed, subjected to individual and group tryout and tested on the sample of 40 IX standard students and found to be an effective and valid material for IX standard students.

BIBLIOGRAPHY

1. Acom, E. M. (2007). Relationship between job factors and employee commitment in private primary schools in greater Kampala district. Unpublished masters (of Arts Educ. Mgt.) dissertation, Makerere University, Kampala, Uganda.
2. Adwete, O. M. (1990). Influence of teacher working conditions on pupil s achievement in primary schools of Jinja and Apac. Unpublished masters (of Arts Educ. Mgt.) dissertation, Makerere University, Kampala, Uganda.
3. Aiftinca, T. (2004) Professionalism, Ethics and Work-Based Learning; British Journal of Educational Studies, 44(2), 168-180
4. Amin, M. E. (2005). Social science research: conception, methodology and analysis. Kampala: Makerere University Printery. 109 Annual report of the education department (1936).
5. Bowman, B. (1989). Self reflection as an element of professionalism. Teachers college record Vol.90; No.3: pp444-450.
6. Boyer, T. (2002). Professions and Professionalization. Cambridge: Cambridge University Press
7. Creswell, J. W. (2003). Research design, qualitative, quantitative and mixed approach (2nd edition). London: Sage publications thousand Oaks,
8. Cheng, Y.C. (1993). Profiles of organizational culture and effective schools. In School effectiveness and school improvement 4, 2: 85 –110.
9. Choy, S., Chan, T., Hun, M. & Bann, T. (1993). America s Teachers: Profile of a Profession. Washington: U.S. Department of Education, National Center for Education Statistics (NCES 93–025).
10. Daulat, R. (1940). Teacher-parent co-operation in Kampala government Indian school. The bulletin of the Uganda education association, February.

11. Dubbledam, J. (1989). The primary school and the community in Mwanza district, Tanzania. Water-noordhoff publishers.

12. Emojong, J. A. (2008 February 23). Tororo to sack poor performing head teachers. Saturday Monitor p. 10.

13. Ejuu, H. (2005). Teachers self-esteem, sex, qualification and level of commitment to teaching. Unpublished masters (of Arts Educ. Mgt.) dissertation, Makerere University, Kampala, Uganda.

14. Enon, J.C. (1998). Educational research, statistics and measurement. Makerere University: Department of Distance Education. 110 Freidson, E. (1994) Professionalism Reborn. Chicago: Chicago University Press.

15. Gay, L. R. (1992). Educational research competencies for analysis and application, (5th ed.). Florida: Macmillan publishing company.

16. Genza, G. M. (2008). The role of administrators in catholic founded secondary schools in the development of students moral character. Unpublished masters (of Educ. Found.) dissertation, Makerere University, Kampala, Uganda.

17. Gonsalves, A. M. (1989). Fagothy s right and reason; Ethics in theory and practice (IXth ed.): Columbus. Merrill publishing company.

18. Government of Uganda, (2005). Ugandan District: Information handbook; expanded edition 2005-2006. Kampala: Fountain Publishers.

19. Howe, R. K. (1986). A conceptual basis for ethics in teacher education. Vol. XXXVII No.3 pp. 5-11

20. Hyland, T. (2002) Education: Theory, practice and performance in teaching: professionalism, intuition and jazz. University of Bolton Journal Articles.

21. Ilukena, A. (1999). Teacher professionalism in Namibia: What went wrong? A speech delivered by Mr. A. Ilukena at the Graduation Ceremony at Caprivi College of Education, 23 April 1999.

22. Joolideh, G. & Yeshodhara, D. (2009). Teacher professionalization and organizational commitment: Evidence from Malaysia. Retrieved February 26, 2007 from the worldwide website: http://chiron.valdosta.edu/whuitt 111 Kanter, A. (1974). Modern times? Work, professionalism and citizenship in teaching. London: Falmer Press.

23. Kamm, F. M. 1996. Morality, Mortality Vol. II: Rights, Duties, and Status. New York: Oxford University Press.

24. Kampala Archdiocesan document (2008). Terms and conditions of service for teachers and other staff members.

3. Effectiveness of Using Multimedia Technology

Chapter - I

Introduction

The imperative character of education for individual growth and social development is now accepted by everyone. Man is highly enterprising being. He is always on the lookout for inventing new innovations in all walks of life. Human like has improved tremendously as a result of the growth in science and technology. Education is a social institution that has also been influenced by technological development. The impact of changes is described as modernization.

Educational technology has great potential for improving the teaching-learning process. Educational technology is the development, application and evaluation of systems, techniques and also aids in the field of human learning. One of the important contributions of educational technology is individualized instruction, which enables is make use of self-instructional programs.

The teacher-centered and group centered approaches are inadequate since they hardly make any provision for individual difference of the learners, the premise is that, strictly speaking no two students in the class are alike and that there are many permutations and combinations of individuals different us.

Education in its general sense is a form of learning in which the knowledge, skills, values, beliefs and habits of a group of people are transferred from one generation to the next through storytelling, discussion, teaching, training, and or research. Education may also include informal transmission of such information from one human being to another. Education frequently takes place under the guidance of others, but learners may also educate themselves (autodidactic learning). Any experience that has a formative effect on the way one thinks, feels, or acts may be considered educational.

Education is commonly and formally divided into stages such as preschool, primary school, secondary school and then college, university or apprenticeship. The methodology of teaching is called pedagogy.

A right to education has been recognized by some governments. At the global level, Article 13 of the United Nations' 1966 International Covenant on Economic, Social and Cultural Rights recognizes the right of everyone to an education. Although education is compulsory in most places up to a certain age, attendance at school often isn't, and a minority of parents chooses home-schooling, sometimes with the assistance of modern electronic educational technology (also called e-learning). Education can take place in formal or informal settings.

Education began in the earliest prehistory, as adults trained the young in the knowledge and skills deemed necessary in their society. In pre-literate societies this was achieved orally and through imitation. Story-telling passed knowledge, values, and skills from one generation to the next. As cultures began to extend their knowledge beyond skills that could be readily learned through imitation, formal education developed. Schools existed in Egypt at the time of the Middle Kingdom.

Plato founded the Academy in Athens, the first institution of higher learning in Europe. The city of Alexandria in Egypt, founded in 330 BCE, became the successor to Athens as the intellectual cradle of Ancient Greece. There, mathematician Euclid and anatomist Herophilus constructed the great Library of Alexandria and translated the Hebrew Bible into Greek. European civilizations suffered a collapse of literacy and organization following the fall of Rome in AD 476.

In China, Confucius (551-479 BCE), of the State of Lu, was the country's most influential ancient philosopher, whose educational outlook continues to influence the societies of China and neighbors like Korea, Japan and Vietnam. Confucius gathered disciples and searched in vain for a ruler who would adopt his ideals for good governance, but his Analects were written down by followers and have continued to influence education in East Asia into the modern era.

After the Fall of Rome, the Catholic Church became the sole preserver of literate scholarship in Western Europe. The church established cathedral schools in the Early Middle Ages as centers of advanced education. Some of these ultimately evolved into medieval universities and forebears of many of Europe's modern universities. During the High Middle Ages, Chartres Cathedral operated the famous and influential Chartres Cathedral School. The medieval universities of Western Christendom were well-integrated across all of Western Europe, encouraged freedom of inquiry, and produced a great variety of fine scholars and natural philosophers, including Thomas Aquinas of the University of Naples; Robert Grosseteste of the University of Oxford, an early expositor of a systematic method of scientific experimentation; and Saint Albert the Great, a pioneer of biological field research. The University of Bologne is considered the oldest continually operating university.

Elsewhere during the Middle Ages, Islamic science and mathematics flourished under the Islamic caliphate established across the Middle East, extending from the Iberian Peninsula in the west to the Indus in the east and to the Almoravid Dynasty and Mali Empire in the south.

The Renaissance in Europe ushered in a new age of scientific and intellectual inquiry and appreciation of ancient Greek and Roman civilizations. Around 1450, Johannes Gutenberg developed a printing press, which allowed works of literature to spread more quickly. The European Age of Empires saw European ideas of education in philosophy, religion, arts and sciences spread out across the globe. Missionaries and scholars also brought back new ideas from other civilizations as with the Jesuit China missions who played a significant role in the transmission of knowledge, science, and culture between China and Europe, translating works from Europe like Euclid's Elements for Chinese scholars and the thoughts of Confucius for European audiences. The Enlightenment saw the emergence of a more secular educational outlook in Europe.

E-learning (or e-Learning) is the use of electronic educational technology in learning and teaching. Information and communication technology (ICT) in education, EdTech, learning technology, multimedia learning, technology-enhanced learning (TEL), computer-based instruction (CBI), computer managed instruction, computer-based training (CBT), computer-assisted instruction or computer-aided instruction (CAI), internet-based training (IBT), flexible learning, web-based training (WBT), online education, online learning, virtual education, virtual learning environments (VLE) (which are also called learning platforms), m-learning, and digital education. In usage, all of these terms appear in articles and reviews; the term "e-learning" is used frequently, but is variously and imprecisely defined and applied.

These alternative terms are all linguistically more restrictive than "educational technology" in that they refer to the use of modern tools, such as computers, digital technology, electronic media, networked digital devices and associated software and courseware with learning scenarios, worksheets and interactive exercises that facilitate learning. However, these alternative names individually emphasize a particular digitization approach, component or delivery method. Accordingly, each conflates to the broad domain of educational technology. For example, m-learning emphasizes mobility, but is otherwise indistinguishable in principle from educational technology.

Advantages of eLearning

There are many advantages to online and computer-based learning when compared to traditional face-to-face courses and lectures.

Advantages of online or computer-based learning

1. Class work can be scheduled around work and family
2. Reduces travel time and travel costs for off-campus students
3. Students may have the option to select learning materials that meets their level of knowledge and interest
4. Students can study anywhere they have access to a computer

and Internet connection

5. Self-paced learning modules allow students to work at their own pace
6. Flexibility to join discussions in the bulletin board threaded discussion areas at any hour, or visit with classmates and instructors remotely in chat rooms
7. Instructors and students both report eLearning fosters more interaction among students and instructors than in large lecture courses
8. E-Learning can accommodate different learning styles and facilitate learning through a variety of activities
9. Develops knowledge of the Internet and computers skills that will help learners throughout their lives and careers
10. Successfully completing online or computer-based courses builds self-knowledge and self-confidence and encourages students to take responsibility for their learning
11. Learners can test out of or skim over materials already mastered and concentrate efforts in mastering areas containing new information and/or skills

Meaning, Definition and Significance of the Environmental Pollution

(a) Meaning

Environmental Pollution refers to any change from natural conditions. It is usually man made. It causes various problems.

(b) Definition

Environmental Pollution is the introduction of contaminants into a natural environment that causes instability, disorder, harm or discomfort to the ecosystem i.e. physical systems or living organisms.

An **Ecosystem** is a biological system consisting of all the living organisms or biotic components in a particular area and the nonliving or abiotic component with which the organisms interact, such as air, mineral soil, water and sunlight.

(c) Significance of the Environmental Pollution

We have significance of the environmental pollution is,

1. Air Pollution
2. Water Pollution
3. Land Pollution
4. Noise Pollution

Type of Pollution

There are many types of pollution we have. Such as,

(a) Air Pollution

Air pollution means the presence of higher amounts of carbon dioxide and carbon monoxide in air. It causes bronchitis and tuberculosis. Air pollution comprises industrial pollution and vehicular pollution. Cement factories, leather tanneries and thermal stations cause industrial pollution. Automobiles cause vehicular pollution.

(b) Water Pollution

Water pollution is another danger. Industries producing paper, leather, soap, etc., Use a lot of water. This water is discharged along with chemicals. Fish is killed by this poisonous water. Animals and human beings are affected by this impure water. Crops are also affected.

(c) Land Pollution

Land pollution is the demolition of Earth's land surfaces often caused by human activities and their misuse of land resources. It occurs when waste is not disposed properly. Health hazard disposal of urban and industrial wastes, exploitation of minerals, and improper use of soil by inadequate agricultural practices are a few factors. Urbanization and industrialization are major causes of land pollution.

(d) Noise Pollution

Noise pollution is equally serious. Any poise should be below a certain level. But loud speakers, automobiles and factories cause heavy noise. People living near airports are affected by noise. Excessive noise causes nervousness, deafness, ulcer, irritability and many other problems.

(e) Thermal Pollution

Thermal pollution is the discharge of waste heat via energy dissipation into cooling water and subsequently into nearby waterways. The major sources of thermal pollution are fossil-fuel and nuclear electric-power generating facilities and, to a lesser degree, cooling operations associated with industrial manufacturing, such as steel foundries, other primary-metal manufacturers, and chemical and petrochemical producers.

(f) Pesticide Pollution

Pesticides are organic and inorganic chemicals originally invented and first used effectively to better the human environment by controlling undesirable life forms such as bacteria, pests, and foraging insects. Their effectiveness, however, has caused considerable pollution.

(g) Radiation Pollution

Radiation pollution is any form of ionizing or nonionizing radiation that results from human activities. The most well-known radiation results from the detonation of nuclear devices and the controlled release of energy by nuclear-power generating plants. Other sources of radiation include spent-fuel reprocessing plants, by-products of mining operations, and experimental research laboratories. Increased exposure to medical X rays and to radiation emissions from microwave ovens and other household appliances, although of considerably less magnitude, all constitute sources of environmental radiation.

Introduction to Multimedia

Multimedia is media and content that uses a combination of different content forms. The term can be used as a noun (a medium with multiple content forms) or as an adjective describing a medium as having multiple content forms. The term is used in contrast to media which use only rudimentary computer display such as text only, or traditional forms of printed or hand-produced material. Multimedia includes a combination of text, audio, still images, animation, video, or interactivity content forms.

Multimedia is usually recorded and played, displayed or accessed by information content processing devices, such as computerized and electronic devices, but can also be part of a live performance. *Multimedia* (as an adjective) also describes electronic media devices used to store and experience multimedia content. Multimedia is distinguished from mixed media in fine art; by including audio, for example, it has a broader scope. The term "rich media" is synonymous for interactive multimedia. Hypermedia can be considered one particular multimedia application.

Special Features of Multimedia

1. Technologically friendly so as to be downloaded and used in any computer either independently or in LAN situation.
2. Learner friendly for easy navigation.
3. Motivation the students
4. Focusing attention
5. Reducing verbalism
6. Inducing greater attention
7. Bring the world into the class room
8. Making abstract concept into concrete
9. Adding interest and involvement

Multimedia Package

Flash 8 certainly bears no resemblance to the first version of flash I worked on way back in 1997. Unlike its predecessor. Flash 8 is truly a solid program with rich features and a sophisticated interface.

Flash 8 now ships in two versions. Flash 8 Basic and Flash 8 Professional. The basic drawing and animation features in both programs are identical, as are the simple scripting capabilities. Flash 8 Basic is an ideal solution for those needing to produce interactive animation that is of simple to medium complexity. In fact, you can even embed video clips into Flash 8 Basic files, so even though the application is "basic" it still has many features you find in the professional version.

Flash 8 professional does all that Flash Basic does and much more. The Flash 8 Professional user may be a web developer, Programmer, Video user, experienced designer, or anyone else who likes to control the more complex elements of Flash design, like scripting. A Flash "power user" would look to the Professional version for the more advanced features it offers. New and intermediate users, whether in Flash Basic or professional version for the more advanced features it offers.

Flash 8 is a powerful application that can be used to create applications, Presentations, games and more. However, when you create a Standalone Applications and publish it is a Projector file; you cannot customize the player to make it appear as though you created a custom application. However, a company called North code (http://www.northcode.com) has developed an application known as SWF studio, which is now in its third iteration. SWF studio is a replacement for the Flash Projector, enabling you to create a standalone custom application. The application takes an SWF file and converts it to a projector, which you can customize with the various tabs present in the application. You can personalize the application by including an icon of your company logo in the title bar and displaying your company name, or for that matter, any other text that will fit in the title bar. You can download a trial version of the application at http://www.northcode.com.

New features in Flash MX enhance the approachability, creativity, and power of Flash. Designers who require a higher level of control and integration with industry-standard design tools now have an unparalleled creative application for creating media-rich content.

Powerful new features build on this creativity, giving application developers access to new capabilities that make Flash MX a robust and exciting application development environment. Developers can work with advanced scripting and debugging tools, built-in code reference, and predefined components to rapidly deploy rich Web applications.

For all flash users

The ability to save Flash MX documents in Flash 5 formats lets you upgrade now and still collaborate with designers who are working on Flash 5 projects.

Accessible content that can be seen and heard by persons with disabilities is now easy to develop, expanding the audience for Flash movies and applications.

Korean and Chinese language support reaches audiences in more of the world. Features like vertical text fields and Unicode support make it easy to create Asian-language content.

For the designer

Flash MX enhances creativity by providing designers with a higher level of control and expanded integration capabilities with a rich set of design tools. New features help designers quickly create a broad range of content. Instead of focusing on how Flash works, they can give more attention to their designs.

Timeline enhancements such as folders for organizing layers, improved pointer feedback, and the ability to resize, cut, and paste multiple frames make it easier to use the Timeline, helping you work faster and with less effort.

Enhanced editing of symbols in place makes document creation easier by letting designers work on symbols in the context of their movies. New controls above the Stage make it easier than ever to edit symbols in place.

Library improvements eliminate production bottlenecks by simplifying the creation and manipulation of library symbols. Moving symbols or folders between Flash documents or creating new library symbols is now as easy as dragging and dropping. The new Resolve Library Conflict dialog box simplifies adding library symbols to a document that has an existing library symbol with the same name.

Shared library assets improve Flash movie authoring by letting you share library assets with other Flash documents, either while authoring, or when a movie is played with the Flash Player. Shared runtime libraries help you create smaller files and easily make updates to multiple documents simultaneously by letting your document show library symbols and shared objects that are stored on an intranet or the Internet. Shared author-time libraries improve your work place by letting you track, update, and swap symbols in any Flash document available on your computer or network.

Workspace enhancements make the Flash MX workspace more manageable and easier to understand for new and veteran designers. The most commonly used features now appear in one context-sensitive

Property inspector, eliminating the need to access many other windows, panels, and dialog boxes Other frequently used features now appear in easily collapsible panels that dock and undock as necessary to conserve screen space. Designers can even save custom panel layouts to personalize their Flash workspace.

New starter templates included with Flash MX simplify the creation of new documents by eliminating many of the common tasks required to start a new document. You can also create your own templates from documents.

Color Mixer improvements make creating, editing, and using colors and gradients easier than ever.

Video support expands the creative possibilities for Flash movies by letting you import video clips in a variety of formats.

Pixel-level editing ads precision and polish to your work by letting you align objects with pixel-level precision in your Flash documents. Precisely place objects or points of objects where you want them to appear in your final movie.

The Break Apart feature makes it easy to make creative edits to individual text characters without having to convert the text to symbols, simplifying the creation of complex designs and animation.

The Distribute to Layers command quickly and automatically distributes any number of selected objects to their own layers.

Movie clip mask layers let you create animated masks by placing a movie clip on a mask layer. You can also use Action Script to create an animated mask with a movie clip.

Enhanced sound controls enhance the production quality of your movies by letting you synchronize movie events with the start or end of sound clips.

For the developer

The powerful Flash MX environment includes enhanced scripting and debugging tools, built-in code reference, and predefined components you can use to rapidly develop rich Web applications.

Enhanced Action Script gives you the ability to dynamically load JPEG and MP3 sound files at runtime, and lets you update your files at any time without having to republish your movie.

Anchor points enhance navigation in Flash movies by letting users use the Forward and Back buttons in their browsers to jump from anchor to anchor.

The improved Action Script editor makes it easier for new and veteran authors to access the full potential of Action Script.

Code hints speed content development of Action Script by automatically detecting what command the user is typing and offering hints to reveal the exact syntax of the command.

Flash components accelerate Web application development by providing reusable drag-and-drop interface elements for Flash content, such as list boxes, radio buttons, and scroll bars.

The improved debugger combines the debugging capabilities already in existence with an Action Script debugger by allowing you to set breakpoints and single-step through the code as it executes.

The object model integrates movie clips, buttons, and text fields into the Action Script object-oriented scripting language.

The event model makes Action Script event handling more powerful and easier to understand. The event model now allows for more sophisticated control over user events, such as mouse movement and keyboard input.

The Live Preview feature for components makes it possible to actively view changes in user interface components within the authoring environment.

Enhanced text support allows for detailed control using Action Script over every property of a text object, including its formatting, size, and layout.

The new drawing API enhances the object-oriented programming power of Action Script by offering a set of shape-drawing capabilities through the Movie Clip object, allowing for programmatic control over the Flash rendering engine.

Strict equality and switch statements allow for concise definition of flow control statements such as if, then, and else, further increasing Action Script support for ECMA-262. See the entries for these statements in the online Action Script Dictionary in the Help menu.

Conversion of String, Array, and XML objects to native objects increases performance by optimizing the Number, Boolean, Object, String, Array, and XML Action Script objects. Performance in the Flash Player is increased as much as 100 times. See the entries for these objects in the online Action Script Dictionary in the Help menu.

SWF Compression uses existing Z-lib compression code to improve download times for complex Flash content.

Macromedia Flash MX movies are graphics, text, animation, and applications for Web sites. They consist primarily of vector graphics, but they can also contain imported video, bitmap graphics, and sounds. Flash movies can incorporate interactivity to permit input from viewers, and you can create nonlinear movies that can interact with other Web applications. Web designers use Flash to create navigation controls, animated logos, long-form animations with synchronized sound and even complete, sensory-rich Web sites. Flash movies use compact vector graphics, so they download rapidly and scale to the viewer's screen size.

You've probably watched and interacted with Flash movies on many Web sites. Millions of Web users have received the Flash Player with their computers, browsers, or system software; others have downloaded it from the Macromedia Web site. The Flash Player resides on the local computer, where it plays back movies in browsers or as stand-alone applications. Viewing a Flash movie on the Flash Player is similar to viewing a DVD on a DVD player-the Flash Player is the device used to display the movies you create in the Flash authoring application.

Flash documents, which have the FLA filename extension, contain all the information required to develop, design, and test interactive content. Flash documents are not the movies the Flash Player displays. Instead, you publish your FLA documents as Flash movies, which have the SWF filename extension and contain only the information needed to display the movie.

Some people think **SWF** stands for "**Shockwave Flash File**." It actually means "**Small Web Format**." A nomenclature perfect for Flash movies, since Flash Player files tend to be smaller than animations generated from other applications.

Scope of the study

Environmental Pollution is prescribed in almost all boards of education at Higher Secondary Level, this study is primarily focused on the awareness of environmental pollution using multimedia package of higher secondary level students. Keeping this view in mind, the researcher has developed Computer Assisted Learning Package in Creating Environmental Awareness to the Learners at Higher Secondary Level Students.

This investigation is restricted to only is higher secondary first year student of Government Higher Secondary School, Karambakudi which is situated in an urban area of Pudukkottai district is constitute the sample.

This is parallel group study which measures the validate multimedia package on the achievement of higher secondary students in creating environment awareness using CAL method.

Statement of the Problem

Pollution is one of the important topics of environmental science. Now days most of the schools and colleges to follow traditional method, to teach important concepts. So that the student do not understand easily. If we are teaching the important topic like pollution through the multimedia package that should be effective by considering the above ideas the researcher selected research topic of the present study is *"Effectiveness of using Multimedia Technology in Creating Awareness on Environment Pollution among XI Standard Students"*.

Operational Definition of key terms used

Development

Development refers to the production of the multimedia which includes story board, video capture editing and final production.

Validation

Validation refers to the assessment of the multimedia in terms of certain identified parameters and establishment of its worthiness based on technical pedagogical and statistical validity.

Multimedia

Multimedia is media and content that uses a combination of different content forms. The term can be used as a noun (a medium with multiple content forms) or as an adjective describing a medium as having multiple content forms. The term is used in contrast to media which use only rudimentary computer display such as text only, or traditional forms of printed or hand-produced material. Multimedia includes a combination of text, audio, still images, animation, video, or interactivity content forms.

Eco System

An **ecosystem** is a biological system consisting of all the living organisms or biotic components in a particular area and the nonliving or abiotic component with which the organisms interact, such as air, mineral soil, water and sunlight

Environmental Pollution

Environmental Pollution refers to any change from natural conditions. It is usually man made. It causes various problems.

Environmental Pollution is the introduction of contaminants into a natural environment that causes instability, disorder, harm or discomfort to the ecosystem i.e. physical systems or living organisms.

Higher Secondary Level

Higher Secondary Level refers to students studying +1 level (XI Standard).

Existing System

There is no common system to provide all the essential information in a city. There is individual system for media telecasting, but they are not providing all the related information to the user. The existing System is not reached. So the peoples are suffered by various pollutions.

Proposed System

The proposed system is designed to overcome the entire problem, which are existed in the existing system. The user shares a common browser, so the entire user can share the information, use the proposed system. Any user of this proposed system can enter new information.

Objectives of the Study

The main objectives are,

1. To find out the awareness of Environment pollution among XI Students.
2. To find out the awareness level of students in understanding the multimedia package for Environmental Pollution in Pre-test of control group on the basis of Gender.
3. To find out the awareness level of students in understanding the multimedia package for Environmental Pollution in Pre-test of Experimental group on the basis of Gender.
4. To find out the awareness level of students in understanding the multimedia package for Environmental Pollution in Pre-test of control group boys and Pre-test of Experimental group boys.
5. To find out the awareness level of students in understanding the multimedia package for Environmental Pollution in Pre-test of control group girls and Pre-test of Experimental group girls.
6. To find out the awareness level of students in understanding the multimedia package for Environmental Pollution in Post-test of control group on the basis of Gender.
7. To find out the awareness level of students in understanding the multimedia package for Environmental Pollution in Post-test of Experimental group on the basis of Gender.
8. To find out the awareness level of students in understanding the multimedia package for Environmental Pollution in Post-test of control group boys and Post-test of Experimental group boys.
9. To find out the awareness level of students in understanding the multimedia package for Environmental Pollution in Post-test of control group girls and Post-test of Experimental group girls.

10. To find out the awareness level of students in understanding the multimedia package for Environmental Pollution in Pre-test of control group and Pre-test of Experimental group.
11. To find out the awareness level of students in understanding the multimedia package for Environmental Pollution in Post-test of control group and Post-test of Experimental group.
12. To find out the awareness level of students in understanding the multimedia package for Environmental Pollution in Pre-test of control group and Post-test of control group.
13. To find out the awareness level of students in understanding the multimedia package for Environmental Pollution in Pre-test of Experimental group and Post-test of Experimental group.

Hypotheses of the Study

1. There is no significant difference between mean score of Pre-test of control group on the basis of Gender in creating awareness on environmental pollution.
2. There is no significant difference between mean score of Pre-test of Experimental group on the basis of Gender in creating awareness on environmental pollution.
3. There is no significant difference between mean score of Pre-test of control group boys and Pre-test of Experimental group boys in creating awareness on environmental pollution.
4. There is no significant difference between mean score of Pre-test of control group girls and Pre-test of Experimental group girls in creating awareness on environmental pollution.
5. There is no significant difference between mean score of Post-test of control group on the basis of Gender in creating awareness on environmental pollution.
6. There is no significant difference between mean score of Post-test of Experimental group on the basis of Gender in creating awareness on environmental pollution.
7. There is no significant difference between mean score of Post-test of control group boys and Post-test of Experimental group boys in creating awareness on environmental pollution.

8. There is no significant difference between mean score of Post-test of control group girls and Post-test of Experimental group girls in creating awareness on environmental pollution.
9. There is no significant difference between mean score of Pre-test of control group and Pre-test of Experimental group in creating awareness on environmental pollution.
10. There is no significant difference between mean score of Post-test of control group and Post-test of Experimental group in creating awareness on environmental pollution.
11. There is no significant difference between mean score of Pre-test of control group and Post-test of control group in creating awareness on environmental pollution.
12. There is no significant difference between mean score of Pre-test of Experimental group and Post-test of Experimental group in creating awareness on environmental pollution.

Limitations of the Study

No research study can be done without certain limitations. Limitations are different types and it would be a good practice to mentions the limitation in the research design. So the present investigation has the following limitations.

1. Since the research is an Experimental study the number of students is 30 from Govt. Hr. Sec. School, Karambakudi.
2. Limited variables have been administered for the study.

Conclusion

Environment education has gained momentum all over the world. To make movement an observable reality in India. Schools, College and Universities should come forward and given environmental education its proper place in teaching, research as well as extension activities in all courses of study. It is only self-motivation and sense of duty in teachers themselves which can bring a grassroots change by bringing changes in knowledge, attitude skill and behavior of masses. Thus, in this chapter, an introduction about the environment and man-made pollution area of the study was given. The next chapter deals with the review of related studies.

Chapter - II

Review of Related Literature

Introduction

Research takes advantages of the knowledge which has accumulated in the pass as a result of constant human Endeavour. It can never be undertaken in isolation of the work that has already been done on the problems which are directly or indirectly related to a study proposed by a researcher.

Review of the related literature, besides allowing the researcher to acquaint himself with current knowledge in the field or area in which the research is being conducted, server the following purposes.

1. To avoid unfruitful and useless problem areas
2. To avoid an intestinal duplication of well established findings.
3. To understand the research methodology which refers to the way the study is to be conducted.
4. To know about the recommendations of previous researchers listed in their studies for further research
5. To know the vast knowledge of the topic of discussion

Research Studies analyzing in Environmental Pollution

There are many factors which affects our environment adversely e.g. over exploitation of resources, population, growth, industrialization , use of synthetic materials etc., Man has started overusing and exploiting the natural resources such as air, water, land, fuels, etc., which in turn cause the depletion or shortage of resources. Over exploitation of the natural resources like forest may result in shortage of fuel ,wood , changed climate, soil erosion , drought, siltation etc.,

The impact of the human activities on environment due to over population is pollution.

Pollution

Undesirable change in the physical, chemical or biological characteristics of air, land, water that affect human life adversely is called "pollution".

The major cause for pollution is enhanced pace of developmental activities and rapid urbanization. The increase in pollution in various environmental media has resulted in deterioration of air and water quality, higher noise levels, increase in vehicular emission etc.

Research Studies Conducted in India

Panda, Subash Chandear and Jayakrishna (2000) investigated the "Effect of Computer Assisted Learning in achieving higher cognitive skills". In this research, they found that the Computer Assisted Learning resulted in greater achievements in all hierarchies of cognitive columns.

Balasubramanian (2000) conducted a study on "Computer Based Instructions in Developing Reading Skills among Primary School Children". He compared the effects of different technologies and found that the reading skills and English pronunciation has improved considerably with computer based instruction.

Subba Rao (2001) ICT has become a necessary part of teaching learning process. The ICT act as a facilitator and aids the teachers. The ultimate beneficiary in the child in the school. Quality education should be the half mark of the entire educational process. To achieve this quality and quality, there should be a healthy and strengthened connectivity and continue among teacher educator, teacher student children.

Preetha Viswanath (2003) investigated on "utilization of internet by Educats". The descriptive and inferential statistics computed revealed that the educants utilized the internet facilities adequately and if was found that the e-mail is the most often used mode of internet and the file transfer and achieve are used by the educants in small number.

Singh (2005): investigated effectiveness of Computer Assisted Instruction for teaching Biology. This study related the following findings are, **(i)** While lecture method was more effective than CAI for teaching cell, CAI was more effective than lecture method for teaching tissues, **(ii)** The gain score of the experimental group were higher than the gains recorded by the control group.

Shankara Rajan (2005) conducted a study on Attitude towards Educational Technology among B.Ed students of Alagappa University. It is found that B.Ed students have favourite attitude towards Educational Technology and they do not differ in their attitude towards Educational Technology on the basis of their gender.

Jaisingh (2007) investigated on development and validated of multimedia content on transport for higher secondary commerce students. The major findings of the study reveal that multimedia content was effective in teaching commerce at secondary level multimedia content which is true.

Karthikeyan (2007) developed and validated and e-content in tamil at secondary level. The major finding of the study revealed that, there is a significant mean difference between the achievement of pre test and post test, there is no significant mean difference between the achievement of rural and urban students.

Shivram (2007) studied the effectiveness and validation of self learning software package in learning physics for XI standard students. The major findings of the study are the Self Learning Software Package in learning physics is effective when compared to the conventional method of chalk and talk. The students who are undergoing computer classes and not undergoing computer classes have the small level of learning physics through SLSP.

Vinothkumar (2007) developed PowerPoint based learning package for XI standard student in botany and its effectiveness. Experimental method was adopted in the study. In this study, 40 XI standard students were selected as sample. The investigator used achievement test as a tool for his study. The pre test conducted for experimental group and control group which received the traditional lecturing method for a particular topic in Botany indicated that there is no significant difference between the two groups in their understanding of the topics "Pollination". The post test conducted for experimental group after using the power point package for the topic "Pollination" indicated that there is marked improvement in the understanding of the particular topic by the experimental group that the pre test performance. In the case of controlled which received the traditional lecture method there is no variation of improvement over pre test performance. Therefore the result prove that the teaching method using power point presentation is more effective tool for teaching the particular topic that the traditional chalk and talk method. It indicates that if the power point package use with the suitable treats and animation use for teaching selected topic in Botany the student can enjoy the learning and enhance the understanding level too.

Muthamil Selvi (2007) conducted research on "Effectiveness of Computer Assisted Instruction in Biological Science at Higher Secondary Level". In this research, she concluded they exits significant difference between the pre-test and post-test scorers of control and experimental group in CAI.

Jeevanandam (2008) conducted a research on "The Effectiveness of Multimedia Package on Chemical Bonding in Chemistry for ninth standard student".

Method : Experimental method

Tool : Questionnaire (30 items)

Finding: The statistical analysis of the scores of the pre-test and post-test revealed the fact that the multimedia package presentation improves the achievement of ninth standard students in Chemistry.

Research Studies Conducted Abroad

As McKnight et al (1991) predicted, hypermedia has become an interface standard, and it is increasingly true that the differences between a learning tool and any other digital information space are difficult to draw firmly. Given this, the literature on user navigation, search performance, reading speed, scanning ability, and so forth can all provide some relevant insight into the actions of learners in hypermedia spaces.

R. Mayer (ed) (1998) The Cambridge Handbook of Multimedia Learning, Hypermedia proponents suggest that its ability to make information available in a multitude of formats, provide individual control, engage the learner, and cater to various learning styles and needs makes it the harbinger of a new learning revolution.

Despite nearly two decades of research on hypertext and hypermedia learning tools, we are still a long way from knowing how best to exploit the power of this technology to support learning. It is clear that large individual differences exist among learners and that the freedom to jump and move at one's own pace through material is not equally beneficial to all. Despite these and other limitations, research is making progress on explaining the relevant phenomena.

Kharalash, Villi (2003) observes that increasing international exchange and co-operative among distance teaching institutions of Europe level and beyond made it increasingly attractive to offer nationally designed courseware additionally in version based on other language.

Padovani, S., and Lansdale, Mark. (2003) has studies "Effect of individualized multimedia instructional modules on the strategic learning strategies of students, enrolled in a university study skills courses." In this study, the researcher revealed that the individually targeted multimedia instructions modules used as a study skills intervention are effective in increasing reported study skill use.

Joy and Shaiju (2004) Development of Computer Assisted Teaching Material in History at Higher Secondary Level and its effectiveness. They concluded that the experimental students obtained significantly higher scores on the performance of reading and writing communication that the control group students.

Anboucavassy (2010) Effectiveness of multimedia in teaching Biological science to IX standard student. In this study, reveals that there is a significant difference in the achievement of the experimental group over the control group IX standard student in biology due to the exposure of multimedia based learning to the experimental group.

Tannenbaum, Robert S. (2010) did a research on computer based technology and its pedagogical utility. In this study, they revealed the following findings were,

1. The concept of smart class room is unfamiliar to most of the higher secondary school teachers.
2. Only 12.67% of higher secondary school teachers are able to handle LCD.
3. Most of the higher secondary school teachers are using computers for educational purposes.
4. Computer is a very helpful device for evaluation but only a small percentage of higher secondary school teachers are using computers for evaluation.

Hilda Mary (2010) did a research computer phobia of IX standard students and their attitude towards educational usage of computer. In this study, the researcher revealed the following findings from the above analysis; the investigator found that the factors like gender, locality of the school and types of management of the schools do not influence the computer phobia of IX standard students and their attitude towards computer usage in education.

Conclusion

The previous studies revels that the CAL was more effective than lecture method for teaching. According to Singh(2005) and Muthamil Selvi(2007) say that Computer Assisted Instruction for teaching Biology is a effective method in classroom teaching.

According to Anboucavassy(2010) effectiveness of multimedia in teaching Biology science to IX standard students, in this study reveals that there is significant difference in the achievement of the experimental group over the control group IX standard students in Biology due to the exposure of multimedia based learning to the experimental group.

Chapter - III

Research Methodology

Introduction

This chapter deals with the plan and procedure that are adopted for the present study. This chapter reveals Objectives, Hypotheses Operational definitional of the key terms, Research Method, Research tool, Variables, Experimentation in Phases, Sample for the study, Development and Validation of Multimedia Package, Construction and Validation of achievement test.

Research Design

1. Selection of dependent variables and categorical variables
2. Construction of tools to measure the environmental awareness of students.
3. Methods of establishing the reliability, validity and item analysis of the tools constructed.
4. Sampling procedure adopted in this study.
5. Scheduling the Experimental method.

Statement of the Problem

Pollution is one of the important topics of environmental science. Now days most of the schools and colleges to follow traditional method, to teach important concepts. So that the student do not understand easily. If we are teaching the important topic like pollution through the multimedia package that should be effective by considering the above ideas the researcher selected research topic of the present study is *"Effectiveness of using Multimedia Technology in Creating Awareness on Environment Pollution among XI Standard Students".*

Objectives of the Study

The main objectives are,

1. To find out the awareness of Environment pollution among XI Students.
2. To find out the awareness level of students in understanding the multimedia package for Environmental Pollution in Pre-test of control group on the basis of Gender.
3. To find out the awareness level of students in understanding the multimedia package for Environmental Pollution in Pre-test of Experimental group on the basis of Gender.
4. To find out the awareness level of students in understanding the multimedia package for Environmental Pollution in Pre-test of control group boys and Pre-test of Experimental group boys.
5. To find out the awareness level of students in understanding the multimedia package for Environmental Pollution in Pre-test of control group girls and Pre-test of Experimental group girls.
6. To find out the awareness level of students in understanding the multimedia package for Environmental Pollution in Post-test of control group on the basis of Gender.
7. To find out the awareness level of students in understanding the multimedia package for Environmental Pollution in Post-test of Experimental group on the basis of Gender.
8. To find out the awareness level of students in understanding the multimedia package for Environmental Pollution in Post-test of control group boys and Post-test of Experimental group boys.

9. To find out the awareness level of students in understanding the multimedia package for Environmental Pollution in Post-test of control group girls and Post-test of Experimental group girls.
10. To find out the awareness level of students in understanding the multimedia package for Environmental Pollution in Pre-test of control group and Pre-test of Experimental group.
11. To find out the awareness level of students in understanding the multimedia package for Environmental Pollution in Post-test of control group and Post-test of Experimental group.
12. To find out the awareness level of students in understanding the multimedia package for Environmental Pollution in Pre-test of control group and Post-test of control group.
13. To find out the awareness level of students in understanding the multimedia package for Environmental Pollution in Pre-test of Experimental group and Post-test of Experimental group.

Hypotheses of the study

1. There is no significant difference between Pre-test of control group on the basis of Gender in creating awareness on environmental pollution.
2. There is no significant difference between Pre-test of Experimental group on the basis of Gender in creating awareness on environmental pollution.
3. There is no significant difference between Pre-test of control group boys and Pre-test of Experimental group boys in creating awareness on environmental pollution.
4. There is no significant difference between Pre-test of control group girls and Pre-test of Experimental group girls in creating awareness on environmental pollution.
5. There is no significant difference between Post-test of control group on the basis of Gender in creating awareness on environmental pollution.
6. There is no significant difference between Post-test of Experimental group on the basis of Gender in creating awareness on environmental pollution.

7. There is no significant difference between Post-test of control group boys and Post-test of Experimental group boys in creating awareness on environmental pollution.
8. There is no significant difference between Post-test of control group girls and Post-test of Experimental group girls in creating awareness on environmental pollution.
9. There is no significant difference between Pre-test of control group and Pre-test of Experimental group in creating awareness on environmental pollution.
10. There is no significant difference between Post-test of control group and Post-test of Experimental group in creating awareness on environmental pollution.
11. There is no significant difference between Pre-test of control group and Post-test of control group in creating awareness on environmental pollution.
12. There is no significant difference between Pre-test of Experimental group and Post-test of Experimental group in creating awareness on environmental pollution.

Operational definition of the key terms

Development

Development refers to the production of the multimedia which includes story board, video capture editing and final production.

Validation

Validation refers to the assessment of the multimedia in terms of certain identified parameters and establishment of its worthiness based on technical pedagogical and statistical validity.

Multimedia

Multimedia is media and content that uses a combination of different content forms. The term can be used as a noun (a medium with multiple content forms) or as an adjective describing a medium as having multiple content forms. The term is used in contrast to media which use only rudimentary computer display such as text only, or traditional forms of printed or hand-produced material. Multimedia includes a combination of text, audio, still images, animation, video, or interactivity content forms.

Eco System

An **Ecosystem** is a biological system consisting of all the living organisms or biotic components in a particular area and the nonliving or biotic component with which the organisms interact, such as air, mineral soil, water and sunlight

Environmental Pollution

Environmental Pollution refers to any change from natural conditions. It is usually man made. It causes various problems.

Environmental Pollution is the introduction of contaminants into a natural environment that causes instability, disorder, harm or discomfort to the ecosystem i.e. physical systems or living organisms.

Higher Secondary Level

Higher Secondary Level refers to students studying +1 level

(XI Standard).

Limitations of the Study

No research study can be done without certain limitations. Limitations are different types and it would be a good practice to mentions the limitation in the research design. So the present investigation has the following limitations.

1. Since the research is an Experimental study the number of students is 30 from Govt. Hr. Sec. School, Karambakudi.
2. Limited variables have been administered for the study.

Research Method

In the present study experimental method was adopted for its suitability and accuracy, the research method is conceptual structural of research procedure which provides planning on selection of samples, data gathering device and data analysis techniques in relation to objectives of research. In order to determine the effectiveness of multimedia package the researcher used pre-test and post test experimental design.

Research tools

The tools used by the researcher consist of multimedia package on environmental pollution and achievement test for pre and post tests.

Construction of Research Tool

The pattern of the test is same as the control and Experimental group. The test consists of twenty five marks. All the Questions are objective type. The question paper consists of three levels. They are knowledge, understanding and application levels.

Samples of the study

30 students of male and female studying in class XI STD of Govt. Higher Secondary School, karambakudi were taken as the sample for analysis.

Description of the research tool and scoring procedure

The researcher has taken only objective type questions. The test paper consist of choose the correct answer. Each question carries one mark. If the answer is correct one mark will be given if not zero.

Pilot Study

A pilot study is an initial investigation to give information that will be necessary when designing a future trial or study. For example a pilot may be used to:

1. Asses the time required to examine each patient,
2. To determine the quality of a proposed questionnaire
3. To estimate the variability of key variables.

Hence the investigator conducted the pilot study in the experiment to determine the quality of the question paper

Validity of the tool

Validity is the extent to which a test is measured what it claims to measure. It is vital for a test to be valid in order for the results to be accurately applied and interpreted. Validity is not determined by a single statistics, but by a body of research that demonstrates the relation between the test and the behavior it is intended to measure.

There are three types of validity:

1. Content Validity
2. Criterion Validity
3. Construct Validity

In the present study **Content Validity** was used

Content validity

When a test has content validity, the items on the test represent the entire range of possible items the test should cover

Reliability of the tool

Reliability has to do with the quality of measurement. In its everyday sense, reliability is the "consistency" or "repeatability" of the measures. The word reliable usually means "dependable" or "trustworthy". In research, the term reliability means "repeatability" or "consistency". A measure is considered reliable if it would give us the same result over and over again (assuming that what we are measuring isn't changing).

There are as many types of reliability as the conditions of the tests are.

Anyhow four general classes of reliability estimates, each of which estimates reliability in a different way are important here.

Variables

In the present investigation is an attempt to determine the development and validation of multimedia package on environmental pollution at Higher Secondary Level, the variables involved are given below.

a) Independent Variable is Multimedia Package

b) Dependent Variable is Achievement in environmental pollution

Flowchart – Research Method

The key components of research procedure are given below.

Experimentation in Phases

Phase : 1

Development of multimedia package on environmental pollution in Higher Secondary Students.

Phase : 2

Conduct pre-test for both control and experimental groups to assess the entry behaviour of the students.

Phase : 3

Create interaction among the students in teaching fundamentals in environmental pollution.

Indentifying the students way of thinking with record to environmental pollution.

Phase : 4

Giving theoretical orientation to experimental group alone on environmental pollution multimedia package.

Phase 5:

1. Teaching students of experimental group with multimedia package and control group with conventional method.
2. Duration of the treatment is two weeks.
3. Fee back was collected from the students.

Phase 6 :

Conducting post-test for both group to assess the performance of them.

Sample for the study

The present research was carried out the Government higher secondary school, Karambakudi. The 30, XI-standard students were selected as a sample by using simple random sampling technique out of them 15-students were in control group and remaining 15-students were in experimental group. All the students were equally matched in terms of their previous knowledge in environmental studies.

Sampling frame for the study

Distribution of sample taken for the present study is given below.

Sl. No.	Group	No. of Students	Total
1.	Experimental Group	15	15
2.	Control Group	15	15
Total			30

Development and Validation of Multimedia Package

The topic environmental pollution was selected by the investigator, for the development of multimedia package after collecting opining from the expert in the field of environmental science.

At the time of developing multimedia package the investigator the following steps were undertaken such as Resource Material collection which is related to specific content area preparation of short learning objectives (SLO), collection of relevant pictures, exercise and editing the learning package, that are given in the appendix.

The learning package was given to experts in the field of environmental science and educational technology. Based on their opinion necessary correction were made in that multimedia package.

Since the investigator implemented the multimedia package for the XI-standard students, it was developed in English. The content and technical validity were established for the multimedia package.

Construction and Validation of Achievement Test

The researcher administered the achievement test with the control group and experimental group. The achievement test consisting of 25 multiple choice items were developed by the investigator, the items consist of knowledge, comprehension, application and skill level. The different achievement test tools were developed by the researcher for the conduct of pre test and post test. After consultation with the experts the scoring were made on the basis of correct answer for each items were given one mark and wrong response for each items zero mark.

Analysis of Data

The term analysis refers to the compilation of certain measures along with searching for pattern and relationships that among groups. For the present study the investigator collected the data from higher secondary school student using the tool developed to find out questionary of sample with the environment awareness of higher secondary school students with environmental pollution reference to home atmosphere.

Statistical Techniques Used

Statistical techniques serve the fundamental purpose of the description and inferential analysis. The following statistical techniques were used in study.

1. Mean (M)
2. Standard Deviation (SD)
3. 't' - test for determine the significance of difference between means of two sub-groups.

Conclusion

In this chapter the methodology of the study was explained in detail. Each and every step was carefully planned and executed. The research strategy and the data collection procedures have been explained. The next chapter deals with the analysis and interpretation of data.

Chapter - IV

Analysis and Interpretation

Introduction

This chapter highlights the result of the present research. The results are presented in a systematic manner after all the Hypotheses of the study are tested and verified by applying suitable statistical techniques such as Mean, SD and 't'-test.

Analysis and interpretation of data forms the prominent part of the research as the data gathering in the research are put under processing in the sector. Only under processing the investigation would be able to present the result of the study to the world.

The data of the present study were collected from 30 students studying in higher secondary school student. Standards have been analyzed by using the following statistical techniques.

The measures of central tendencies and the measures deviation are computed and the values of the mean and standard deviation are used to describe the properties of the particular samples and these descriptive statistics are used to reduce the bulk for a data of manageable size.

Analysis of Data

The term analysis refers to the compilation of certain measures along with searching for pattern and relationships that among groups. For the present study the investigator collected the data from higher secondary school student using the tool developed to find out questionary of sample with the environment awareness of higher secondary school students with environmental pollution reference to home atmosphere.

Hypotheses Testing

NULL HYPOTHESIS: 1

There is no significant difference between mean score of Pre-test of control group on the basis of Gender in creating awareness on environmental pollution.

Table: 1

Sl.No.	Testing of the group	N	Mean	SD	't' Value	Level of Significance
1.	Pre-test Control Group Male	7	9.8	8.7	0.9	Not Significant
2.	Pre-test Control Group Female	8	7.3	1.3		

Table Value at 0.05 level = 2.16.

The above table shows that the computed't' value 0.9 is less than critical value 2.16 at 0.05 level and hence it is not significant. Consequently, the null hypothesis is **accepted**. And it can be said there is no significant difference in the awareness of Environmental pollution mean score among XI standard students on the basis of Pre - test control group of Male and Female.

NULL HYPOTHESIS: 2

There is no significant difference between mean score of Pre-test of Experimental group on the basis of Gender in creating awareness on environmental pollution.

Table: 2

Sl.No.	Testing of the group	N	Mean	SD	't' Value	Level of Significance
1.	Pre-test Experimental Group Male	8	6.8	5.8	1.3	Not significant
2.	Pre-test Experimental Group Female	7	10.14	3		

Table Value at 0.05 level = 2.16.

The above table shows that the computed't' value 1.3 is less than critical value 2.16 at 0.05 level and hence it is not significant. Consequently, the null hypothesis is **accepted**. And it can be said there is no significant difference in the awareness of Environmental pollution mean score among XI standard students on the basis of Pre - test experimental group of Male and Female.

NULL HYPOTHESIS: 3

There is no significant difference between mean score of Pre-test of control group boys and Pre-test of Experimental group boys in creating awareness on environmental pollution.

Table: 3

Sl.No.	Testing of the group	N	Mean	SD	't' Value	Level of Significance
1.	Control Group	7	9.8	8.7	0.8	Not significant
2.	Experimental Group	8	6.8	5.8		

Table Value at 0.05 level = 2.16.

The above table shows that the computed't' value 0.8 is less than critical value 2.16 at 0.05 level and hence it is not significant. Consequently, the null hypothesis is **accepted**. And it can be said there is no significant difference in the awareness of Environmental pollution mean score among XI standard students on the basis of Pre - test experimental group and control group boys.

NULL HYPOTHESIS: 4

There is no significant difference between mean score of Pre-test of control group girls and Pre-test of Experimental group girls in creating awareness on environmental pollution.

Table: 4

Sl.No.	Testing of the group	N	Mean	SD	't' Value	Level of Significance
1.	Control Group	8	7.3	1.3	5	Not significant
2.	Experimental Group	7	10.4	3		

Table Value at 0.05 level = 2.16.

The above table shows that the computed't' value 5 is greater than critical value 2.16 at 0.05 level and hence it is significant. Consequently, the null hypothesis is **rejected**. And it can be said there is significant difference in the awareness of Environmental pollution mean score among XI standard students on the basis of Pre - test experimental group and control group girls.

NULL HYPOTHESIS: 5

There is no significant difference between mean score of Post-test of control group on the basis of Gender in creating awareness on environmental pollution.

Table: 5

Sl.No.	Testing of the group	N	Mean	SD	't' Value	Level of Significance
1.	Post-test Control Group Male	7	15.8	8.1	0.01	Not significant
2.	Post-test Control Group Female	8	15.7	19.2		

Table Value at 0.05 level = 2.16.

The above table shows that the computed't' value 0.01 is less than critical value 2.16 at 0.05 level and hence it is not significant. Consequently, the null hypothesis is **accepted**. And it can be said there is no significant difference in the awareness of Environmental pollution mean score among XI standard students on the basis of Post - test control group of Male and Female

NULL HYPOTHESIS: 6

There is no significant difference between mean score of Post-test of Experimental group on the basis of Gender in creating awareness on environmental pollution.

Table: 6

Sl.No.	Testing of the group	N	Mean	SD	't' Value	Level of Significance
1.	Post-test Control Group Male	7	15.8	8.1	0.01	Not significant
2.	Post-test Control Group Female	8	15.7	19.2		

Table Value at 0.05 level = 2.16.

The above table shows that the computed't' value 0.14 is less than critical value 2.16 at 0.05 level and hence it is not significant. Consequently, the null hypothesis is **accepted**. And it can be said there is no significant difference in the awareness of Environmental pollution mean score among XI standard students on the basis of Post - test experimental group of Male and Female.

NULL HYPOTHESIS: 7

There is no significant difference between mean score of Post-test of control group boys and Post-test of Experimental group boys in creating awareness on environmental pollution.

Table: 7

Sl.No.	Testing of the group	N	Mean	SD	't' Value	Level of Significance
1.	Control Group	7	15.8	8.1	0.4	Not significant
2.	Experimental Group	8	18.75	19.5		

Table Value at 0.05 level = 2.16.

The above table shows that the computed't' value 0.4 is less than critical value 2.16 at 0.05 level and hence it is not significant. Consequently, the null hypothesis is accepted. And it can be said there is no significant difference in the awareness of Environmental pollution mean score among XI standard students on the basis of Post - test experimental group and control group boys.

NULL HYPOTHESIS: 8

There is no significant difference between mean score of Post-test of control group girls and Post-test of Experimental group girls in creating awareness on environmental pollution.

Table: 8

Sl.No.	Testing of the group	N	Mean	SD	't' Value	Level of Significance
1.	Control Group	8	15.7	19.25	0.5	Not significant
2.	Experimental Group	7	20	6.2		

Table Value at 0.05 level = 2.16.

The above table shows that the computed't' value 0.5 is less than critical value 2.16 at 0.05 level and hence it is not significant. Consequently, the null hypothesis is **accepted**. And it can be said there is no significant difference in the awareness of Environmental pollution mean score among XI standard students on the basis of Post - test experimental group and control group girls.

NULL HYPOTHESIS: 9

There is no significant difference between mean score of Pre-test of control group and Pre-test of Experimental group in creating awareness on environmental pollution.

Table : 9

Sl.No.	Testing of the group	N	Mean	SD	't' Value	Level of Significance
1.	Control Group	15	8.5	6.9	0.33	Not Significant
2.	Experimental Group	15	8.4	11		

Table Value at 0.05 level = 2.05.

The above table shows that the computed 't' value 0.33 is less than critical value 2.05 at 0.05 level and hence it is not significant.

Consequently, the null hypothesis is accepted. And it can be said there is no significant difference in the awareness of Environmental pollution mean score among XI standard students on the basis of Pre - test of control group and experimental group.

NULL HYPOTHESIS: 10

There is no significant difference between mean score of Post-test of control group and Post-test of Experimental group in creating awareness on environmental pollution.

Table : 10

Sl.No.	Testing of the group	N	Mean	SD	't' Value	Level of Significance
1.	Control Group	15	.15.8	14	0.5	Not Significant
2.	Experimental Group	15	19.33	13.8		

Table Value at 0.05 level = 2.05.

The above table shows that the computed 't' value 0.5 is less than critical value 2.05 at 0.05 level and hence it is not significant. Consequently, the null hypothesis is accepted. And it can be said there is no significant difference in the awareness of Environmental pollution mean score among XI standard students on the basis of Post - test of control group and experimental group.

NULL HYPOTHESIS: 11

There is no significant difference between mean score of Pre-test of control group and Post-test of control group in creating awareness on environmental pollution.

Table : 11

Sl.No.	Testing of the group	N	Mean	SD	't' Value	Level of Significance
1.	Pre – test	15	8.5	6.9	2.6	Significant
2.	Post - test	15	15.8	14		

Table Value at 0.05 level = 2.05.

The above table shows that the computed 't' value 2.6 is greater than critical value 2.05 at 0.05 level and hence it is significant. Consequently, the null hypothesis is **rejected**. And it can be said there is significant difference in the awareness of Environmental pollution mean score among XI standard students on the basis of control group of Pre-test and Post test.

NULL HYPOTHESIS: 12

There is no significant difference between mean score of Pre-test of Experimental group and Post-test of Experimental group in creating awareness on environmental pollution.

Table : 12

Sl.No.	Testing of the group	N	Mean	SD	't' Value	Level of Significance
1.	Pre – test	15	8.4	11	2.7	Significant
2.	Post - test	15	19.33	13.8		

Table Value at 0.05 level = 2.05.

The above table shows that the computed 't' value 2.7 is greater than critical value 2.05 at 0.05 level and hence it is significant. Consequently, the null hypothesis is **rejected**. And it can be said there is significant difference in the awareness of Environmental pollution mean score among XI standard students on the basis of Experimental group of Pre-test and Post - test.

Conclusion

Thus the scores obtained by the XI standard students of Karambakudi Govt School were put into differential analysis. The findings, recommendations and suggestions that are brought by the study are enlisted in a detailed manner in the next Chapter-V.

Chapter - V

Summary and Conclusion

Introduction

This chapter summarizes the work done, discusses the meaning of research results, addresses the consequences of the result by relating them to the more general conceptual frame work of the research topic and offers suggestions and recommendation for the application and utility of research results.

In the previous chapters, the relevant theoretical aspects and different stages development and validation and appropriate methodology and procedure were presented. This chapter is devoted for presenting the most significant element of the research outcome. Any research is evaluated on the basis of the objectives formulated prior to the experimentation, the accurate procedure adopted and the clear outcome of the research. In this chapter, the focus of attention is on the results or outcomes of the research and implications. The outcomes of any research are to be judged on the purpose or objectives of the study. Hence in the beginning, the objectives are restated, followed by the whole procedure of the study, which is helpful to conceive the outcome from its absolute essence.

Need and Significance of the study

System analysis is a process of gathering and interpreting facts, diagnosing problems and the information to recommend improvements on the system. It is a problem solving activity that requires intensive communication between the system users and system developers.

System analysis is concerned with becoming aware of the problem, identifying the relevant and most decisional variables, analyzing and synthesizing the various factors and determining and an optimal or at least a satisfactory solutions or program of action.

Observation was done to a great extend to see difficulties of the processes and the time delay in finding results. Accurate study was conducted to know the system in a better manner.

One of the main tasks of education in a modern society is to keep pace with this advance in knowledge. Thus new technology and strategies are essential to satisfactorily solve the new problems in the field of education for teaching and learning process.

Scope of the study

Environmental Pollution is prescribed in almost all boards of education at Higher Secondary Level, this study is primarily focused on the awareness of environmental pollution using multimedia package of higher secondary level students. Keeping this view in mind, the researcher has developed Computer Assisted Learning Package in Creating Environmental Awareness to the Learners at Higher Secondary Level Students.

This investigation is restricted to only is higher secondary first year student of Government Higher Secondary School, Karambakudi which is situated in an urban area of Pudukkottai district is constitute the sample. This is parallel group study which measures the validate multimedia package on the achievement of higher secondary students in creating environment awareness using CAL method.

Statement of the Problem

Pollution is one of the important topics of environmental science. Now days most of the schools and colleges to follow traditional method, to teach important concepts. So that the student do not understand easily. If we are teaching the important topic like pollution through the multimedia package that should be effective by considering the above ideas the researcher selected research topic of the present study is *"Effectiveness of using Multimedia Technology in Creating Awareness on Environment Pollution among XI Standard Students"*.

Objectives of the Study

The main objectives are,

1. To find out the awareness of Environment pollution among XI Students.
2. To find out the awareness level of students in understanding the multimedia package for Environmental Pollution in Pre-test of control group on the basis of Gender.
3. To find out the awareness level of students in understanding the multimedia package for Environmental Pollution in Pre-test of Experimental group on the basis of Gender.
4. To find out the awareness level of students in understanding the multimedia package for Environmental Pollution in Pre-test of control group boys and Pre-test of Experimental group boys.
5. To find out the awareness level of students in understanding the multimedia package for Environmental Pollution in Pre-test of control group girls and Pre-test of Experimental group girls.
6. To find out the awareness level of students in understanding the multimedia package for Environmental Pollution in Post-test of control group on the basis of Gender.
7. To find out the awareness level of students in understanding the multimedia package for Environmental Pollution in Post-test of Experimental group on the basis of Gender.
8. To find out the awareness level of students in understanding the multimedia package for Environmental Pollution in Post-test of control group boys and Post-test of Experimental group boys.
9. To find out the awareness level of students in understanding the multimedia package for Environmental Pollution in Post-test of control group girls and Post-test of Experimental group girls.

10. To find out the awareness level of students in understanding the multimedia package for Environmental Pollution in Pre-test of control group and Pre-test of Experimental group.
11. To find out the awareness level of students in understanding the multimedia package for Environmental Pollution in Post-test of control group and Post-test of Experimental group.
12. To find out the awareness level of students in understanding the multimedia package for Environmental Pollution in Pre-test of control group and Post-test of control group.
13. To find out the awareness level of students in understanding the multimedia package for Environmental Pollution in Pre-test of Experimental group and Post-test of Experimental group.

Major Findings

1. There is no significant difference between mean score of Pre-test of control group on the basis of Gender in creating awareness on environmental pollution.
2. There is no significant difference between mean score of Pre-test of Experimental group on the basis of Gender in creating awareness on environmental pollution.
3. There is no significant difference between mean score of Pre-test of control group boys and Pre-test of Experimental group boys in creating awareness on environmental pollution.
4. There is significant difference between mean score of Pre-test of control group girls and Pre-test of Experimental group girls in creating awareness on environmental pollution.
5. There is no significant difference between mean score of Post-test of control group on the basis of Gender in creating awareness on environmental pollution.
6. There is no significant difference between mean score of Post-test of Experimental group on the basis of Gender in creating awareness on environmental pollution.
7. There is no significant difference between mean score of Post-test of control group boys and Post-test of Experimental group boys in creating awareness on environmental pollution.

8. There is significant difference between mean score of Post-test of control group girls and Post-test of Experimental group girls in creating awareness on environmental pollution.
9. There is significant difference between mean score of Pre-test of control group and Pre-test of Experimental group in creating awareness on environmental pollution.
10. There is no significant difference between mean score of Post-test of control group and Post-test of Experimental group in creating awareness on environmental pollution.
11. There is no significant difference between mean score of Pre-test of control group and Post-test of control group in creating awareness on environmental pollution.
12. There is no significant difference between mean score of Pre-test of Experimental group and Post-test of Experimental group in creating awareness on environmental pollution.

Research Implication

The multimedia package to increased motivation to learn and increased retention of information. The students were found to be really motivated by the multimedia package and they retained a good memory of the multimedia package learned.

The multimedia package contained so many visuals (animations & images) that made the abstract ideas concrete before the students and hence the effectiveness of their learning is found to be high.

It is found that the role of teacher is less in this particular instructional method (multimedia package). He/she has to give some guidelines only in the beginning before the programme is administered to the students.

While administering the multimedia package, which is a self-instructional learning strategy to the students, it is found that multimedia package promotes active participation and encourages vigilance.

The multimedia package is found to have a beneficial effect on the learner achievement as a result of the unique combination of tutorial interactive and visual capabilities.

New instructional techniques of assisting student through computer are to be explored by the teachers and researchers continuously.

New patterns of Computer Assisted Learning and its uses can lead to a wholly new organizational and administrative system for improving the effectiveness of the total educational enterprise.

Suggestions for further Research

In the present study, the developed multimedia package is validated based on the performance of 30 students in the achievement test for the multimedia package. If a larger sample with a wider area could be chosen in a further research study, it will substantiate the validity of these findings.

Auto instructional package like multimedia package can be developed by the teachers and lecturers as a set of activities integral to the syllabus, textbooks and curriculum complexes.

Instead of trying to present routine lesson through multimedia package, teacher and lecturer can present in a better way by including demonstration, complicated experiments, visual excursions to for off places and current events.

Experimental studies can be carried out to examine on different aspect of environmental pollution. Since multimedia package is a new phenomenon in the field of instructional technology, there is a wide horizon of possibilities for further researches in this area.

Conclusion

Pollution is a man-made problem. Increase in global population, increasing demands for a newer material has resulted in the enormous growth of technology. This in turn can be attributed to the environmental pollution that we are facing today. The rise of multimedia and an electronic content (multimedia package) is a new paradigm for education and training in the knowledge society.

Empowered by technological advancements which gives the modern instructional technology a pew lock. The development of educational content in time with the changing times has become a major responsibility of the modern teacher who has to face a new learner in a new environment. The role of qualitative multimedia package assumes critical necessity and value to boost and spread modern instructional technology. However the development multimedia package is not an easy task. If calls forth the coming together of both the educationists and the technologists. Simply, the development of a multimedia package is not enough. We should keep an eye on the various stages of the multimedia development to ensure whether the developed content is valid and suits so the needs of the learner.

BOOK REFERENCES

1. Aggarwal.Y.P (1998), "Statistical Methods Concepts, Application and Computation" Sterling Publishers Pvt. Ltd., New Delhi.
2. Bartlett, R. M., S. Cheng, & J. Strough (2000) "Multimedia versus traditional course instruction in undergraduate introductory psychology", Washington.
3. Bhatnagar (2005) "Research in Education" (Fifth Edition), R.Lall Book dept near Govt. Inter College, Meerut.
4. Burke Lisa A. and Karen E. James. (2008) "PowerPoint-Based lectures in business education of student-perceived novelty and effectiveness".
5. Craig, Russel J. and Joel H. Amernic (2006) "PowerPoint presentation technology and the dynamics of teaching. Innovation in Higher Education"
6. Wutoh, Rita et.al (2004) "A review of internet based continuing medical education", journal of continuing education in the health professions.
7. Kevin Knight (2005), "Macromedia Flash MX 2004", Flipping Book publishers, Washington.
8. Mayer, Richard E. (2005) "The Cambridge handbook of multimedia learning" New York.
9. Mehrotra.P (2007) "Analysis of Global Environmental Pollution", BPB publication, Nehru Place, New Delhi.
10. Nasr Y.M. Omar (2009) "Environmental Pollution Analysis", Neel Kamal Publications Pvt.Ltd.New Delhi.
11. Norman, Gronlund and Robert, Linn (1990), "Measurement and evaluation of Technology" (Sixth Edition) Macmillan.

12. Rick Darnell (2002), "HTML", Penguin *Books publishers,* England.

13. Sampath et. al (1990) "Introduction to Educational Technology",

14. Sterling Publishers Pvt. Ltd, New Delhi.

15. Scott Urman (2009) , "Macromedia Flash8", Flipping Book publishers, Washington JOURNALS

16. Hilda Mary (2010) "Computer phobia of IX standard students and their attitude towards educational usage of computer" institute of advanced study in education Chennai.

17. Keen, Desmond (2002) "The future of learning: From e-learning to m-learning", information analysis, opinion papers.

18. Kimmelman, Paul and Kroeze, David (2002) "Achieving world class school" Mastering school improvement using a genetic model", books, Guides-Non-Classroom.

19. Lam Paul and McNaught, Carmel (2007) "Management of an e-learning evaluation project. The e-learning model", Journal of interactive learning research.

20. Little john, Allison et al. (2008) "Characterizing Effective e-Learning Resources", Computer & Education.

21. Nimavathi and Ganadeven (2009) "Developing study habits through multimedia program" Department of Education. Annamalai University, Tamil Nadu.

22. Ryan, Malcolm and Hall, Lynda (2001) "Multimedia, Teaching and Training: A first look at principal, issues and implications" information analysis" Speeches/meeting Papers

23. Sathis kumar and Rezene Habtemariam (2010) Learning with multimedia, A constructive cooperative approach in Education" Eritrea institute of technology, mai-Nefhi, Asmara, Eritrea, N.E.Africa.

24. Singh, Mukhbir (2002) "e-Learning translates to experimental learning in a communication theory class.", Reports – Evaluative; Speeches/Meeting papers.

25. Vinothkumar (2007) "An innovative computer assisted instructional programme" Jamil University, Thanjavur, Annamalai University, Chidambaram.

4. Effectiveness of Teaching Metonymy in Modern Techniques

Chapter-I

INTRODUCTION

The status of the teacher reflects on Socio-cultural ethos of a society. The government and the community should create conditions that will help teachers to have motivation and inspiration in a constructive and create lines. Teachers should have the freedom activates relevant to the needs and capabilities of and the concerns of the community. If at all, we want to provide quality education, teachers should involve in teaching, learning process and at the end allow them to have created thinking. Teachers who involve in technical programmes is quite different from other learning process, though teachers are not having adequate responsible, they should involve in the role of supervisor and guide. His role is to provide chance learners to have independent learning experiences can be given to student, in varieties of Educational Technological programmes and activities.

These programmes are essential for providing effective input by the teacher to the students. Therefore teachers is considered on a spectator of teaching and how he is effectively involving in teaching - learning process by using video programmes to the students. In this process of video programmes. Teacher have to concentrate on adequate improve, future use of teaching. It is an essential task of the teachers to use variety of video instruction spending upon the learners in teaching - learning process. But students are willing to learn through video instruction, now there is not awareness in many schools and colleges. So the teachers in and to provide teaching learning process and to provide suitable suggestion to improve the teaching - learning process by using variety of video instruction in effectively and to involve students in teaching - learning process for effective learning. This study has been under taken by the educational and the title of researchers.

Stress is a state of mind which reflects certain biochemical reactions in the human body and is projected by a sense of anxiety, tension and depression and is caused by such demands by the environmental forces or internal forces that cannot be met by the resources available to the person. The intensity of such demands that require a readjustment of resources or operational styles would determine the extent of stress. Such environmental events or conditions that have the potential to induce stress are known as "Stressors" the stress created by desirable and successful effects is called "eustress" and the stress created by undesirable outcomes is known as "distress" it is primarily the distress form of stress which requires examination and steps to cope with it.

It is important to deal with stress at an early stage. Early warning sign such as headaches, back pain, irritability, and insomnia, absenteeism from work or alcoholism should be taken seriously; otherwise they could lead to serious emotional disorders as well as physiological problems such as ulcers and heart diseases. When stress is left untreated for a long time, it can develop into anxiety and depression.

"Selye" postulated a 'general adaptation syndrome' of somatic systems caused by 'non- specific stresses'. It involved three stages.

1. Alaram reaction- when an initial shock phase of lowered resistance is followed by counter – shock during which an individual' defense mechanisms are activated.
2. Resistance – it is a stage of maximum adaptation when the individual restores the equilibrium.
3. Exhaustion – if the stress continues or the defense mechanism falters, the individuals moves to this stage.

Feeling stressed is a danger signal a sign that you are reaching the limits of your resources. Stress is not only bad for health but also causes inefficiency and worsening of relationships. The danger is that when under stress we tend to ignore our health and put our relationships under increasing strain. This sets up a vicious cycle because poor health and poor relationships then add to the stress.

EDUCATION

Education is not a new concept. It is as old as human race. Its importance and magnanimity have been keenly realized since the dawn of human Civilization. The biped animal human being is the best and finest creation of God on earth. His life is pious and praiseworthy God has unequally endowed man with certain race qualities which are not found other animate bodies. Man is amenable. He applies his reasoning power. Since education and philosophy are concerned with man and his life. It is philosophers who take a lion's share in the educational Concern.

MEANING AND DEFINITION OF EDUCATION

The act or process of education and the result of education as determined by the knowledge, skill or discipline of character is acquired and the process is unending. The act or process or training by prescribed or customary course of study or discipline-as, as education for the bar or the pulpit-has a finishing point and we say the student has finished his education.

The destiny of India is now being shaped in her classrooms (Kothari-1966). Education is the most essential human value knowledge is developed through literacy and education.

Definition

According to education aims to seek and cultivate new knowledge to engage vigorously and fearlessly in the pursuit of truth and to interpret old knowledge and benefits in the light of new needs and discoveries -

J.C.Aggarwal

Writes the education if the process of living through a continuous reconstruction of experience. It is the development of all these capacities in the individual which will enable him to control his environment and fulfill his responsibilities- **John dewey.**

Education meets the immediate needs of a child and also prepares him for his future life. It develops all his intellectual and emotional powers so that he is able to meet the problems of life squarely and solve them successfully. It also develops the social qualities of service, tolerance, co-operation and fellow feeling. "Education is a key that open the eyes of a person towards the brightness of the world"- **Dr.Rathakrishnan.**

"The central task of education is to implant a will and facility for learning. It should produce not learned but learning people. The truly human society is a learning society where grandparent's parents and children are students together"-**Eric hoffer**

"No one has yet realized the wealth of sympathy, the kindness and generosity hidden in the soul of a child. The effort of every true education should be to unlock that treasure"-**Emma goldman.**

"The only purpose of education is to teach a student how to live his life-by developing his mind and equipping him to deal with reality. The training he needs is theoretical. i.e. conceptual. He has to be taught to think to understand, to integrate and to provide. He has to be taught the essentials of the knowledge discovered in the past and he has to be to be equipped to acquire further knowledge by his own effort"- **Ayn rand**

"The aim of education should be to teach us rather how to think than what to think rather to improve our minds. So as to enable us to think for ourselves than to load the memory with the thoughts of other men"- **Bill beattie**

THE CONCEPT OF EDUCATION

The word education is derived from two Latin words. They are edure and educare. Educare means to bring up and nourish. Educare means to bring forth and propulsion from internal to external. Education is the modification of behavior in a controlled environment. The term education in the widest sense may be held to include the whole process of development through which a human being passed from infancy to maturity.

Education is the aggregate of all the processes by means of which a person develops abilities, attitudes and other forms of behavior of positive value in the society in which he lives.

Gandhiji defined education in the following quote by education I mean an all round drawing out of the best in child and man body, mind and spirit.

NEED OF EDUCATION

Across countries education plays a vital role not only in acquiring knowledge but also inculcating social, ethical, moral and spiritual values. In our model, schooling teaches people to interact with others and raises the benefits of civic participation including voting and organizing. Education raises the benefits of civic participation. Education is able to instill in the child a sense of maturity and responsibility in bringing in him the desired changes. According to this needs and demands of ever changing society of which he is an integral part.

IMPORTANCE OF EDUCATION

The importance of education is quite clear. Education is the knowledge of putting one's potentials to maximum use. One can safely say that a human being is not in the proper sense complete till he is educated.

The second reason for the importance of education is that only through the attainment of education, man is enabled to receive information from the external world to acquaint himself with past history and receive all necessary information regarding the present. Without education main is as through in a closed room and with education he finds himself in room with all its windows open towards outside world.

GRAMMAR

Grammar is the theory of language and the study of organisation of communicative words into sentences. Plato and his pupil Aristotle were the first to take up this subject seriously.

Sweet has defined grammar as, "the practical analysis of a language, its anatomy" According to Champman, "Grammar is a study of Communicative language by specialists, made in order to establish the rules and principles which are followed more or less unconsciously or instinctively by the native speakers" Grammar has three different meanings.

i. It is the set of formal patterns in which the words of a Communicative language are arranged in order to convey larger meanings.
ii. It is the branch of linguistic science which is concerned with the description, analysis and formalization of formal Communicative language patterns,
iii. It is linguistic etiquette.

The Objectives of Teaching Grammar

1. To develop students' insight into the structures of Tamil language.
2. To enable the-students to assimilate the correct Tamil language and Grammar.
3. To teach grammar as a rule-governed behaviour.
4. To develop their mental abilities of reasoning and correct observation.
5. To develop a scientific attitude in pupils about the language.

TYPES OF GRAMMAR

1. Prescriptive Grammar

It is also called formal or theoretical grammar. It is the old traditional grammar. In it the main emphasis is on rules and forms. It prescribes its norms upon the language users. It is traditional in approach. It does not allow changes in language, whereas change in rules is a must.

2. Descriptive or Functional Grammar

Its main emphasis is on the functional side of the language. It describes the behaviour of the language. It changes along with the change in language.

3. Structural Grammar

C.C. Fries an American Linguist founded this type of grammar. The grammar is taught on the basis of structure of sentences. The structural grammarians prefer to study the grammatical forms (structures) of the Communicative language before considering their lexical meaning

4. Transformational- Generative:

Its emphasis is laid upon the sentences. The grammarians of this school recognize that there are sentences basic to the language, sentences from which all others are derived. The approach here is characterized by abstraction. The components of this sort of grammar are phonological, syntactic and geomantic.

5. Communicative Grammar:

This type of grammar is functional and task-based. The grammarians of this school focus their attention on meaning rather than on form of expressions. In the divergent situations they describe the communicate value and significance of each utterance or expression. Most of these grammarians prefer fluency in the use of language to accuracy.

Prescriptive - Formal Grammar

Grammar is the theory of language and the study organisation of words into sentences. Plato and his pupil Aristotle were the first to take up this subject seriously.

Sweet has defined grammar as, "the practical analysis of language, its anatomy" According to Champman, Grammer is a study of language by specialist, made in order to establish the rules and principles which are followed more or less unconsciously or instinctively by the native speakers" Grammar has three different meanings.

i. It is the set of formal patterns in which the words of a Communicative language are arranged in order to convey larger meanings.
ii. It is the branch of linguistic science which is concerned with the description, analysis and formalization of formal language patterns.
iii. It is linguistic etiquette.

Communicative Grammar

This type of grammar is functional and task-based. The grammarians of this high school focus their attention on meaning rather than on form of expressions. In the divergent situations they describe the communicate value and significance of each utterance or expression. Most of these grammarians prefer fluency in the use of language to accuracy.

Principles of Teaching Grammar

The following principles should be borne in mind while teaching grammar.

1. In the beginning stages, a separate grammar book need not be introduced. Let the pupils unconsciously absorb grammatical items as contained in the reader.
2. Grammar should not be begun on abstract lines and abstract principles as pupils may not understand.
3. Grammar principles should begin with language. It must correlate speech", in which a sentence is a unitary whole with reading. After the students have listened to it, try to guide them to deduce the pattern which we want them to use.
4. Try to teach grammar and usage. Simultaneously with their own examples and make them listen to as many usages as possible.
5. Attention should be paid on meaning of the structure rather than on grammatical points unless they are interfering with the communication of meaning.
6. Grammar should be taught as an intellectual exercise. Its aim is to make skilful (pupils) users of the language. So they should be taught to use the structures of Tamil correctly rather than to just label them.
7. Students must be in a position to use the grammatical patterns skillfully and build us their own structures. Mere knowledge of the names of material alone is not sufficient.
8. According to McGregor, "If we are to teach the grammar of Tamil realistically and truthfully, then we must help our pupils to understand the concept "idioms and phrases, idioms in language" because all languages are different total means which they employ to convey meaning. Idioms point out different expressions

because they indicate the way of expressing an idea which is peculiar to one Communicative language.

Organization of Grammar Learning

The stages suggested here constitute a general frame work which consists of four stages.

1. Perception
2. Understanding
3. Absorption
4. Demonstration

Perception

We can begin the class by presenting a passage in which the grammatical item or structure appears. We can enable the learners to perceive the form and meaning of the item either in speech or writing or in both. The learners may be asked to read aloud, read silently repeat, copy and reproduce instances of the use of the item within the present text.

Understanding

In this stage we can facilitate the learners to move away from the context and focus on the grammatical item itself. We can enable them to understand what the item looks like and means and how it sounds and functions. We can explain what rules govern them. We should not involve the learners with jargons or grammatical terms more then what is necessary. Sometimes we can use the learner's first language to explain so that they could make generalizations about the item.

Absorption

At this stage, we enable the learner's to-do a series of varied exercises based on the grammatical item. They should practice the item both in the classroom and at home. Discrete items as well as transformation exercises can be thought. Even communicative tasks can be given.

Demonstration

In this stage, we should administer tests to the learners so that they can demonstrate how well they have learnt item. If we could induct proper techniques and well designed activities into grammar teaching students could realize that grammar could also be as fiction. They will begin to love grammar.

METHODS OF TEACHING GRAMMAR

The Traditional Method

Rules, examples and exercises on grammar are explained for the pupils. The teacher tells a definition or a rule to the students. For e.g.: He says, "A noun is a name of the person, place or thing". He gives examples of nouns Then he refers to an exercise and ask the pupils to point out the nouns in it the pupils have to memorize the definition of noun. The same procedure is followed for teaching others parts of speech. When pupils are well, acquainted by these, the teacher then introduces them to rules regarding the change of voice, transformation and analysis of sentences, singular and plural nouns etc. Pupils commit these rules to memory and solve the exercises given in the text books on grammar.

The Informal Method

Here teaching of grammar is taught not by rules but by usages. By continuous practice of using words while speaking, writing and reading, grammar can be taught. This method explains correct usage informally during correction work. This method is a necessity in early stages when the pupils have not mastered enough of vocabulary and yet are baffling with speech.

The Inductive - Deductive Method

This method is thought to be the first method, because it is based on some educational principles. In-fact this method is used to teach science and as grammar is a science of language, it is successfully used for teaching grammar. But it will not be appropriate to teach them as such, as pointed out by Thomson and Wyatt, "Even when the facts are discovered inductively, the knowledge acquired has to be applied deductively, or it is apt to be forgotten for lack of use.

A. Inductive Process

Presentation of Examples and Illustrations

Analysis of Examples

Generalization

The Rules

B. Deductive Process

Application of the Rule

Practice

TESTING GRAMMAR AND USAGE

Construction of test items

1. A list of specifications of the grammar skill showing the aspects of the skill and the specific language elements to be tested.
2. A rough inventory of the areas of grammar to be tested. Specifications of grammatical skill.
3. Recognition of structure which insides recognition of grammatical forms.
4. Production of structure which includes production of (a correct grammatical forms.
5. Correction of grammatical errors

Supposing you have chosen as your specification recognition of grammatical forms in the area of non-finite forms of verbs such as gerunds, infinitives and participles, you have to select a problem in that area which will provide a basis for your test-item For example, there is a class of transitive verbs (dislike, enjoy, avoid, keep, etc) which are followed only by the-ing form, and not the infinitive. A test-item may be based on problem.

METONYMY

Western culture studied poetic language and deemed it to be rhetoric. A. Al-Sharafi supports this concept in his book Textual Metonymy, "Greek rhetorical scholarship at one time became entirely poetic scholarship. Philosophers and rhetoricians thought that metaphors were the primary figurative language used in rhetoric. Metaphors served as a better means to attract the audience's attention because the audience had to read between the lines in order to get an understanding of what the speaker was trying to say. Others did not think of metonymy as a good rhetorical method because metonymy did not involve symbolism. Al-Sharafi explains, "This is why they undermined practical and purely referential discourse because it was seen as banal and not containing anything new, strange or shocking."

Greek scholars contributed to the definition of metonymy. For example, Isocrates worked to define the difference between poetic language and non-poetic language by saying that "prose writers are handicapped in this regard because their discourse has to conform to the forms and terms used by the citizens and to those arguments which are precise and relevant to the subject-matter. In other words, Isocrates proposes here that metaphor is a distinctive feature of poetic language because it conveys the experience of the world afresh and provides a kind of de-familiarization in the way the citizens perceive the world." Democritus described metonymy by saying, "Metonymy, that is the fact that words and meaning change." Aristotle discussed different definitions of metaphor, regarding one type as what we know to be metonymy today.

Latin scholars also had an influence on metonymy. Auctor's treatise Rhetorica ad Herennium states metonymy as, "the figure which draws from an object closely akin or associated an expression suggesting the object meant, but not called by its own name". Auctor describes the process of metonymy to us saying that we first figure out what a word means. We then figure out that word's relationship with other words. We understand and then call the word by a name that it is associated with. "Perceived as such then metonymy will be a figure of speech in which there is a process of abstracting a relation of proximity between two words to the extent that one will be used in place of another." Cicero viewed metonymy as more of a stylish rhetorical method and described it as being based on words, but motivated by style.

Metonymy is one of the basic characteristics of cognition. It is extremely common for people to take one well-understood or easy-to-perceive aspect of something and use it to stand either for the thing as a whole or for some other aspect or part of it. ... The kind [of metonymic models] of most interest for [categorization] are those in which a member or subcategory can stand metonymically for the whole category for the purpose of making inferences or judgments.

Metonymy of Definition

It is a figure of speech that replaces the name of a thing with the name of something else with which it is closely associated. We can come across examples of metonymy both from literature and in everyday life.

Metonymy is often confused with another figure of speech called synecdoche. They resemble each other but are not the same. Synecdoche refers to a thing by the name of one of its parts. For example, calling a car "a wheel" is a synecdoche. A part of a car i.e. "a wheel" stands for the whole car. In a metonymy, on the other hand, the word we use to describe another thing is closely linked to that particular thing, but is not a part of it. For example, "Crown" which means power or authority is a metonymy.

Metonymy is different from a metaphor. A metaphor draws resemblance between two different things as in "You are sunlight and I moon" - Sun and Moon from Miss Saigon. Sunlight (and moon) and human are two different things without any association but it attempts to describe one thing in terms of another based on a supposed similarity. Metonymy, however, develops relation on the grounds of close associations as in "The White House is concerned about terrorism." The White House here represents the people who work in it.

Examples of Metonymy in Everyday Life

We use metonymy frequently in our everyday life. For a better understanding, let us observe a few metonymy examples:

1. England decides to keep check on immigration. (England refers to the government.)
2. The suits were at meeting. (The suits stand for business people.)
3. The pen is mightier than the sword. (Pen refers to written words and sword to military force.)
4. The Oval Office was busy in work. ("The Oval Office" is a metonymy as it stands for people at work in the office.)
5. Let me give you a hand. (Hand means help.)

Metonymy Examples from Literature

The given lines are from Shakespeare's "Julies Caesar" Act I.

"Friends, Romans, countrymen, lend me your ears."

Mark Anthony uses "ears" to say that he wants the people present there to listen to him attentively. It is a metonymy because the word "ears" replaces the concept of attention.

This line is from Margaret Mitchell's novel "Gone with the Wind".

"I'm mighty glad Georgia waited till after Christmas before it secedes or it would have ruined the Christmas parties."

Scarlett uses "Georgia" to point out everything that makes up the state: citizens, politician, government etc. It is a metonymy extremely common in the modern world, where a name of a country or state refers to a whole nation and its government. Thus, it renders brevity to the ideas.

These lines are taken from "Out, Out" by Robert Frost.

"As he swung toward them holding up the hand

Half in appeal, but half as if to keep

The life from spilling"

In these lines, the expression "The life from spilling" is a metonymy that refers to spilling of blood. It develops a link between life and blood. The loss of too much blood means loss of life. These lines are from the poem "Yet Do I Marvel".

"The little buried mole continues b'ind,

Why flesh that mirror Him must someday die,"

Countee Cullen uses "flesh" to represent human and questions God why we have to die when we are created in His likeness.

These lines are from Lycidas written by John Milton.

"But now my oat proceeds,

And listens to the herald of the sea

That came in Neptune's plea,

He asked the waves, and asked the felon winds,

What hard mishap hath doomed this gentle swain?"

In the above-mentioned lines, John Milton uses "oat" for a musical instrument made out of an oak-stalk. Thus, "oat" represents the song that the poet is composing next to the ocean.

Metonymy Function

Generally, metonymy is used in developing literary symbolism i.e. it gives more profound meanings to otherwise common ideas and objects. By using metonymy, texts exhibit deeper or hidden meanings and thus drawing readers' attention. In addition, the use of metonymy helps achieve conciseness. For instance, "Rifles were guarding the gate" is more concise than "The guards with rifles in their hands were guarding the gate."

Furthermore, metonymy, like other literary devices, is employed to add a poetic color to words to make them come to life. The simple ordinary things are described in a creative way to insert this "life" factor to the literary works.

Metonymy is a figure of speech in which a thing or concept is called not by its own name but rather by the name of something associated in meaning with that thing or concept. The words "metonymy" and "metonym" come from the Greek: metonymia, "a change of name", from, meta "after, beyond" and - onymia, a suffix used to name figures of speech, from onyma or onoma, "name".

For instance, "Wall Street" is often used metonymously to describe the U.S. financial and corporate sector, while "Hollywood" is used as a metonym for the U.S. film industry because of the fame and cultural identity of Hollywood, a district of the city of Los Angeles, California, as the historical center of film studios and film stars. The national capital is often used to represent the government or monarchy of a country, such as "Washington" for United States government or "Downing Street" for the Government of the United Kingdom.

Metonymy and related figures of speech are common in everyday talk and writing. Synecdoche and metalepsis are considered specific types of metonymy. Polysemy, multiple meanings of a single word or phrase, sometimes results from relations of metonymy. Both metonymy and metaphor involve the substitution of one term for another. In metaphor, this substitution is based on some specific analogy between two things, whereas in metonymy the substitution is based on some understood association or contiguity.

American literary theorist Kenneth Burke described metonymy as one of four "master tropes": metaphor, a substitute for perspective; metonymy, a substitute for reduction; synecdoche, a substitute for representation; and irony, a substitute for dialectic. He described these tropes and the way they overlap in *A* Grammar of Motives.

In addition to its use in everyday speech, metonymy is a figure of speech in some poetry and in much rhetoric. Greek and Latin scholars of rhetoric made significant contributions to the study of metonymy.

Meaning relationships

This section needs additional citations for verification. Please help improve this article by adding citations to reliable sources. Unsourced material may be challenged and removed. (December 2013)

Synecdoche, wherein a specific part of something is used to refer to the whole, or the whole to a specific part, usually is understood as a specific kind of metonymy. However, sometimes people make an absolute distinction between a metonymy and a synecdoche, treating metonymy as different from, rather than inclusive of, synecdoche. There is a similar problem with the use of simile and metaphor.

Metalepsis is also closely related to metonymy. Much as synecdoche, it is sometimes understood as a specific kind of metonymy. Metalepsis is a figure of speech in which a word or a phrase from figurative speech is used in a new context. The new figure of speech refers to an existing one.[9] For example, in the idiom lead foot, meaning someone who drives fast, lead is a heavy substance, and a heavy foot on the accelerator pedal would cause a vehicle to go quickly. The use of "lead foot" to describe a person follows the intermediate substitution of "lead" for "heavy". The figure of speech is a "metonymy of a metonymy".

The concept of metonymy also informs the nature of polysemy, i.e., how the same phonological form (word) has different semantic mappings (meanings). If the two meanings are unrelated, as in the word pen meaning both writing instrument and enclosure, they are considered homonyms.

Within logical polysemies, a large class of mappings may be considered to be a case of metonymic transfer (e.g., chicken for the animal, as well as its meat; crown for the object, as well as the institution). Other cases wherein the meaning is polysemous, however, may turn out to be more metaphorical, e.g., eye as in the eye of the needle.

Metaphor and metonymy

Metonymy works by the contiguity (association) between two concepts, whereas the term metaphor is based upon their analogous similarity. When people use metonymy, they do not typically wish to transfer qualities from one referent to another as they do with metaphor. There is nothing press-like about reporters or crown-like about a monarch, but "the press" and "the crown" are both common metonyms. Some uses of figurative language may be understood as both metonymy and metaphor; for example, the relationship between "a crown" and a "king" could be interpreted metaphorically

The Two examples using the term "fishing" help clarify the distinction. The phrase "to fish pearls" uses metonymy, drawing from "fishing" the idea of taking things from the ocean. What is carried across from "fishing fish" to "fishing pearls" is the domain of metonymy.

Kinds of Metonymy

A special case of metonymy, part for the whole, is known as is synecdoche:

1. The automobile is clogging our highways. (= the collection of automobiles)
2. We need a couple of strong bodies for our team. (= strong people)
3. There are a lot of good heads in the university. (= intelligent people)
4. I've got a new set of wheels. (= car, motorcycle, etc.)
5. We've got some new blood in the organisation. (= new people)

There are, however, plenty of other kinds of metonymy

They are "different kinds of processes. Metaphor is principally a way of conceiving of one thing in terms of another, and its primary function understands. Metonymy, on the other hand, has primarily a referential function, that is, it allows us to use one entity to *stand for* another. But metonymy is not merely a referential device. It also serves the function of providing understanding. For example, in the case of the metonymy the part for the whole there are many parts that can stand for the whole. Which part we pick out determines which aspect of the whole we are focusing on. When we say that we need some "good heads" on the project, we are using "good heads" to refer to "intelligent people". The point is not just to use a part (head) to stand for a whole (person) but rather to pick out a particular characteristic of the person, namely, intelligence, which is associated with the head. The same is true for other kinds of metonymies. ...

Thus metonymy serves some of the same purposes that metaphor does, and in somewhat the same way, but it allows us to focus more specifically on certain aspects of what is being referred to. It is also like metaphor in that it is not just a poetic or rhetorical device. Nor is it just a matter of language. Metonymic concepts are part of the ordinary, everyday way we think and act as well as talk.

TECHNIQUES OF USING VISUAL AIDS

The teacher should plan the routine of the use of visual aids is the class. He should classify all the available aids and check to find out that they are ready for use without much delay. The teacher may give a brief talk about the aids and the type of information they will provide and thus prepare the children before using the particular visual aids. The purpose of using the visual aids should be known to the children. Over enthusiasm in using visual aids leads to waste of precious teaching time.

The teacher should be careful in selecting the visual aids so that it will fit the need. Only when there is a need, visual aids should be used. Perfuse use of visual aids leads to confusion and thus jeopardize the entire teaching process. The visual aids presented should bring out student reaction so that the teacher is able to judge the use of visual aids. The teacher should be use various types of visual aids and see that the class is able to judge the visual aids used in the class clearly.

NEED FOR THE STUDY

1. Since video instruction is considered as the latest and most effective innovation in the field of education particularly programmes for Effectiveness of Teaching Metonymy the study is needed in the present contest.
2. In this way learning metonymy is provided learner centered programme are needed in the present context.
3. Multimedia is effective utilize in the video programmes which guarantees minimum level of learning on the part of the learners.
4. This study is undertaken by the researcher to stress the point of effective learning which is needed for the students to improve the knowledge in Teaching Metonymy spelling video, sources and hence. It is conceded as a needful one to bring and change in the field of education particularly in conducting teaching - learning process effectively.
5. To create awareness on video instruction particularly among IXth standard students, investigator felt that the study is need one.

SIGNIFICANCE OF THE STUDY

Due to educational technological advances in class practices, every teacher is expected to use these technologies to enhance his class room teaching. Hence video assisted instruction plays a vital role in the improvement of classroom teaching. In particular Effectiveness of Teaching Metonymy in modern Techniques can easily be improved through this way.

OPERATIONAL DEFINITIONS OF THE KEY TERMS USED

1. Tamil

Tamil languages are a First language in India. It is also a link language, and library language. Language serves as a means of communication. There are two modes of expression / available for a user of any language. One is known as speech and the other is writing.

2. Metonymy

Metonymy makes written communication easy. It also establishes to a large extent a person's educational level. The better we spell, the move we are likely to know. Good Metonymy carries with it social prestige. If one's Teaching Metonymy is poor and earless, communication suffers because the reads will be puzzled to understand the word.

3. Video

Video has become a very useful aid for the teaching of Tamil. The largest technique of language teaching now is adopted on the Video. Listening to video lessons in Tamil helps in developing correct pronunciation, listening with comprehension, acquaintance with different kinds of conversational English and dialogues. It also enriches the vocabulary. Video refers to the storage of visuals and their display in a television type screen.

4. Video Assisted Instruction

Unlike the traditional method it is very effective innovative method in teaching Tamil Teaching Metonymy. When we use this method of teaching, the students will be as positive learner. In Class room teaching, video acts as a tutor or tool in the hands of the language teacher.

5. Effectiveness

Effectiveness means that entry behaviours and exist behavior of IXth standard students in understanding the Teaching Metonymy in modern Techniques.

6. IX th Standard Students

They are in age group of 12 to 13. And they are in. pre adolescence period and their behavior pattern as follow as:

Usually, by this age children begin to attend to school where they are made to learn various and the teachers as well as the school environment generate pressures on them to work hard in order to perform well parents also now begin to make demands upon the children to lend their hand with household duties or in some cases saddle them with occupational responsibilities. The children have also to complete with their peers in terms of ability and productivity in school and also in their school situation.

Now in case the child performs well in school, home or in other social environment or is admired for his intellectual or motor pursuits he will be likely to develop a sense of achievement.

Such a child will consequently be motivated to work harder and achieve more in terms of competency be motivated to work hander and achieve more in terms of competency and productivity. On the other hand, if his performance remains inferior to that of his pars or he does not satisfy his teachers and parents with his performance, he may begin to look down upon himself and develop a sense of inferiority.

STATEMENT OF THE PROBLEMS

The Problem of the study is stated as *"A Study on Effectiveness of teaching Metonymy in modern Techniques among IX th Standard Students in Devakottai Educational District.*

LIMITATION OF THE STUDY

1. The study is restricted to IXth standard students Karaikudi, Devakkottai Educational District.
2. The researcher conducted research only 25 students.
3. Investigator conducted the class only in Teaching Metonymy
4. 25 Students in controlled group and 50 students in compartmental group

OBJECTIVES OF THE STUDY

1. To find out the significant difference between the mean scores of pre-test and post-test performance of controlled group in the understanding of Metonymy of teaching.
2. To find out the significant difference between the means scores of pre-test and post-test performance of Experimental group in the understanding of Metonymy of teaching.
3. To find out the significant difference' between the means scores of pre-test of controlled group and experimental group in the understanding of Metonymy of teaching.
4. To find out the significant difference between the means scores of post-test of controlled group and experimental group in the understanding of Metonymy of teaching.

5. To find out the significant difference in the means scores of post test of experimental group in the understanding of Metonymy of teaching in respect of boys and girls.
6. To find out the significant difference in the means scores of post test of experimental group to the understanding of Metonymy of teaching of in respect of Educated and illiterate parents.
7. To find out the significant different between the means scores of post test if experimental group in the understanding of Metonymy of teaching of in respect of rural and urban students.

HYPOTHESES

1. There is no significant difference between the means scores of pre-test and post-test performance of controlled group in the understanding of Teaching Metonymy in modern techniques among IX th Standard Students.
2. There is no significant difference between the means scores of pre-test and post-test performance of Experimental group in the understanding of Teaching Metonymy in modern techniques among IXth Standard Students.
3. There is no significant difference between the means scores of pre-test performance of Controlled and Experimental group in the understanding of Teaching Metonymy in modern techniques among IXth Standard Students.
4. There is no significant difference between the means scores of post-test performance of Controlled and Experimental group of the understanding of Teaching Metonymy in modern techniques among IXth Standard Students.
5. There is no significant difference between the means scores of post-test performance of Experimental group of the understanding of Teaching Metonymy in modern techniques among IXth Standard Students in the respect of boys and girls.
6. There is no significant difference between the means scores of post-test performance of Experimental group of the understanding of Teaching Metonymy in modern techniques among IXth Standard Students in the respect of Student's parents Education.

7. There is no significant difference between the means scores of post-test performance of Experimental group of the understanding of Teaching Metonymy in modern techniques among IXth Standard Students in the respect of rural and urban students.

SCOPE OF THE STUDY

1. Technological input can be given in teaching - learning process, Instead of conducting the classes by conduct in a traditional way.
2. Knowledge in metonymy can be improved through modern techniques.
3. Learners freedom can be given by using video instruction programmes. Because it stress the effective learning under the guidance of teachers based no learners capacity.

CONCLUSION

Education is vital for the development of any country. Teachers in the educational system play a significant role. They are dispensers of knowledge in the teaching - learning process. The academic achievement of the learners largely lies on the teachers instructional delivery system.

If the teachers combine newer technologies in their instruction, these will be a significant improvement in the academic performance of the learners. But it is noted that some teachers exhibit resistance towards video. This study attempts to find out the video instruction usage problems among the IXth Standard Students in Karaikudi, Devakkottai Educational District.

Chapter - II

Review of The Related Literature

INTRODUCTION

According to **Charter V.Good,** "The keys to the vast store house of published literature may open doors to sources of significant problems and explanatory hypotheses and provide helpful orientation for definition of the interpretation of results. In order to be creative and original, one must read extensively and critically as a stimulus to thinking".

According to **W.R. Borg**, "the literature in any field forms the foundation upon which all future work will be built. It we fail to build the foundation of Knowledge provided by the review of literature our work is likely to be shallow and native and will often duplicate work that has already been done better by someone else".

NEED OF REVIEW OF LITERATURE

The review of literature is essential due to the following reasons.

1. It is very essential for ever investigator to be up-to-date in his information about the literature, related to his own problem already done by others. It is considered the most important prerequisite to actual planning and conducting the study.

2. It provides as source of problem of study an analogy may be drawn for identifying and selecting his own problem of research. The researcher formulates his hypothesis on the basis of review of literature. It also provides the rationale for the study. The results and findings for the study can also be discussed at length.
3. One of the early steps in planning a research work is to review research done previously in the particular area of interest and relevant area quantitative and qualitative analysis of this research usually gives the worker an indication of the direction
4. It avoids the replication of the study of findings to take an advantage from similar of related literature as regards to methodology, techniques of data collection, procedure adopted and conclusions drawn. He can justify his own Endeavour in the field.
5. The review of literature indicates the clear picture of the problem to be solved. The scholarship in the field can be developed by reviewing the literature of the field.

BJECTIVES OF REVIEW OF LITERATURE

The review of literature serves the following purposes in conducting research work:

1. It provides theories, ideas, explanations' or hypothesis which may prove useful in the formulation of a new problem.
2. It provides the sources for hypothesis. The researcher can formulate research hypothesis on the basis of available studies.
3. It indicates whether the evidence already available solves the problem adequately without requiring further investigation. It avoids the replication.
4. It suggests method, procedure sources of data and statistical techniques appropriate to the solution of the problem.
5. It locates comparative data and findings useful in the interpretation and discussion of results. The conclusions drawn in the related studies may be used as the subject for the findings of the study.

6. It helps in developing experts and general scholarship of the investigator in the area investigated.
7. It contributes towards the accurate knowledge of the evidence or literature in one's area of activity is a good avenue towards making oneself. This knowledge is an assert ever after wards, whether one is employed in an institution of higher learning or a research organization.

PURPOSE OF THE REVIEW OF LITERATURE

Review of the related literature besides, to allow the researcher to acquaint himself with current knowledge in the field or area in which he or she is going to conduct his or her research, serves the following specific purposes.

1. The review of related literature enables the researcher to define the limits of the field. It helps the researcher to delimit and define his problem. The knowledge of related literature brings the researcher up to data on the work which others have done and them to state the objectives clearly and concisely
2. By reviewing the related literature the researchers can avoid unfruitful and useless problem areas. He can select those areas in which positive findings are likely to result and his Endeavour's would be likely to add to the knowledge in a meaningful way.
3. Through the review of related literature the researcher can avoid unintentional duplication of well established findings. It is no use of replicate a study when the study when the stability and validity of its result have been clearly established.
4. The review of related literature gives the researcher an understanding of the research methodology which refers to the way the study is to be conducted. It help the researcher to know about the tools and instruments which proved to be useful and promising the previous studies. The advantage of the related literature is also to provide insight into statistical methods through which validity of results is to be established.
5. The final and important specific reason for reviewing the related literature to know about the recommendations of previous

researcher for further research which they have listed in their studies.

Bruce W.Tuckman (1978) has enumerated the following purposes of the review.

1. Discovering important variable.
2. Distinguishing what has done from what needs to be done.
3. Synthesizing the available studies to have perspective
4. Determining meanings relevance of the study and relationship with the study and its deviation from the available studies.

Edward 1. Vockell (1983) has pointed out the following two purposes:

1. The main purpose of this review is to put the hypothesis to be examined in the research report into its proper context.
2. Secondary purposes of this part of the report are to provide readers with guidelines regarding where they can look to find more information and to establish the author's credential by letting readers know that the researcher is aware of what has been giving on with regard to the current and related topics.

The review of literature provides some insight regarding strong points and limitations of the previous studies. It enables him to improve his own investigation.

STUDIES CONDUCTED IN INDIA

1. **Urmil katoch (2010)** in his article "developing speaking Tamil skills in Indian students" communicative language is a window that opens to the outside world. As a language teacher, have been working on many projects to develop the skills among the India students the skills among the Indian and puppetry students practice speaking Tamil. Enacting drama/ short skills through puppet show builds confidence and poise to emerge successful in group discussion /seminars/ debates and interviews. Language teachers to adopt these techniques promote speaking skills in Tamil to overcome the inhibition of speaking in Tamil of Indian.

2. **Mahar attar and s.s. chopra (2010)** in their article "Language Teaching in India" the position of -Tamil in India gaining more and more impetus. The need of Tamil in India is for a variety of purpose such as education, business and administration hence the teaching and learning of Tamil has increased the nominally. But in order to teach a communicative language more effectively, and toward the goal of proficient, it is necessary for prospective teachers to be conversant with the theories, approaches and methods of teachers to be conversant with the theories, approaches and methods of teaching i.e. what should be taught. The attitude that communicative language teachers had, towards teaching methods and classroom techniques varied, when the teacher centered

3. **Thirumalai M.S (2009)** in his study on "teaching Tamil to speakers of other language". This is an introductory course on teaching English to speakers of other languages. The goal of this experimental text is to introduce the students to some basic ideas, method, and tools of teaching Tamil as a communicative language.

4. **Savitra.M (2009)** "Teaching Tamil as a mother language using communicative language teaching - an evaluation of practice in India" this paper traces the history of communicative language teaching (CLT) reasons for communicative language teaching in America and Europe, CLT theory and the advent of CLT in India. The reasons for CLT being popular are critically analyzed and evaluated. The implementation of CLT in India - its success and failure - is discussed. Suggestions for making CLT a success in India are discussed.

5. **Murali. M (2009)** in his study on "teaching Tamil as a communicative language in India" majority of the students are coming from village and also their parents are farmers and uneducated. If the nature fails, survival of the formers will be questionable. Hence the students are mentally discouraged due to the family conditions. In the second category, the students are enough background in basic education since their parents all educated and they don't find much difficulty is pursuing their

higher education. The finding of the study that the only thing is that they have to be given training in oral communication also. Hence, a common programmed for communicative language teaching must be female in the pre - schooling itself.

6. **Rama Meganathan (2009)** in his article "communicative language education in rural school of India" that the increasing demand for Tamil both as a language and as a medium driven by the instrumental motivation has compelled most governments at the state level to introduce Tamil as a language from class one while the demand increase on the one hand, the quality of communicative language education is our state schools, more particularly in rural schools, presents an abysmal picture. The 'divide' between the urban and rural is further contributed by the way communicative language education is making it way medium of instruction.

7. **Chandra Sekaran. T (2008**) made an attempt to his study of "Family environment in relation to study habits and Academic Achievement among highest secondary science group's students on Thanjavur Education District" .the investigator selected 430 students consist of 235 boys and 195 girls. Investigator finding revealed that study habits expected influence academic achievement in case of science students both male and female. circles to your speaking skills for decent job, want to impress a girl, or desire respect society, everything

8. **Emilia Stopar (2008)** An Analysis of Form and function in Course plans and teaching materials in the subject of communicative language for Upper Secondary school. This essay deals with the communicative approach towards learning communicative language. The aim is to investigate how and why form and/or function are stressed in course plans in the subject of communicative language intended for the first year of upper secondary school and how the content of these plans are mirrored in teaching materials.

9. **Maria Edvardsson (2008)** A study of conversational topic shifts among communicative language learners of Tamil studies carried out by different scholars have shown that the social roles society

assigns to women and men create differences in how the genders use language. However, there is little previous research in the domain of gender and topic shift or initiation.

10. **Ravi (2008)** in his article titled " parents personality development and Academic performance to students" in the journal "journal of psychological researches" at Namakkal and found that parents involvement could help the students improve their socialization and academic achievement performance and school authorities should take necessary acts for the parents involvement in the conformity behaviours and education of the children.

11. **Revathi Viswanathan (2008)** conducted a study on "Recent impacts of internet on -communicative language training in India". The study discusses the impact of the internet in education in India, in general and in communicative language education in particular.

12. **'Sanjay Kumar and Praveen Raj (2008)** conducted a study on "IGNOU Edusat, GD and GV- Assessment study". Qualitative and Qualitative study was conducted. The awareness of teachers was also assessed with face to face interviews, open ended and closed ended questions. The sample was selected using stratified sampling techniques. The study threw light on the teachers, awareness of Edusat, Gyan Darshan and Gyan Vani.

13. **Sree Priya Ashok (2008)** in her article titled "parent child interaction and academic achievement in kinder garden, primary and middle school". **"Indian journal of applied psychology"** at Kodaikanal and emphasized that parent child interacting helps to enhance the academic performance of the child and the training given to the parent will have the desire result of improving the scholastic achievement of the children and it revealed that there was no significant difference between parent child interaction and academic achievement in boys but significant difference was seen in girls.

14. **Nicola Belsey (2007)** titled "communicative activity in the Tamil classroom". The purpose of this essay is to investigate year 5 pupils' evaluation of their own abilities regarding Tamil and to

see if this is reflected in an individual's communicative activity and participation in the lesson. This essay also poses the question if it is possible to increase communicative activity in the lesson through a three - week programme of interactive exercises designed to emulate the criteria of the syllabus and the National test.

15. **Bernad John Poole (2007)** in his study on "technology integrated Education: the Indian Experience" a context for the ensuring discussion of the extent to which modern computer based information and communication technologies (ICT) in India are integrated into primary Secondary and tertiary teaching and learning. The researcher concludes with a set of recommendations for successful technology integrated education.

16. **Chose, S. (2007)** looked into, the reporting in Tamil Nadu. The survey goes-beyond education and covers programmes on health agriculture and adult, education, It was found that although time-duration of the programmes was generous, the telecast did not come at a convenient hour with the result that the targeted audience had to miss the probrammes. A conspicuous neglect was pointed out in the training of teachers, both in writing radian scripts and in utilizing school broadcasts. All teachers agreed that school broadcasts were useful and helpful to students.

17. **Benjamin and Sivakumar (2006)** conducted a study, "Multimedia Enhances Effective Self-Learning". They in their study emphasizes the need and importance on learning through multimedia CD-based self-learning and dwells on the quality as well as quantity of teaching and learning bringing forth the need the significance of learning science through self-learning with the help of multimedia CD-based courseware.

18. **R.K.Singh (2005)** titled "teaching Tamil for specific purposes" an evolving experience Tamil for specific purposes (ESP) is a learner - centered approach to teaching Tamil as a communicative language. It fulfills the needs of adult learners who need to learn a communicative language for use in their specific fields, such as science, technology, medicine, leisure, and academic learning.

19. **Sobhana. N (2003)** in her article titled "Communicative competence in Tamil "as everybody knows that language is a means of communication, it is the medium and instrument through which thoughts, ideas and feelings are transmitted from one person to another. The importance of Tamil- is such that if under sentimental urges we give it up, we would cut ourselves off from the living stream of ever growing knowledge.
20. **Joseph C.Mukalel (1998)** in his article titled "communicative language teaching" communicative language teaching today has assumed dimensions that go for beyond the grid of an ordinary classroom teacher unless he is willing to apply his mind in a professional manner for enhancing the quality of his classroom teaching. This is true chiefly because an area like ELT has become a highly specialized on with components and implications well grounded on language teaching.

STUDIES CONDUCTED IN ABROAD

1. **Glover (2011)** in his article "communicative language teaching materials: theory and material" is a very useful for all teachers of Language experienced teachers looking for more specialized help with lesson planning or understanding course or involve with materials writing teaching materials covered in the text books. Of course, text books are covered but so are idea, worksheet, specific experience another one also covers the production and publication of materials.
2. **Laura Catherine Smith, Norbert Schmitt (2010)** in his article "Instructed communicative language vocabulary learning" this article -overviews current research on communicative language vocabulary learning. It concludes that a large 942— vocabulary is necessary to function in language: 8000-9000 word families for teaching, and perhaps as many as 5000-7000 families for oral discourse. In addition, a number of word knowledge aspects need to be learned about each lexical item. Taken together, these amounts to a substantial lexical learning challenge, one which many/most learners fail to meet.

To facilitate adequate vocabulary learning, four vocabulary learning partners (students, teachers, materials writer, and researchers) need to contribute to the learning process. Vocabulary learning programs need to include both an explicit, intentional learning component and a component based around maximizing exposure and incidental learning, the four learning strands (meaning -focused input, meaning - focused output, language focused learning, and fluency development) suggested by Nation (2001) provide a structure by which to integrate intentional and incidental learning is to increase the amount of engagement learners have with experiments. All four learning partners need to acknowledge the incremental nature of vocabulary learning, and to develop learning programs which are principled, long term and which recognize the richness and scope of the lexical knowledge that needs to be mastered.

1. **Lee, Jeong. Ah (2009)** in his study on "teacher's sense of efficacy in teaching language perceived communicative language proficiency and attitudes towards the communicative language". The present study by adopting the notion of teachers sense of efficacy as the theoretical framework, has explored Korean A ri 1/4A-cict elementary school teacher confidence in teacher Language. The study has also examined teacher's attitudes towards the communicative language and the current Korean elementary Language Education policy and practices a teachers communicative language proficiency and respectively. It was found that teaches communicative language were the significant predicators, Language teaching specific efficacy beliefs or confidences. Several important theoretical and practical implications of teacher development and policy making in the Korean elementary language educational context have emerged from the present study.
2. **Natasa Indihar Chaucer (2009)** conducted a research study on "Developing speaking skills in the young learners in the classroom" at Slovenia emphasized that young learners in the communicative classroom should get as many speaking time should slowly but steadily raise so as to prepare them for various communicative situations keeping in mind that each classroom offers a wide range of learners differencing in their abilities knowledge confidence, motivation and learning styles, a teacher should provide them with a proper environment that would help

them develop their skills, in depend of their basic characteristics and diversity.

3. **Meredith Rowe and Susan Golder - Medow (2009)** in their article titled "Early gesture selectively predicts later language learning" in the journal "Development science" at U.S.A and emphasized that particular milestone in vocabulary and sentence complexity at the age by watching how children move their hands two years later.
4. **Rachel (2008)** in her study on" Development linguistic ability and early language exposure " for more than 100 years, the scientific and educational communities have the thought that age is critical to the outcome of language learning, but whether the onset and type of language experienced during early life affects the ability to learn communicative language is unknown. Here we show that deaf and learning individuals exposed to language to infancy perform comparably will in learning a new language later in life, Whereas deaf individual with little language experience in early life perform poorly, regardless of whether the cater language was speaking or signed. These findings show that language learning ability is determine by the onset of language experience during early brain development, in depend of the specific form of the experience.
5. **Wang, Chuang (2004)** they conducted their studies on "Self - Regulated Learning strategies and self - efficacy beliefs of children learning as a communicative language" strategies in the process of learning social cognitive and socio - cultural perspective of self regulation, recent studies of students self efficacy beliefs and language learners willingness to communicate this study provides a "thick description" of bowl Chinese children's behalf out associated with self-efficacy beliefs and strategy age across home-base and school based context. Participants reported self efficacy beliefs across a variety of language learning tasks in listening, speaking, reading and writing. These findings have extended scholarly work on children's self efficacy beliefs and their use of language learning strategies in the context of communicative language acquisition. The implication of this study

also extend to language class room teaching since teachers may better understand their students self-efficacy and the impact of self- efficacy study they may incorporate SRL-strategies specific to communicative language learning in the curriculum and enhance students self-efficacy by providing accurate and continuous feedback to the students.

6. **Capraco, Fernado (2003)** in his study "Educational studies; Human Science" the purpose of this journal study was to described and explore the communicative language learning experience of perspective international teaching assistants (ITAS) in an intermediate SE course in order to improve the teaching and learning in SE course. Five Asian students' volunteers were selected to participate on the study these finding yielded conclusion. First, reflection activities should be an important part of ITA, SE course. Second ITA learners need to be encouraged to make positive changes in their thinking and attitude about learning SE, because these changes seem to have a beneficial effect on their languages learning.
7. **'Richards and Rodgers (2001),** in his article titled "Communicative Language teaching" has considered the best approach rather than a method. It refers to a diverse set of principles that reflect a communicative view of language and language learning and that can be used to support a wide variety of Classroom procedures.
8. **Richards and Rodgers (2001)** also quoted **Johnson (1984)** and **Littlewood (1984)** consider an alternative learning theory that they also see as compatible with CLT, there is a skill learning model of learning. **Longman** dictionary of language teaching and applied Linguistics defines the communicative Approach communicative language teaching as "an APPROACH to foreign or second language teaching which emphasizes that the goal of language learning is communicative competence." (Richards et al 1992:65)
9. **Freeman (2000),** in his article titled "communicative Language Teaching (CLT) aims broadly to apply the theoretical perspective of the Communicative Approach by making communicative competence the goal of language teaching and by acknowledging

the independence of language and communication.

10. **Brown (2000),** in his article titled "communicative competence is relative, not absolute, and depends on the cooperation of all the participants involved."
11. **Warschauer &Kern, (2000)** Stemming from the socio-cognitive perspective of the socio- linguistic theory, with an emphasis on meaning and communication, and a goal to develop learners' "communicative competence", communicative Language Teaching (CLT) approach evolves as a prominent language teaching method and gradually replaced the previous grammar-translation method and audio-lingual method. Since the concept of "communicative competence" was first introduced by Hymes in the mid-1960s, many researchers have helped develop theories and practices of communicative language teaching approach.
12. **Li (1998)** reported that all teachers who attended in-service teaching training in South Korea considered that the major constraint of implementing CLT is their own deficiency of communicative language.
13. **Thompson (1996)** in the application of the communicative language teaching (CLT) method in the classroom, there are still several misconceptions about what it involves. Since the main goal of CLT is communicative competence and its emphasis is on communication, several theorists and teachers stats that CLT does not involve teaching grammar at all.
14. **Willbrand M.L. & Riecke R.D. (1983) as 'Teaching oral communication in Elementary schools'** defined 'oral communicate ion' as the process of interaction through heard and spoken messages in a variety of situations. And instruction which integrates the teaching of listening and speaking over various situations has been termed "the communicative approach to language teaching.

CONCLUSION

The review gave lot of insight to the investigator in selecting the research problem and suitable methodology. The research gap was also identified on the basis of the review. The methodology adopted by the researcher in this study was discussed in the following chapters.

Chapter-III

Methodology

INTRODUCTION

The present chapter 'Methodology' explains the detailed account of the following title of the problem, definition of key terms with operational definitions, objectives, hypothesis, assumption of the study, delimitation of the study, planning research in stages and selection of sample.

METHODS AND ITS PROCEDURE

For this research parallel group design was adopted. All the 50 students studying in IXth standard in the Karaikudi where the subjects of Experiment, after administering validated pre-test selected techniques were implemented by the investigator. The investigator divided the students into two groups named as Controlled Group and Experimental Group. Each group has consisted 25 students whose are selected randomly. The controlled group, pre-test was conducted by the investigator. He/she was given the treatment through the traditional method during the period of 1 week. Then, post-test was conducted to the controlled group. Followed by, the pre-test was conducted for Experimental group. Then the treatment was given for Experimental group for duration of 16 periods over 8 days. Each period extended for about 45 minutes and treatment was given on daily 2 periods allotted for Tamil which was used for data collection through video Assisted Instruction. Giving illustration for play way method such as joining words drills, identifying missing letters, by showing video clips, detecting errors of metonymy like APPLE with its picture and identifying errors and memorizing it clearly. Lastly, the investigator was conducted the post-test as per the same pattern but in different questions.

STATEMENT OF THE PROBLEM

The title of the present investigation is precisely stated thus, *A Study on Effectiveness of Teaching Metonymy in Modern Techniques among IXth standard students in Devakkottai Educational District.*

Operational Definition of The Key Terms Used

Tamil

Tamil languages are a First language in India. It is also a link language, and library language. Language serves as a means of communication. There are two modes of expression / available for a user of any language. One is known as speech and the other is writing.

Metonymy

Metonymy is often confused with another figure of speech called synecdoche. The resemble each other but are not the same. Metonymy is different from a metaphor.

Metonymy makes written communication easy. It also establishes to a large extent a person's educational level. The better we spell the move we are likely to know. Good Metonymy carries with it social prestige. If one's Teaching Metonymy is poor and earless, communication suffers because the reads will be puzzled to understand the word.

Video

Video has become a very useful aid for the teaching of Tamil. The largest technique of language teaching now is adopted on the Video. Listening to video lessons in Tamil helps in developing correct pronunciation, listening with comprehension, acquaintance with different kinds of conversational English and dialogues. It also enriches the vocabulary. Video refers to the storage of visuals and their display in a television type screen.

Video Assisted Instruction

Unlike the traditional method it is very effective innovative method in teaching Tamil Teaching Metonymy. When we use this method of teaching, the students will be as positive learner. In Class room teaching, video acts as a tutor or tool in the hands of the language teacher.

Effectiveness

Effectiveness means that entry behaviours and exist behavior of IXth standard students in understanding the Teaching Metonymy in modern Techniques.

IXth Standard Students

They are in age group of 12 to 13. And they are in. pre adolescence period and their behavior pattern as follow as:

Usually, by this age children begin to attend to school where they are made to learn various and the teachers as well as the school environment generate pressures on them to work hard in order to perform well parents also now begin to make demands upon the children to lend their hand with household duties or in some cases saddle them with occupational responsibilities. The children have also to complete with their peers in terms of ability and productivity in school and also in their school situation.

Now in case the child performs well in school, home or in other social environment or is admired for his intellectual or motor pursuits he will be likely to develop a sense of achievement.

Such a child will consequently be motivated to work harder and achieve more in terms of competency be motivated to work hander and achieve more in terms of competency and productivity. On the other hand, if his performance remains inferior to that of his pars or he does not satisfy his teachers and parents with his performance, he may begin to look down upon himself and develop a sense of inferiority.

OBJECTIVES OF THE STUDY

1. To find out the significant difference between the mean scores of pre-test and post-test performance of controlled group in the understanding of Metonymy of teaching.
2. To find out the significant difference between the means scores of pre-test and post-test performance of Experimental group in the understanding of Metonymy of teaching.
3. To find out the significant difference' between the means scores of pre-test of controlled group and experimental group in the understanding of Metonymy of teaching.
4. To find out the significant difference between the means scores of post-test of controlled group and experimental group in the understanding of Metonymy of teaching.
5. To find out the significant difference in the means scores of post test of experimental group in the understanding of Metonymy of teaching in respect of boys and girls.
6. To find out the significant difference in the means scores of post test of experimental group to the understanding of Metonymy of teaching of in respect of Educated and illiterate parents.
7. To find out the significant different between the means scores of post test if experimental group in the understanding of Metonymy of teaching of in respect of rural and urban students.

HYPOTHESES

1. There is no significant difference between the means scores of pre-test and post-test performance of controlled group in the understanding of Teaching Metonymy in modern techniques among IX th Standard Students.
2. There is no significant difference between the means scores of pre-test and post-test performance of Experimental group in the understanding of Teaching Metonymy in modern techniques among IXth Standard Students.
3. There is no significant difference between the means scores of pre-test performance of Controlled and Experimental group in

the understanding of Teaching Metonymy in modern techniques among IXth Standard Students.

4. There is no significant difference between the means scores of post-test performance of Controlled and Experimental group of the understanding of Teaching Metonymy in modern techniques among IXth Standard Students.
5. There is no significant difference between the means scores of post-test performance of Experimental group of the understanding of Teaching Metonymy in modern techniques among IXth Standard Students in the respect of boys and girls.
6. There is no significant difference between the means scores of post-test performance of Experimental group of the understanding of Teaching Metonymy in modern techniques among IXth Standard Students in the respect of Student's parents Education.
7. There is no significant difference between the means scores of post-test performance of Experimental group of the understanding of Teaching Metonymy in modern techniques among IXth Standard Students in the respect of rural and urban students.

LIMITATIONS OF THE STUDY

1. The study is restricted to IXth standard students Karaikudi, Devakkottai Educational District.
2. The researcher conducted research only 25 students.
3. Investigator conducted the class only in Teaching Metonymy
4. 25 Students in controlled group and 50 students in compartmental group

RESEARCH METHOD

The investigator employed experimental method to collect data from the students who are studying in middle-schools-located in Karikudi are in order to find out the effectiveness of Video -Assisted Instruction to improve the metonyms Vidco, LCD, Computer Assisted instruction.

EXPERIMENTAL METHOD AND EXPERIMENTAL DESIGNS

Experimental Method

Experimental design is a blueprint of the procedure that enables the researches to test hypothesis by reading valid conclusions about relationship between the independent and dependent variables. "Experiment means a scientific test to find out or prove something"- **Chakara Warthy**

Experimentation In Phases

The Experiment is conducted in two phase.

I. Conducting the pre-test

II. Conducting the post-test

For this research parallel group design was adopted. All the 50 students studying in IXth standard in the Karaikudi where the subjects of Experiment, after administering validated pre-test selected techniques were implemented by the investigator. The investigator divided the students into two groups named as Controlled Group and Experimental Group. Each group has consisted 25 students whose are selected randomly on the basis of pre achievement test scores controlled group, pre-test was conducted by the investigator. The Investigator was given the treatment through the traditional method during the period of 1 week. Then, post-test was conducted to the controlled group. Followed by, the pre-test was conducted for Experimental group. Then the treatment was given for Experimental group for a duration of 16 periods over 8 days. Each period extended for about 45 minutes and treatment was given on daily 2 periods allotted for Tamil Teaching Metonymy which was used for data collection through video Assisted Instruction.

The investigator gave training in metonymy through video assisted instruction in addition with teaching metonymy.

1. Show the Video Clips in order to understand the vocabulary with correct metonymy
2. To memorize the metonymy and to say it repeatedly,
3. To enable the students to come forward and tell the answer in front of the students,

4. To divide the students into three groups conduct Teaching metonymy
5. To create their interest to observe video clips and to say the right answer, To give a number of cards to arrange the vocabularies with correct spelling.

Phases of Experiment

1. Construction of question paper covering Bloom's taxonomy in the areas of knowledge, understanding, Application and skills.
2. Conducting pre-test
3. Assessing pre-test
4. Constructing post-test question paper
5. Assessing the post-test.

RESEARCH TOOL

The investigator himself developed a research tool which is indicated below. A questionnaire on *"A Study on Effectiveness of teaching metonymy in modern Techniques among IXth Standard Students in Devakkottai Educational District."* Self made tool has been made by the members, expert's critized the tool and they have given suggestion for improvement in the tool. The suggestion was incorporated in the tool.

CONSTRUCTION OF RESEARCH TOOL

In the process of construction the investigator referred few books on advanced Educational Technology, Journals and Encyclopedia to identify the *"A Study on Effectiveness of Teaching metonymy in modern Techniques among IXth Standard Students in Devakkottai Educational District."* and their different dimensions. After identify the different dimensions, the investigator has gone through in each and every dimensions and its related video instruction in the field of improving spelling knowledge.

After identifying the different items of effectiveness of video assisted instruction with the help of teacher's performance, the investigator met few experts in the fields of educational psychology and examines each and every topics that are selected as item for the research tool. Then the investigator also identified few improvement of video instruction related to improving the Teaching metonymy knowledge by having test with the students who are studying Karaikudi.

Selection of Sample

The investigator taken all the 50 students studied in IXth standard at Baima for investigation. The whole samples was divided into two groups by giving numerical order one and two. Odd numbers are named as controlled group. Even numbers are named as Experimental Group. Each group consists of 25 students randomly in intellectual capacity.

Description of Research Tool and Scoring Procedure

The investigator developed two questionnaires for pre-test and post-test. The questionnaires comprise the following items. Some items are followed for post-test including new vocabularies. The items are frame work of the same questions but the vocabularies testing the spelling were used differently. The pre-test questionnaires were administered among 10 students at Karaikudi as a pilot study. Some corrections are made according to difficulties faced by the above students. Then the questionnaire was presented to eminent language experts and corrective measures have been undertaken by the investigator under the guide and instruction of the above experts.

Pattern of Question Paper

The investigator developed 2 questionnaires for pre-test and post-test. In pre-test and post-test questions included are capital letters (2mark) missing letters (1 marks), opposite words (2 marks), feminine and plurals (8 marks), words building (2 marks) prefix and suffix (5 marks), look at the picture and find out the vocabularies (5 marks), combine the pictures to form compound words (5 marks), write the word to equal pictures in the blank and choose the best

Scoring

For objective type questions if answer is correct one mark will be given, if not zero will be given. For other questions, the marks will be given based upon their performance.

Technical Validity of CD

To measure the validity of the tool, the investigator was the CD. in front of the experts in research and that display instruction tool was appreciated and accepted by the experts.

Validation of Tools

Validity and reliability are two important characteristics of measuring tool. Validation refers to the accuracy with which a tool measures which it is supported the measure. A test is said to be valid if it meets the purpose of which it is designed content validity is used.

Content validity of a test is determined by finding out how will the test content represent the subject matter and situation upon which the test is supposed to be content validity of this diagnostic test is established to the experts opinion.

The content validity in determined by the fact that adequately covers both the content and objectives of the subject matter with which the tools is used. As per this statement said, possess diagnostic test, remedial teaching since the experts gave their concurrent for the content validity of the tools.

Reliability of the Tool

The reliability of the tool refers to the consistency of measurement observed for the same individual on different occasions or with different set of equivalent items. A test is a reliable to the extent that is measures accurately upon repeated administration.

There are four procedures in common use for computing reliability of the test following are the four methods of establishing reliability.

1. Test-pre-test
2. Alternative or parallel forms
3. Split half method
4. Rationale equivalences

The investigator adopted split half method and found that the reliability score from

$$R=2r/1+r$$
$$= 2x0.09/1+0.9$$
$$= 0.9$$

Pilot Study

The pilot study is conducted at the rudimentary stage of entering into the data collection which is done by the investigator before the actual data collection process. The main purpose of conducting the study is to get some prominary ideas about the present research and with the help of the above ideas the researchers plan is entire work to collect objective data in the present research process.

Sampling Techniques Used

For this research parallel group design was adopted. All the 50 students studying in IXth standard in where the subjects of Experiment, after administering validated pre-test selected techniques were implemented by the investigator. The investigator divided the students into two groups named as Controlled Group and Experimental Group. Each group has consisted 25 students whose are selected randomly. The controlled group, pre-test was conducted by the investigator. The investigator was given the treatment through the traditional method during the period of 1 week. Then, post-test was conducted to the controlled group. Followed by the pre-test was conducted for Experimental group. Then the treatment was given for Experimental group for duration of 16 periods over 8 days. Each period extended for about 45 minutes and treatment was given on daily 2 periods allotted for Tamil which was used for data collection through video Assisted Instruction.

ANALYSIS OF DATA

The marks incurred by each student in each task are tabulated from which mean score and standard deviation is collected and 't' value used to find out impact of the session. In this study suitable statistics technique are used.

STATISTICAL TECHNICAL USED

The investigator selected experimental design for this study. The investigator decided to have parallel group method. At the end, post-test was conducted on both groups. Then the investigator tabulated the pre-test and post-test scores of control and experimental groups. The mean and standard deviation of pre-test and post-test scores of both groups were computed. The investigator applied correlated group formulas 't' test in order to compare the difference between the mean scores of the both groups in pre-test and post-test.

CONCLUSION

An attempt is made to develop the Teaching metonymy of the students in Tamil through video assisted instruction.

Chapter - IV

Analysis and Interpretation of Data

INTRODUCTION

The present chapter 'Analysis and Interpretation data' explains the detailed account of the following title of the data analysis, statistical techniques used, mean, standard deviation, 't' -test, hypothesis testing a longer with diagrams and conclusion.

DATA ANALYSIS

The investigator selected experimental design for this study. The investigator decided to have parallel group study. The investigator administered a pre-test for controlled group and after that the investigator was given traditional treatment through traditional method post-test was conducted and valued the answer script. Then the investigator implemented the experimental treatment in experimental group the pupils for one week after conducted the pre-test as per the above group. At the end post-test was conducted and valued.

Then the investigator tabulated the pre-test and post-test scores of control groups and experimental group. The mean and standard deviation of pre-test and post-test scores of both groups were computed.

The investigator applied correlated group formulas 't test in order to compare the difference between the mean scores of the both group in pre-test and post-test.

STATISTICAL TECHNIQUES USED

In the present study the investigator followed the statistical procedures mentioned earlier to analyze the data and to arrive the meaningful conclusions. The 't' value has been used to find out the significance of the difference between the mean scores of attitude of the whole sample and the sub sample.

1. Gender
2. Parents Qualification
3. Native Place

MEAN ($\acute{X}$)

The mean of a distribution is commonly understood as the arithmetic average. The term grade point average, familiar to student is a mean value. It is computed by dividing the sum of all the scores by the numbers of scores. Formula is,

$$\acute{X} = \frac{\Sigma fx}{N}$$

Where x = mean

Σ = Sum of

X = Scores in a distribution

N = Number of Scores

f = Frequency

STANDARD DEVIATION (ó)

The standard deviation, the square root of the variance, is most frequently used as a spread or dispersion of scores in a distribution. The formula for standard deviation is

$$S.D = C.Ix\sqrt{\left[\frac{\Sigma\Sigma fd^2}{N}\right] - \left[\frac{\Sigma fd}{N}\right]}$$

't'-TEST

The test of significance of the difference between two means is known as t-test. It involves the computation of the ratio between experimental variance (Observed difference between two sample means) and error variance (the sampling error factor)

When small samples are involved, the t-test is used to determine statistical - significance, rather than normal probability table. This concept of small sample size was developed around 1915 by William Sealy Gusset, consulting tacticians for Guinness Bublin, Ireland. Gusset's - distribution table. The t-critical values necessary for rejection of a null hypothesis are higher for small samples of a given level of significance. Each t-critical value for rejection is based upon the appropriate number of degrees of freedom.

The t-test would be based upon this formula.

$$t = \frac{M_1 M_2}{SE_D}$$

$$SE_D = \sqrt{\frac{SD_1^2}{N_1} + \frac{SD_2^2}{N_2}}$$

$df = (N_1 - 1) + (N_2 - 1)$

M_1, M_2 – Mean Values

SD_1, SD_2 – Standard Deviation

N_1, N_2 – Number of Students

HYPOTHESES TESTING

Hypotheses – 1

There is no significant difference between the means scores of **pre-test and post-test** performance of **controlled group** in the understanding of Teaching Metonymy in modern techniques among IX th Standard Students.

Table- 1

't' value of the scores of the control Group Pre-test and Post-test

S. No	Group	Test	Number	Mean	S.D.	't' value	Level of Significance at 0.05
1	Control Group	Pre-test	25	22	10.29	2.03	Significan
		Post-test	25	27.84	10.07		

It is inferred that since the calculated value 2.03 is greater than the table value of 2.01 at 0.05 level of significance. There is significant difference between pre-test and post-test performance of control group. Hence the hypothesis framed by the investigator is **rejected.**

This implies that pre and post test mean scores of control group under consideration is statistically significant.

HYPOTHESES - 2

There is no significant difference between the means scores of **pre-test and post-test** performance of **Experimental group** in the understanding of Teaching Metonymy in modern techniques among IXth Standard Students.

Table - 2

't' value of the scores of Experimental Group Pre-test and Post-test

S. No	Group	Test	Number	Mean	S.D.	't' value	Level of Significance at 0.05
1	Experimental Group	Pre-test	25	29.6	9.82	3.88	Significant
		Post-test	25	39.4	7.93		

It is inferred that since the calculated value 3.88 is greater than the table value 2.01 at 0.05 level of significance. There is significant difference between the mean scores of pre-test and post-test performance of Experimental group. Hence the hypothesis framed by the investigator is **rejected.**

This implies that pre and post test mean scores of experimental group under consideration is statistically significant.

HYPOTHESES – 3

There is no significant difference between the means scores of **pre-test** performance of **Controlled and Experimental** group in the understanding of Teaching Metonymy in modern techniques among IXth Standard Students.

Table - 3

't' value of the scores of the Control and Experimental Groups Pre-test

S. No	Group	Test	Number	Mean	S.D.	't' value	Level of Significance at 0.05
1	Control Group	Post-test	25	22	10.29	2.77	Significant
2	Experimental Group		25	29.6	9.82		

It is inferred that since the calculated value 2.77 is greater than the table value 2.01 corresponding at 0.05 level of significant. There is significant difference between the mean scores of Control and Experimental group performance of Pre-test in the understanding as Metonymy in modern Techniques. Hence the hypothesis framed by the investigator is **rejected.**

This implies that pre test of control and experimental group do differ significantly.

HYPOTHESES - 4

There is no significant difference between the means scores of **post-test** performance of **Controlled and Experimental group** of the understanding of Teaching Metonymy in modern techniques among IXth Standard Students.

Table - 4

't' value of the scores of the Control and Experimental Groups Post-test

S. No	Group	Test	Number	Mean	S.D.	't' value	Level of Significance at 0.05
1	Control Group	Post-test	25	27.84	10.07	4.52	Significant
2	Experimental Group		25	39.4	7.93		

It is inferred that since the calculated value 4.52 is greater than the table value of 2.01 corresponding at 0.05 level of significant. There is significant difference between the mean scores of Control and Experimental group performance of Post – test. Hence the hypothesis framed by the investigator is **rejected.**

This implies that the post test means scores of control and experimental group under consideration is statistically significant.

HYPOTHESES - 5

There is no significant difference between the means scores of **post-test** performance of Experimental group of the understanding of Teaching Metonymy in modern techniques among IXth Standard Students in the respect of boys and girls.

Table - 5

't' value of the scores of the Experimental Groups Post-test

S. No	Group	Test	Variables	Number	Mean	S.D.	't' value	Level of Significance at 0.05
1	Experimental Group	Post-test	Boys	15	38.5	8.44	0.60	Not Significant
			Girls	10	40.4	7.34		

It is inferred that since the calculated value 0.60 is less than the table value of 2.07 corresponding at 0.05 level of significance. There is significant difference between in the mean scores of post-test of experimental group in the understanding of Metonymy in Modern Techniques in respect of boys and girls. Hence the hypothesis framed by the investigator is **accepted.**

This implies that both boys and girls do not differ significantly at the post-test level.

HYPOTHESES - 6

There is no significant difference between the means scores of **post-test** performance of Experimental group of the understanding of Teaching Metonymy in modern techniques among IXth Standard Students in the respect of Student's parents Education.

TABLE - 6

't' Value of the scores of the Experimental Groups Post-Test

S. No	Group	Test	Variables	Number	Mean	S.D.	't' value	Level of Significance at 0.05
1	Experimental Group	Post-test	Literate Parents	15	42.3	8.37	1.84	Not Significant
			Illiterate Parents	10	36.4	7.49		
			Girls					

It is inferred that since the calculated value 1.84 is less than the table value of 2.07 corresponding at 0.05 level of significance. There is significant difference between in the mean scores of post-test of experimental group in the understanding of metonymy in modern Techniques among IXth standard students in respect of literate and illiterate parents. Hence the hypothesis framed by the investigator is **accepted.**

This implies that both educated parents and illiterate parents do not differ significantly at the post-test level

HYPOTHESES - 7

There is no significant difference between the means scores of **post-test** performance of **Experimental** group of the understanding of Teaching Metonymy in modern techniques among IX th Standard Students in the respect of rural and urban students.

Table - 7

't' value of the scores of the Experimental Groups Post-test

S. No	Group	Test	Variables	Number	Mean	S.D.	't' value	Level of Significance at 0.05
1	Experimental Group	Post-test	Rural	9	35.61	8.66	2.74	Significant
			Urban	16	43.54	6.84		

It is inferred that since the calculated value 2.74 is Greater than the table value of 2.07 corresponding at 0.05 level of significance. There is significant difference between in the mean scores of post-test of experimental group in the understanding of metonymy in modern Techniques in respect of rural and urban area students. Hence the hypothesis framed by the investigator is **rejected.**

This implies that both rural and urban do differ significantly at the post-test level

CONCLUSION

In this chapter Analysis and Interpretation of the research have been discussed. Findings and Conclusion of the research will be given in the upcoming chapter.

Chapter - V

Summary of Findings and Conclusion

INTRODUCTION

The knowledge and technology based society requires individuals who are able to think critically about complex issues, analyse and adapt to new situations, solve problems of various kinds and communicate their thinking effectively. The study of Metonymy equips students with conceptual skills that are essential for successful and rewarding participation, with in a sufficient knowledge with in a society. To learn metonymy in a way that will serve they well throughout their life.

RESTATEMENT OF THE PROBLEM

The present study has attempted to improve the students Teaching of Metonymy through the video assisted instruction.

STATEMENT OF THE PROBLEM

"A Study On Effectiveness Of Teaching Metonymy In Modern Techniques Among Ix Th Standard Students In Devakkottai Educational District."

LIMITATION OF THE STUDY

1. The study is restricted to IXth standard students Karaikudi, Devakkottai Educational District.
2. The researcher conducted research only 25 students.
3. Investigator conducted the class only in Teaching Metonyms
4. 25 Students in controlled group and 50 students in compartmental group

OBJECTIVE OF THE STUDY

1. To find out the significant difference between the mean scores of pre-test and post-test performance of controlled group in the understanding of Metonymy of teaching.
2. To find out the significant difference between the means scores of pre-test and post-test performance of Experimental group in the understanding of Metonymy of teaching.
3. To find out the significant difference' between the means scores of pre-test of controlled group and experimental group in the understanding of Metonymy of teaching.
4. To find out the significant difference between the means scores of post-test of controlled group and experimental group in the understanding of Metonymy of teaching.
5. To find out the significant difference in the means scores of post test of experimental group in the understanding of Metonymy of teaching in respect of boys and girls.
6. To find out the significant difference in the means scores of post test of experimental group to the understanding of Metonymy of teaching of in respect of Educated and illiterate parents.
7. To find out the significant different between the means scores of post test if experimental group in the understanding of Metonymy of teaching of in respect of rural and urban students.

HYPOTHESES

1. There is no significant difference between the means scores of pre-test and post-test performance of controlled group in the

understanding of Teaching Metonymy in modern techniques among IX th Standard Students.

2. There is no significant difference between the means scores of pre-test and post-test performance of Experimental group in the understanding of Teaching Metonymy in modern techniques among IXth Standard Students.
3. There is no significant difference between the means scores of pre-test performance of Controlled and Experimental group in the understanding of Teaching Metonymy in modern techniques among IXth Standard Students.
4. There is no significant difference between the means scores of post-test performance of Controlled and Experimental group of the understanding of Teaching Metonymy in modern techniques among IXth Standard Students.
5. There is no significant difference between the means scores of post-test performance of Experimental group of the understanding of Teaching Metonymy in modern techniques among IXth Standard Students in the respect of boys and girls.
6. There is no significant difference between the means scores of post-test performance of Experimental group of the understanding of Teaching Metonymy in modern techniques among IXth Standard Students in the respect of Student's parents Education.
7. There is no significant difference between the means scores of post-test performance of Experimental group of the understanding of Teaching Metonymy in modern techniques among IXth Standard Students in the respect of rural and urban students.

MAJOR FINDINGS

The video assisted instruction techniques implemented by the investigator have significantly improved the performance of IXth standard students in identifying errors in teaching of metonymy.

1. The calculated value 2.03 is greater than the table value of 2.01 at 0.05 level of significance. There is significant difference between

pre-test and post-test performance of control group. Hence the hypothesis framed by the investigator is **rejected.**

2. The calculated value 3.88 is greater than the table value of 2.01 at 0.05 level of significance. There is significant difference between the mean scores of pre-test and post-test performance of experimental group. Hence the hypothesis framed by the investigator is **rejected.**

3. The calculated value 2.77 is greater than the table value of 2.01 corresponding at 0.05 level of significant. There is significant difference between the means scores of Control and Experimental group $_t$ performance of pre-test in the understanding of teaching of metonymy. Hence the Hypothesis framed by the investigator is **rejected.**

4. The calculated value 4.52 is greater than the table value of 2.01 corresponding at 0.05 level of significance. There is significant difference between the means scores of control & Experimental group performance of post - test. Hence the hypothesis framed by the investigator is **rejected.**

5. The calculated value 0.60 is less than the table value of 2.0 f corresponding at 0.05 level of significance. There is no significant difference between in the mean scores of post-test of experimental group in the understanding of teaching of metonymy respect of boys and girls. Hence the hypothesis framed by the investigator is **accepted.**

6. The calculated value 1.84 is less than the table value of 2.07 corresponding of significance 0.05 level. There is no significant difference between the mean scores of post-test of Experimental group in the understanding of teaching of metonymy among IXth standard students in respect of literate parents and illiterate parents. Hence the hypothesis framed by the investigator is **accepted**

7. The calculated value 2.74 is greater than the table value of 2.07 corresponding at 0.05 level of significance. There is significant difference in the means scores of post-test of Experimental group in the understanding of teaching of metonymy in respect of rural

and urban area students. Hence the hypothesis framed by the investigator is **rejected.**

DESCRIBE

The findings of this study were supported by similar findings of the studies in these techniques carried out by Mohan (1982), Jothi (1985), Baskaran, Herbert S. (1989), Sudarkkodi (1990), Ramamoorthy (1992), Kumar (1997), Allavandar (2003), Prasanna kumar (2003), G.Anbalagan (2003), Shubhra (1984), Ann and V.S (1985), Rohtas Singh (1995), Manjunath Govlat (2002), Levy and Olive (2002), Hartman (2008).

RECOMMENDATIONS

1. Teacher should be aware of the importance teaching of metonymy in improving academic achievements of the students.
2. Teachers should check every student individually to make sure whether the students follow the rules regarding identifying errors in Teaching of metonymy by video assisted instruction techniques or not.
3. The techniques can be adapted to high school students.
4. The curriculum should be designed in such away so as to give more importance for Teaching of metonymy.
5. Special classes to develop skills of language may be conducted at school level. More attention should be given for Teaching of metonymy.
6. Skill assessment programme may be organized periodically with the help of language teachers.

EDUCATIONAL IMPLICATIONS OF THE STUDY

The school education department may be provided with certain motivation programmes to the students exclusively in Teaching of metonymy.

Teachers using tried out in the present study techniques can help the students in identifying errors in metonymy correctly.

Lack of technical instruction limits children's clarity of expression; So by providing continuous training to improve their Teaching of metonymy.

Language clubs and labs may be established under the guidance of teachers of Tamil at every school.

Periodical orientation programs may be conducted for Tamil teachers with the specific skill developing themes.

SUGGESTIONS FOR FURTHER STUDY

1. Studies can be done on other & language such as listening, speaking and reading.
2. Studies similar to the present one can be conducted at high school student's levels IXth standard.
3. The study can be extended on a large sample including other classes.
4. A follow up study can be undertaken to improve the academic achievement of the students.
5. A survey study can be undertaken to assess the awareness of students and teachers on video instruction.
6. The same study can be alone on Tamil Languages.

CONCLUSION

Metonymy is one of the promotes logicality thinking and reasoning abilities. In this final chapter a brief summary of the present study has been outlined the major find is of the study which is more highlighted.

BIBLIOGRAPHY

1. Aggawal T.C.(1975) "Education Research" New Delhi, Arya Bok Department.
2. Allen L.Edward (2007) "Statistical Design and Analaysis", Mac Millan Publications.
3. Alderson, J.C. & Urquhart, A.H (1984) "Reading in a Foreign Language", London; Longman.

4. Allavandar (2003), Investigated the selected variable related to Tamil reading competency Annamalai University.
5. Ann and V.S. (1985), Factors that affect the orthography in English and Diagnosis of Spelling Mistakes in the writing of class XI students. Chatterji B (1987), The interference of cognitive development in the Middle School Children.
6. Bartram,M., & Parry, A (1986) "Penguin Elementary Reading Skills" Lonon; Penguin. Bright, J.A., MC Gregor, G.P.(1970)" teaching English as a second Language", London; Longman.
7. Blank, Andreas (1997). Prinzipien des lexikalischen Bedeutungswandels am Beispiel der romanischen Sprachen. Walter de Gruyter. ISBN 978-3-11-093160-0.
8. Brocon,J.D (1988) "Understanding Research in Second Language Learning", Cambridge; Cambridge University Press.
9. Chacho.C (1964) "Reading Comprehension in Teaching Reading, Oxford: IBH Publication. De LeeUW, M (1964), "Read Better, Read Faster", London Penguin.
10. Corbett, Edward P.J. (1998) [1971]. Classical Rhetoric for the Modern Student (4th ed.). New York: Oxford University Press. ISBN 978-0-19-511542-0.
11. Dirven, René (1999). "Conversion as a Conceptual Metonymy of Event Schemata". In K.U. Panther and G. Radden. Metonymy in Language and Thought. John Benjamins Publishing. pp. 275–288. ISBN 978-90-272-2356-2.
12. Della – Piana G.M (1968) "Reading Diagnostic and prescription. An introduction", INC, New York.
13. Eapen, Lalitha (2000) "Developing Writing Skills" in Methods of Teaching Tamil CIEFL Course Book, Block III, CIEFL, Hyderabad.
14. Evangeline Arulselvi (2007) "Teaching of Tamil" Saratha Pathippagam, Chennai.
15. Grzega, Joachim (2004). Bezeichnungswandel: Wie, Warum, Wozu? Ein Beitrag zur englischen und allgemeinen Onomasiologie. Heidelberg: Universitätsverlag Winter.ISBN 978-3-8253-5016-1.

16. Fass, Dan (1997). Processing Metonymy and Metaphor. Ablex. ISBN 978-1-56750-231-2

17. Kothari C R (1984) "Research Methodology and Methods of Techniques" Wiley Eastern Ltd., New Delhi.

18. Khare. M (1966), Traditional and structural approaches to teaching of Tamil with reference to their learning out comes.

19. Manjunath Goulat (2002), Reading errors analysis of IV standard Tamil students in Kannada language.

20. Patel MM (1981) Developing and trying out the scheme of improving the expression of through in mother tongue for std VIII.

21. Prasannakumar (2003), Investigated the reading interest as a determination of comprehension level in -Tamil among secondary school students.

22. Van Dalen, Deohold B, (1966) "Understanding Educational Research", Prentice Hall of India Privated Ltd., New Delhi.

23. W.Best (2007) "Research in Education" 9th Edition, Prentice - Hall of India P.Ltd., New Delhi.

5. Role of Television Programmes in Language Understanding

Chapter - I

INTRODUCTION

Education is a rope that can carry us to greatness. It is one of the most importance things in life because without education you can't contribute to the world or earn money and lack knowledge. Knowledge is power. So the most basic thing to know about the importance of education is to research its benefits or how it will brighten up human life.

The education is the process of instruction aimed at the all round development of individuals, providing. The necessary tools and knowledge to understand and participate in day to day activities of today world.

Keeping the importance of man to the social well-being. Educationists contemplated of education are conservation, communication, to the young generation, interpretation and innovation of culture of a society.

EDUCATIONAL RESEARCH

Research is a logical and systematic search for new and useful information on a particular topic. It is an investigation of finding solutions to scientific and social problems through objective and systematic analysis. It is a search for knowledge, that is, a discovery of hidden truths. Here knowledge means information about matters. The information might be collected from different sources like experience, human beings, books, journals, nature, etc.

A research can lead to new contributions to the existing knowledge. Only through research is it possible to make progress in a field. Research is indeed civilization and determines the economic, social and political development of a nation. The results of scientific research very often force a change in the philosophical view of problems which extend far beyond the restricted domain of science itself.

Research is done with the help of study, experiment, observation, analysis, comparison and reasoning. Research is in fact ubiquitous.

The prime objectives of research are,

(1) To discover new facts.

(2) To verify and test important facts.

(3) To analyze an event or process or phenomenon to identify the cause and effect relationship.

(4) To develop new scientific tools, concepts and theories to solve and understand scientific and nonscientific problems.

(5) To find solutions to scientific, nonscientific and social problems

MEANING OF EDUCATION

The act or process of education and the result of education, as determined by the knowledge, skill or discipline of character is acquired and the process is unending.

The Destiny of India is now being shaped in her classrooms **(Kothari-1966).** Education is the most essential human value. Knowledge is developed through literacy and education.

DEFINITION OF EDUCATION

J.C. AGGARWAL (1987), Education aims to seek and cultivate new knowledge, to engage vigorously and fearlessly in the pursuit of truth and to interpret old knowledge and benefits in the light of new needs and discoveries.

JOHN DEWEY writes the Education is the process of living through a continuous reconstruction of experience. It is the development of all these capacities in the individual, which will enable him to control his environment and fulfill his responsibilities.

Education meets the immediate needs of a child and also prepares him for his future life. It develops all his intellectual and emotional powers, so that he is able to meet the problems of life squarely and solve them successfully.

It also develops the social qualities of service, tolerance, co-operation and fellow feeling. Education is a key that open the eyes of a person towards the brightness of the world.

Indian Thinkers

According to Aurobindo Ghosh thinks of education as "helping the growing soul to draw out that is in itself."

According to "By education" says Mahatma Gandhi, "I mean an all-round drawing out of the best in child and man-body, mind and spirit".

Foreign Thinkers

Pestalozzi "Education is natural, harmonious and progressive development of man's innate power".

John Lock' "Plants are developed by cultivation and men by education".

ROLE OF TELEVISION IN THE FIELD OF EDUCATION

Television has been given considerable importance in many countries as a source and a tool of teaching. The success stories of using television for education in many countries has negated the concept that television is basically on entertainment oriented medium and it is hostile to thoughts. Television is adaptable and can follow different approaches when used in the different educational situations. The medium is used for formal, non-formal and informal education. To support formal education, television usually function as supportive and reinforcement tool. Television can be attached with school curriculum and time tables. When systematically organized it takes the form of school broadcast. In non-formal education, television has a more specific role to play. When used as a part of multi-media communication tool, television can directly or indirectly teach the subject matter.

Importance of television to communicate information, idea, skills and attitudes has been affirmed by researches. You should attempt to study various reports published on educational television in different countries in different situations. In the words of Director BBC "next to home and school believe television to have a more profound influence on human race than any other medium of communication."

If media is to work as an effective teaching tool then certainly it is helping hand towards, achieving the aim and objectives of education. Media is an agent of boost cultural economic and social development activity. Television, as an important mass medium disseminates education through formal and information methods.

Television also continues to benefit the masses by making them conscious of the environment, rights, duties and privilege. It is a source of teaching etiquettes, language skills, hobbies, social relations and religious believes.

Role of television is neither fixed nor easily tangible and measurable. The role is directly related to the question of how the planners are serious and determined to use television. The role could either be enormous or, on the contrary very meager depending upon the specific tasks and available resources. Generally television can help to achieve the following objectives:

1. Social quality in education
2. Enhance quality in education
3. Reduce dependency on verbal teaching and teachers
4. Provide flexibility of time and space in learning.

5. Stimulates learning
6. Provide mass education opportunities.

As far the impact of education television it should rather be studied in more narrow and specific areas. In the world of scram; TV is more effective in teaching mathematics, science and social studies. Where as history, humanities, and literature has not benefited from this medium the same degree. The impact of television on macro level should be studied in three areas namely;

1. Teacher's Competencies
2. Student's Competencies
3. Effects on general viewers

EDUCATIONAL PROGRAMMES OF AIOU

AIOU is a distance learning institution. Students in this system are not supposed to come at campus for class study. However, the "open learning system" of AIOU is not absolutely parallel to that of independent studies by the private and external students who are registered with the boards or universities and appear only for the final examination. They get degree on successful completion of terms. AIOU learning system is more systematic and disciplined.

For the purpose of educational programme of AIOU, electronic media is used for a variety of purposes depending on the requirement of the courses and teaching methodologies. Follow is the summary of various uses of television;

1. To show practical application of principle already written in the textbooks and to show the laboratory work and demonstrations.
2. To humanize distance education and to improve language skills and teaching skills by showing model teaching techniques.
3. To show real life situation and microscope things on magnified scale
4. Animations, dramatic presentations, slow motions and case studies.

AIOU has so far produced more than four hundred television programmes and many non-broadcast audio-visual cassettes. Slide tapes and flip charts are also used as visual media. Television is used in sciences, technical and vocational subjects. The demonstration through television helps to substitute the laboratory experiments. In social science and language, television is used to show real life situation. Television also helps to understand information, which is too complex for the written or spoken explanation.

Technology has changed the life of the language teacher. It has increased the range of resources which teachers can use; it has facilitated display of these resources in ways which eases the task of the teacher; and it has facilitated access to these resources in a way which means that learning can take place beyond the classroom. First, the tape recorder has brought sound to the classroom for nearly half a century: as a mainstay of audio-lingual approaches, audio recordings have become a TESOL institution, a companion to any serious course book, and a focus of teaching skills in initial teacher training courses. Second, the computer is a more recent development, and, although there are still many questions about ways to harness its potential, is fast becoming an essential tool of the trade. Television, a technology which combines sound and visual information and presents language use in rich social and cultural contexts, has not had the same impact as these technologies. The aim of this article is to explore the potential of television and set out a framework for using television material in language learning and teaching. tape recorder and the computer in language teaching and learning. In social life more generally however, the advent of television has had a strong impact, changing how people live their lives in ways comparable to the development of radio/recorded sound, and of digitized information technology. There are a number of possible reasons for this lack of impact on TEFL practice:

Video has not been associated with a specific approach to language teaching, such as audio recording for audio-lingual and communicative methods, and computers in Computer Assisted Language Learning (CALL); Television and video have become associated with language learning without a teacher, rather than in classroom contexts;

Television and video involve a combination of aural and video data which present challenges for comprehension in ways which data input through these channels separately does not;

Television requires machines for recording and playback, which are resource demands many teaching centers have not been able to meet, and course book series have not assumed;

Television represents a form of popular culture, and language teaching has traditionally been associated with the study of literature and other forms of high culture

Television as authentic data presents language in culturally-specific contexts which can be difficult for learners in other language contexts to understand or appreciate.

A FOCUS ON LANGUAGE USE

The focus here is the development of listening comprehension skills, particularly the skills required where aural data is augmented by visual data in ways which both facilitate comprehension and present information overload challenges.

A Focus on Language Forms

The focus here is the phonological, lexical and grammar (morphology and syntax) forms of the language. Typically, in a communicative teaching framework, the focus on forms is developed after the comprehension stage.

Television as social practice: Activities in this column explicitly exploit television literacy, instinctive understanding of the purpose and context of events such as sports interviews, interactions in drama programmes, and politeness (or increasing, absence thereof) in game shows. The learning derives from analysis of language to understand how intentions are realized and identities are performed. The three rows in the table present three contexts of language teaching and learning:

1. whole class;
2. project-based; and
3. Individualized learning.

These are not wholly separate contexts: rather, they represent classroom organizational perspectives for the teacher, which become organically blended as activities develop and learning journeys progress.

THE SATELLITE INSTRUCTIONAL TELEVISION PROGRAMME (SITE)

The satellite instructional television experiment (SITE) was a large scale experiment conducted by the Government of India in the use of the Satellite for instructional purposes. During August 1, 1975 and July 30, 1976 the Indian Space Research Organization (ISRO) Jointly with Doordarshan, the Indian Television authority, broadcast instructional television programmes through a satellite. The experiment was designed to expose people of far-flung rural areas particularly those poorly served by other means of communication to educational television programmes. The daily broadcast time of four hours was divided between primary school students in the morning and general audiences in the evening. The site programmes were aimed at to transform rural communities by educating them about various socio-economic schemes and enlarging the base of people's involvement in development plans.

The programmes telecast for adult viewers were of three types.

1. News relating to the incidents of national importance,
2. Instruction-oriented programmes for dissemination of up-to-date knowledge relating to improved practices in agriculture, health, hygiene, family planning, nutrition, and
3. Some recreational programmes interspersed with instructional ones.

OBJECTIVE OF THE PROGRAMME

The major objective of the SITE programme was to help people in their developmental endeavours. As students's morning programme formed an important component of the SITE, educational advancement was emphasized more than anything else. It was expected that the educational television programme would bring about improvement both in quality and quantity of education. The programme envisaged to achieve the following expected outcomes:

1. There would be more enrolment, more regular attendance and less dropout, as the students would feel attracted to the school through this programme.
2. Students would develop receptivity to the new ideas and activities when they get exposed to various external stimuli of the immediate and distant environment.

3. They would form good health habits which would consequentially help the students in their academic achievement.
4. This would help them develop proper attitudes, interests and values as are conducive to social harmony and democratic growth.
5. They would develop interest for living objects and be conscious of the need for conservation of wild life and forests.
6. They would develop scientific attitude as a result of observing natural phenomena, doing experiments themselves, skilful questioning and analyzing facts and figure.
7. They would develop awareness about different community development programmes, so that their participation in them would be promoted.
8. Students's interest and awareness in proper utilization of nature resources would be increased as a result of their understanding.
9. They would develop the ability of coordinating visual and auditory reception.
10. They would develop the feelings of national and international understanding

INSTRUCTIONAL TV

Instructional television (ITV) boomed in the 1950s and 1960s, fueled by funding from government and private foundations. Programming often took the form of taped lectures designed for replay to a classroom or by individual students. But by the mid-60s, interest had declined, largely due to "mediocrity in the instructional quality of these programs" (Marshall, 2001). Many reasons were cited for instructional TV's lack of impact in the schools, among them teacher resistance, equipment expense, and inflexibility of the content. As Marshall (2001) points out, "Rather than enhancing and extending the good things already happening in the traditional classroom, instructional television mirrored classroom teaching practices, replacing the classroom teacher with a televised version."

EDUCATIONAL TV

Fortunately, at about the same time that ITV was waning, programs like Sesame Street were coming into being, giving rise to a new category educational television which attempted to complement, not compete, with the classroom. As is often the case with new technologies, applications of the television medium emerged in ways that were unanticipated at its advent. As one noted educational economist comments, "...claims...have been made for every new instructional technology (motion pictures, radio, television, videocassettes, videodisks, and computers) which heralded them as having revolutionary implications for education. In every case their educational impacts fell short of that [early] promise... They simply did not evolve in the ways that were predicted" (Levin, 1988).

The answer is just about all of them. Teacher surveys show that television is most commonly used for instruction in science, the language arts (reading and English), and social studies, with health/nutrition and math uses also widely reported (CPB, 1997). While less than half of math teachers reported using video, it was the most requested subject for new programming. It's worth noting that some of the benefits of classroom television are difficult to quantify from a research perspective as they introduce educational experiences that would otherwise be impossible to reproduce in another medium. Thus, it can be difficult to create valid comparisons as "these media can take viewers to places in the world that they could not otherwise experience, bring distinguished experts into the classroom, and allow demonstrations not generally possible or too dangerous to perform within a classroom" (Wetzel, 1994). That said, the examples below are intended to show the wealth of applications that teachers of many disciplines and of elementary, middle, and high schools students have found for classroom television.

TV IN LANGUAGE ARTS

Alex (1988) in a survey of the literature has found wide use of video as a tool for motivating writing: language arts teachers have successfully used film, news stories, even soap operas to organize writing activities for students at a variety of levels from elementary grades up through college, and in advanced through remedial levels.

Williams (2001) observes that students bring deep experience in television to the classroom. He notes these literacies "...can be gateways to otherwise hidden student knowledge about the society and culture at large," and calls on teachers to "make students aware of how experience with any form of communication, be it television or print, leads to a deeper, critical enjoyment of that form and ability to use it more effectively for their own goals.

Linebarger (2001), in a study of second-graders, has found increased word recognition, comprehension, and identification of critical story elements when television with captions is used as a supplement to print-based reading instruction.

Flood (1995) offers several ways to use television "texts" to enrich language arts instruction: literary classics;

1. as presentations of background information and context;
2. to foster reader-response approaches to understanding literature, especially when video and print-based texts are compared; and
3. to develop communication skills as students learn to interpret visual messages.

PROMOTING MEDIA LITERACY

The role of the teacher is critical to the effective use of television in school settings. But the attitudes and frameworks that students bring to their viewing can matter just as much.

Paris (1997) has identified the dual nature of student perceptions of television, observing that students's familiarity with video "can make film and video a powerful pedagogical tool." Yet, he also notes that same familiarity can lead to a casual attitude toward the visual content, and might "reinforce passive viewing and unquestioning acceptance" (Paris, 1997). The solution here, he advocates, is the development of critical viewing skills. (For more on his proposed frameworks, designed for use in the social studies curriculum, see the section below, "Using Classroom Television to Support Specific Academic Disciplines.

WATCHING TELEVISION FOR LANGUAGE LEARNING

One of television's most obvious characteristics is its visual aspect. Humans intuitively grasp the power of images to convey meaning, as can be seen in the old adage that values a picture at a thousand times the value of a word. Research in the past two decades has proven what we intuitively know: our brains deal with images differently than print (Merringoff, 1983).

Words are processed in the neocortex where the higher thinking capability of the brain resides. Pictures, however, are handled in the limbic system, rapidly, and trigger instinct, emotion, and impulse (Bergsma, 2002). Because brains are programmed to remember experiences that have an emotional component, television has a powerful ability to relay experience through the emotions evoked by images (Noble, 1983). Television, of course, offers information in multiple forms: images, motion, sound and, at times, text.

The richness of these forms of information benefits learners, by enabling them "...to learn through both verbal and visual means, to view actual objects and realistic scenes, to see sequences in motion, and to view perspectives that are difficult or impossible to observe in real life" (Wetzel, 1994). Early fears that these multiple channels might overtax the viewer's capacity for comprehension seem to have been unfounded, and now most researchers agree that "...when presented together, each source provides additional complementary information," thus increasing the chances that comprehension will take place (Kozma, 1991). Watching television may seem a very simple act, but it actually involves a rather complicated thinking process. Like any communications medium, the content of television is composed of symbols, in the form of discrete units of information. As literate humans our cognitive task is to decode those symbols.

But with broadcast television, the symbols are more transient, more fleeting than with static media like books or pictures. Thus, television offers a "window of cognitive engagement." The degree of openness of that window is conditioned by the quality of interaction between viewer and the visual medium.

Viewers of television generally have less control over the flow of information than with more static media, their ability to "recall" or go back to passages that they may not have grasped the first time is more limited than with still media. While VCRs and other playback technologies have obviously made this less of a factor, in school settings, videos still tend to be a one-to-many broadcast.

Since viewers have limited control of the flow of information, comprehension is importantly linked to their ability to stay engaged with the medium.

Researchers have accordingly devoted much attention to the subject of attention; that is, to how and why viewers stay attuned to the content flow from the screen. And because television draws on two sensory channels, comprehension also depends on the viewer's ability to simultaneously process both audio and visual tracks (Anderson, 1983).

By adjusting the pacing, sequencing, and relative priority of the two information channels, and manipulating of the program's formal features, video producers are able to affect viewer attention, and can thereby affect the learning potential of the program

TAMIL LANGUAGE

Tamizh is a Dravidian language spoken predominantly by Tamil people of Tamil Nadu and Sri Lanka. It has official states in the Indian status in the Indian states of Tamil Nadu, Puducherry and national language of Srilanka and one of the official languages of medium of education in Malaysia along with English, Malay and Mandarin. It is also chiefly spoken in the states of kerala, Puducherry and Andaman and Nicobar Islands as a secondary language and by minorities in Karnataka and Andhra Pradesh. It is one of the 22 scheduled languages of India and was the first Indian language to be declared a classical language by the Government of India in 2004. Tamil is also spoken by significant minorities in Malaysia, England, Mauritius, Canada, South Africa, FIJI, Germany, Philippines, United states, Netherlands, Indonesia, Reunion and France as well as emigrant communities around the world.

Tamil is one of the longest surviving classical languages in the world. 2,200-year-old Tamil-Brahmi inscription have been found on Samanamalai. It has been described as "the only language of contemporary India which recognizably continuous with a classical past .The variety and quality of classical Tamil literature has led to it being described as "one of the great classical traditions and literatures of the world". Tamil literature has existed for over 2000 years. The earliest period of Tamil literature, Sangam literature, is dated from ca. 300BC-AD 300. It has the oldest extant literature amongst other Dravidian languages. The earliest epigraphic records found on rock edicts and hero stones date from around the 3rd century BC. More than 55% of the epigraphically inscriptions (about 55,000) found by the Archaeological Survey of India are in the Tamil language. Tamil language inscriptions written in Brahmi script have been discovered in Sri Lanka, and on trade goods in Thailand and Egypt. The two earliest manuscripts from India, acknowledged and registered by UNESCO Memory of the World register in 1997 and 2005, were in Tamil.

In 1578, Portuguese Christian Missionaries published a Tamil prayer book in old Tamil script named 'Thamniraan Vanakkam', thus making Tamil the first Indian language to be printed and published. Tamil Lexicon, published by the University of Madras, is the first among the dictionaries published in any Indian language. Tamil is used as a sacred language of Ayyavazhi and in Tamil Hindu traditions of Shaivism and Vaishnavism. According to a 2001 survey, there were 1,863 newspapers published in Tamil, of which 353 were dailies.

CLASSIFICATION

Tamil belongs to the southern branch of the Dravidian languages, a family of around 26 languages native to the Indian sub continent. It is also classified as being part of a Tamil language family, which alongside Tamil proper, also includes the languages of about 35 ethno-linguistic groups such as the

The closest major relative of Tamil is Malayalam; the two began diverging the 9th century CE. Although many of the differences between Tamil and Malayalam demonstrate a pre-historic split of the western dialect, the process of separation into a distinct language, Malayalam, was not completed until sometime in the 13th or 14th century.

Origin of Tamil in Hinduism

According to Hindu legend, Tamil, or personification from Tamil Tay (Mother Tamil), was created by Shiva. The Tamil god Murugan and the sage Agastya brought it to people.

According to linguists like Bhadriraju Krishnamurti, Tamil, as a Dravidian language, descends from Proto-Dravidian, a Proto-language. Linguistic reconstruction suggests that Proto-Dravidian was spoken around the third millennium BC, possibly in the region around the lower Godavari river basin in peninsular India. The material evidence suggests that the speakers of Proto-Dravidian were of the culture associated with the Neolithic complexes of South India. The next phase in the reconstructed proto-history of Tamil is Proto-South Dravidian. The linguistic evidence suggests that Proto-South Dravidian was spoken around the middle of the second millennium BC, and that proto-Tamil emerged around the 3rd century BC. The earliest epigraphic attestations of Tamil are generally taken to have been written shortly thereafter among Indian languages. Tamil has the most ancient non-Sanskritised Indian literature. Scholars categories the attested history of the language into three periods, Old Tamil (300 BC-AD 700), Middle Tamil (700-1600) and Modern Tamil (1600-present). During a recent excavation at Quseir-al-Qadim, Egyptian pottery dating back to first century BC was discovered with ancient Tamil Brahmi inscriptions.

Indians today might like to stereotype Gujaratis as the nation's most mercantile community, but at one point around 2,000 years ago, Tamil was the lingua frame of traders across the South East Asian seas.

"You get a sense of the role of yearly and medieval merchant guilds in the Deccan and Tamil Nadu and Kerala" Guy said in a conversation with Scroll in. "You know how common they are in India, but then you find their inscriptions in places like Sumatra and. It is astonishing how they got around. They were busy boys, travelling far like and wide" research started with a highly acclaimed exhibition curate last year at the Metropolitan Museum of Art in New York "Lost Kingdoms. Hindu-Buddhist Sculpture of Early Southeast Asia, 5th to 8th Century" had 160 sculptures, gathered for the first time in such numbers, from museums and collections across India, Cambodia, Indonesia, Thailand and Vietnam.

Gold Obsession

Around the first millennium, Tamil traders dominated the seas, inscriptions suggest, though they would later give way to Bengalis and Guajarati's from India and Arabic would eventually become the language of the region's merchants Gold was more or less what Tamil merchants wanted at that time. Inscriptions suggest that the traders of South India were hoarders of precious metals, even as they paid their debts with textiles such as painted cotton kalamkaris and iron."India retains the biggest private stores of gold in the world, and mostly in female hands".

It is true now and it always has been true. "India was notorious for demanding to settle its foreign debts in precious metals and owed everyone for their trade. Even the Romans were upset at having to buy muslins with precious metals. Making sure they always had the better deal, in South East Asia, Indian traders imported spices such as cloves and nutmeg in return for kalamkaris, painted cottons.

The earliest extant literary works and their commentaries celebrates the Pandiyan Kings for the organization of long-termed Tamil Sangams, which researched, developed and made amendments in Tamil language. Even though the name of the language which was developed by these Tamil Sangams is mentioned as Tamil, the exact period when the name "Tamil" came to be applied to the language is unclear, as is the precise etymology of the name. The earliest attested use of the name is found in Tholkappiyam, which is dated as early as 1st century BC. Southworth suggests that the name comes from tam-mil>tam-il 'self-speak', or 'one's own speech'.(see Southworth's derivation of Sanskrit term for "other" or Mleccha) Kamil Zvelebil suggests an etymology of tam-il, with tam meaning "self" or "one's self", and "-il" having the connotation of "unfolding sound". Alternatively, he suggests a derivation of tamil < tam-il < * tav-il, meaning in origin "the proper process (of speaking)".

The Tamil Lexicon of University of Madras defines the world 'Tamil' as 'sweetness' S.V.Subramarammar and , an suggest the meaning ' sweet sound' from' -'sound'.

OLD TAMIL LANGUAGE

The earliest records in old Tamil are short inscription from around the 2nd century BC in caves and on pottery. These inscriptions are written in a variant of the Brahmi script called Tamil Brahmi. The earliest long text in old Tamil is the Tolkappiyiyam, an early work on Tamil grammar and poetics, whose oldest layers could be as old as the 1st century BC. A large number of literary works in old Tamil have also survived. These include a corpus of 2,381 poems collectively known as Sangam literature. These poems are usually dated to between the 1st and 5th centuries AD, which makes them the oldest extent body of secular literature in India. Other literary works in old Tamil include

Thirukural, Silappatikaram and Manimekalai, and a number of ethical and didactic texts, written between the 5th and 8th centuries.

NEED OF THE STUDY

Teachers have been highly creative in their use of television in the classroom, and perceive it to have contributed to significant learning gains in their students. According to educator surveys and research, educational television: Reinforces reading and lecture material, Aids in the development of a common base of knowledge among students, Enhances student comprehension and discussion, Provides greater accommodation of diverse learning styles, Increases student motivation and enthusiasm, Promotes teacher effectiveness viewing by planning ahead to consider instructional goals, Preparing by previewing the program, Determining the setting and length of the video, Setting clear expectations for students, Encouraging student participation through, setting the context before viewing, pausing during the program to ask key questions and flag priority topics, promoting reflection through post-viewing discussion and assignments, Connecting post-viewing activities to hands-on or real-world experiences.

Busy teachers today can use all the help they can get. Broadcasters can facilitate teaching with television by making their program options more flexible, more aligned with core curricula, and more supported by other learning materials and resources.

To achieve the greatest impact on student learning, broadcasters might consider providing high quality professional development for teachers in effective classroom integration of multimedia. Today's students are immersed in media. Students under six spend an average of two hours a day with screen media, more than twice the amount of time they spend being read to or reading. About 25% of students this age are already active computer users, while about the same percentage has a TV, VCR, or video game player in their bedroom. Having grown up with television themselves, their parents trust in the educational value of their students media interactions, with 78% reporting that their students model prosaically behavior from their viewing. As another researcher has noted "...because of the ubiquitous presence of television in students daily lives, the medium has become a major socialize and educator of students".

These findings support the common observation that television is already an important and widely used instructional resource. As the presence of broadband, digital media, and streaming video increases, the likelihood is that video will become an even more essential classroom resource. Thus the study was undertaken to find the Role of Television Programmes in Understanding Tamil Language for VIIIth Standard Students.

SCOPE OF THE STUDY

Today's students are growing up surrounded by television and video. Visual media is already an essential component of classroom instruction, with almost all teachers employing video in some form in their teaching. As the presence of broadband, digital media, and streaming video increases, the likelihood is that video will become an even more essential classroom resource. Classroom resources these days must be backed by research. As a result, scientifically-based research is more important in education than ever before. This report focuses on television research to demonstrate television's positive effect on student achievement. A set of practical recommendations are also provided so that broadcasters and educators can maximize the effectiveness of video in the classroom.

STATEMENT OF THE PROBLM

The present investigation is entitled as *"A Study on the Role of Television Programmes in Understanding Tamil Language for VIIIth Standard Students".*

OBJECTIVES OF THE STUDY

The objective of this present study will gives the detailed analysis of the research on "Study on the Role of Television Programmes in Understanding Tamil Language". The present study will helpful in understanding ability towards Tamil learning.

The findings of the study will help the people to know various positive aspects of Understanding Tamil Language. This will make the school students effective in understanding through Television programme.

The objectives of the overall studies are;

1. To find out the significant difference in the mean scores of Role of Television Programmes in Understanding Tamil Language for

VIIIth Standard Students in terms of their Gender as Male and Female.

2. To find out the significant difference in the mean scores of Role of Television Programmes in Understanding Tamil Language for VIIIth Standard Students in terms of their Type of School as Government and Aided.
3. To find out the significant difference in the mean scores of Role of Television Programmes in Understanding Tamil Language for VIIIth Standard Students in terms of their Type of School as Aided and Private.
4. To find out the significant difference in the mean scores of Role of Television Programmes in Understanding Tamil Language for VIIIth Standard Students in terms of their Type of School as Private and Government.
5. To find out the significant difference in the mean scores of Role of Television Programmes in Understanding Tamil Language for VIIIth Standard Students in terms of their Locality as Rural and Urban.
6. To find out the significant difference in the mean scores of Role of Television Programmes in Understanding Tamil Language for VIIIth Standard Students in terms of their Parent Educational Qualification as Educated and Un-educated.
7. To find out the significant difference in the mean scores of Role of Television Programmes in Understanding Tamil Language for VIIIth Standard Students in terms of their Parent Occupation as Self Employment and Government Job.
8. To find out the significant difference in the mean scores of Role of Television Programmes in Understanding Tamil Language for VIIIth Standard Students in terms of their Parent Occupation as Government Job and Private Job.
9. To find out the significant difference in the mean scores of Role of Television Programmes in Understanding Tamil Language for VIIIth Standard Students in terms of their Parent Occupation as Private Job and Government Job.

10. To find out the significant difference in the mean scores of Role of Television Programmes in Understanding Tamil Language for VIIIth Standard Students in terms of their Parent Annual Income as Above 50000 and Below 50000.

HYPOTHESES OF THE STUDY

The Hypotheses should be framed according to the Variables chosen to find the Role of Television Programmes in Understanding Tamil Language for VIIIth Standard Students. *'A hypothesis could be defined as an expectation about event based on generalization of the assumed relationship between variable'.*

Hypothesis means subject to the verification and statement about solution of the problem.

The Hypothesis of the present study is to find the difference in the mean scores of Role of Television Programmes in Understanding Tamil Language for VIIIth Standard Students.

1. There is no significant difference in the mean scores of Role of Television Programmes in Understanding Tamil Language for VIIIth Standard Students in terms of their Gender as male and female.
2. There is no significant difference in the mean scores of Role of Television Programmes in Understanding Tamil Language for VIIIth Standard Students in terms of their Type of School as Government and Aided.
3. There is no significant difference in the mean scores of Role of Television Programmes in Understanding Tamil Language for VIIIth Standard Students in terms of their Type of School as Aided and Private.
4. There is no significant difference in the mean scores of Role of Television Programmes in Understanding Tamil Language for VIIIth Standard Students in terms of their Type of School as Private and Government.
5. There is no significant difference in the mean scores of Role of Television Programmes in Understanding Tamil Language for

VIIIth Standard Students in terms of their Locality as Rural and Urban.

6. There is no significant difference in the mean scores of Role of Television Programmes in Understanding Tamil Language for VIIIth Standard Students in terms of their Parent Educational Qualification as educated and Un-educated.
7. There is no significant difference in the mean scores of Role of Television Programmes in Understanding Tamil Language for VIIIth Standard Students in terms of their Parent Occupation as Self Employment and Government Job.
8. There is no significant difference in the mean scores of Role of Television Programmes in Understanding Tamil Language for VIIIth Standard Students in terms of their Parent Occupation as Government Job and Private Job.
9. There is no significant difference in the mean scores of Role of Television Programmes in Understanding Tamil Language for VIIIth Standard Students in terms of their Parent Occupation as Private Job and Government Job.
10. There is no significant difference in the mean scores of Role of Television Programmes in Understanding Tamil Language for VIIIth Standard Students in terms of their Parent Annual Income as Above 50000 and Below 50000.

LIMITATIONS OF THE STUDY

The investigation on the Role of Television Programmes in Understanding Tamil Language for VIIIth Standard Students is limited to 300 data collected in and around Pudukkottai District.

The present educational study survey was conducted to VIIIth standard students only.

The present educational survey was conducted in 2014- 2015 only.

CONCLUSION

The present study consists of the introduction and the overview of all the chapters. It tells the need and the pedagogical importance of the present study.

Chapter - II

Review of Related Literature

INTRODUCTION

According to Water Borg, "The literature in any field forms the foundation upon which all further work will be built." Research takes advantage of the knowledge which has accumulated in the past as a result of constant human endeavor. It can never be undertaken in isolation of the work that has already been done on the problems which are directly or indirectly related to a study proposed by a researcher.

A careful review of the research journals, books, dissertations, thesis and other sources of information on the problem to be investigated is one of important steps in the planning of any research study. The importance of review of related literature or related studies cannot be denied in any research. Such literature provides the researcher with the footprints of earlier travellers gone ahead on the same route; they save her from the pitfalls and help her in removing the hindrances, which are likely to come in her way.

Related literature works as a guide-post not only with regard to quantum of work done in the field, but also enables us to perceive the gap and lacuna in the concerned field of research. Review of the related literature, besides, allowing the researcher to acquaint herself with current knowledge in the field or area in which he/she is going to conduct her research, serves many purposes.

The review of related literature enables the researcher to define the limits of her field. By reviewing the related literature the research can avoid unfruitful and useless problem areas.

The review of related studies is an exacting piece of work calling for a deep insight and clear-cut perspective of the overall field. It is a crucial step which invariably minimizes the risk of the dead ends, rejected topics, rejected studies, wasted efforts, trial and error activity and even more important, erroneous findings based on a faulty research design.

The review of literature also promotes greater understanding of the problem and its crucial aspects and ensures the avoidance of unnecessary duplication. Emphasizing the importance of survey of related literature, **C. V. Goods** and others mentioned, "The competent physicians must keep constantly abreast of the latest discoveries in the field of medicine, the successful lawyer mist be able to locate the information pertaining to the case in hand; obviously, the careful student of education, a researcher and investigator should become familiar with the location and use of sources of educational information".

THE PURPOSE OF THE REVIEW OF LITERATURE

1. It helps the research worker to find out what is already known, what others have attempted to find out, what methods of attack have been promising of disappointing and what problems remain to be solved. It shows whether the evidence already available, solves the problem adequately without further investigation.
2. It is the basis of most of the research projects in various sciences and humanities. It forms the foundation upon which all future work will be built.
3. It enables her to know the means of getting to the frontier in the field of her research. Unless she has learnt what others have done had what still remains to be done, he cannot develop a research project that will contribute something to the knowledge existing in her field.

4. It furnishes her with indispensable suggestion about comparative data, good procedures, likely methods and tried techniques.
5. Through it she will also know in detail about all related research projects in progress which are completed or reported.
6. The insight into the methods, measures etc. employed by others will lead to significant improvement of her research design. It makes her alert to research possibilities that have been overlooked and research approaches that have proved to be sterile.
7. It provides ideas, theories, explanations, hypotheses and methods of research, valuable in formulating and studying the problem.
8. It helps in locating comparative date useful in the interpretation of results.
9. It prevents pointless repetition of research.

Keeping in view the importance of review of related studies the investigator reviewed the related literature. It is based on the material like Survey of Research, Research Journals, Research Abstracts and Encyclopaedias available in different national level libraries, universities, Educational Research Centres of the country and abroad as well as studies available on website have been discussed under the following categories:

1. Studies conducted in India
2. Studies conducted in Abroad

STUDIES CONDUCTED IN INDIA

Chaudhary, S. and Garg, S. (2014) conducted a study on Using Satellite-Based Networks for Capacity Building and Education for All: A Case Study of Rajiv Gandhi Project for EDUSAT-Supported Elementary Education. One of the serious problems associated with Indian school education has been high dropout rate. The reasons are many and varied but the major constraints are: non-availability of adequate number of competent and trained teachers in most of the schools and separate room for each class. To overcome such problems and increase equitable access to all, it was considered prudent to use capabilities of satellite based teaching-learning. This network was also to be used for capacity building of in-service teachers. So an indigenously built, dedicated satellite for education—Educational Satellite (EDUSAT)—was launched on September 20, 2004, which supports one national hub and five regional hubs. This paper discusses the case study cf Rajiv Gandhi Project for EDUSAT-Supported Elementary Education (RGPEEE) project for imparting value added education and professional development of in-service teachers. The project was implemented by Indira Gandhi National Open University (IGNOU). More than 862 schools in four Hindi speaking states chosen on the basis of physical contiguity were networked through 850 ROTs and 12 SITs. In the first phase (pilot), the project focused mainly on Sidhi district, inhabited mainly (90%) by tribal population and one of the most educationally less-developed districts of Madhya Pradesh. Through ten orientation programmes, 868 teachers and functionaries associated with the project were oriented at different levels to familiarize them in imparting instruction through EDUSAT and their role and responsibility in facilitating child learning. They were also trained in developing content for tele-teaching; development of knowledge repositories as effective and sustainable sources of courseware. Feedback studies undertaken to judge the effectiveness of EDUSAT reveal that it is being well received and making steady progress towards improvement in attendance and academic achievement of students and creation of better learning-environment in schools.

Bhattacharya, B. (2013) conducted a study, Engineering Education in India-The Role of ICT. Engineering education in India has witnessed a major change over the past few years. Substantial increase in the demand for high-quality education has led to the adoption of Information and Communication Technologies for extending the outreach of education. This paper presents a review of some of these technology-enhanced initiatives already taken up by the government of India, as well as by some of the leading institutions in the country. Important developments include the National Programme on Technology Enhanced Learning (NPTEL), the use of an educational satellite called the EDUSAT and various other approaches such as the use of "virtual classrooms" and "virtual laboratories." The paper goes on to discuss some of the problem areas in the present mode of dissemination and deployment; some possible future trends and modalities are also outlined. These include blending collaborative learning with interactive technology-enhanced learning initiatives and finding ways of providing support for learners' queries.

Dash, M. K. (2013) attempted to study the effectiveness of EDUSAT for improving learning achievements of high school students. The programme of Sarva Shiksha Abhiyan (SSA) aims of providing access to quantity education to all and improving professional competencies of various categories of teachers. Distance Education Programme (DEP) under SSA is a special component to supplement the traditional approach particularly for in-service teacher education programme. Implementation of EDUSAT through Rajiv Gandhi Project for EDUSAT Supported Elementary Education (RGPESEE) is a challenge in the light of optimum utilization of communication technology for improving learning of students at elementary level. This study focused on reflectiveness of implementation of EDUSAT on improving learning achievement of primary students. At the same time, attempt has been taken to compare learning achievement of students at primary grade. The findings of the study aimed at development of innovative strategies for effective implementation of EDUSAT in improving learning of students at elementary level and achieving the target of improving quality of elementary education all over the country.

Desai, V. et al. (2013) studied the enhancement of primary education using EDUSAT and found out that due to the non-availability of required number of trained and expert teachers' knowledge-divide exists between students population of urban and rural/remote areas. To bridge this gap Distance Learning or Tele-education is the best option. During the study it was decided to provide a Tele-education network in and around the Sidhi district of Madhya Pradesh, with uplink and studio facility (Hub) at Jabalpur (MP) and around 700 receive only terminals (ROTs) in various schools and it was found that it enhances achievement of high school learners.

Rout, S. K. (2012) conducted a study of the Utilization Educational Media at Primary Stage". This study examined the existing status and utilization of educational radio and television programmes produced by Central Institute of Educational Technology (CIET), National Council of Educational Research and Training (NCERT) New Delhi and broadcasted through Gyan Vani (educational FM radio channel V for Educational Radio (ER) programmes and DD-1 (National TV Channel), Gyan Darshan (Educational free cable channel) for Educational Television (ETV) programmes respectively. A sample of 60 schools run by Municipal Corporation of Delhi (MCD) was randomly selected from three educational zones in Delhi. Views and opinions on the utilization of educational radio and television programmes were collected through questionnaires and opinionnaire. The results revealed that only 50 per cent schools have been utilizing educational radio programme, while 27 per cent schools have been utilizing educational television programme. Further, regularly / occasionally listening and viewing schools of these media were unsystematic in the process of utilization. It was found after close scrutiny of collected data from the headmasters/ headmistress (HMs), teachers, students and informal observation done by the investigator that the genuine cause of non-utilization of educational mass media was apathetic attitude of the teachers than anything else, though they showed positive attitude towards them on pen and paper. The attitude of schools regularly / occasionally utilizing (listening and viewing) media programme were found to be casual.

Arulchelvan, S. and Viswanathan, D. (2010) attempted to find out the variations in the pattern of usage of TV among students of different demographic characteristics. The focus of the study was to trace the pattern of TV viewing and usages among graduate students, especially with regard to the exposure, access, purpose of use, perceived benefits.

Phalachandra Bhandigadi, NCERT, (2010) conducted a study on impact of EDUSAT on school students and teachers and found out that the students have benefited from the video programmes delivered through the Satellite. The benefit gained is in terms of gain in knowledge and understanding of the content, improvement in attendance and holding attention and interest in viewing programmes.

Dogra, S and Gulati, A. (2008) conducted a study, Learning Traditions and Teachers Role: The Indian Perspective. In this paper, the authors discuss about the Indian learning traditions and the role played by teachers in imparting education. They discuss the efforts played by government in enhancing education, Non-Governmental Organizations (NGOs) contribution in spreading literacy, various learning traditions from past to present such as “Gurukula, Kautilya”, participative learning. Further, they highlighted the educational technologies used like EDUNET, E-campus and EDUSAT in various schools giving the example of Delhi Public School (DPS) and open learning trends of India. Furthermore, they discussed the role of a teacher in Indian tradition and in modern education with the examples of Guru Gobind Singh Indraprastha University and Indian Institute of Technology Kharagpur. The paper concludes with the remarks of the authors in which they suggest to reframe the educational policy, emphasize on enhancing professional education in government institutions and universities and development of industry-academia partnership.

Pillay, G. S. and Anandan, K. (2008) made an analysis of the educational video programmes produced in India at the higher educational level. The survey revealed that very few video programmes were produced in subjects like law, anthropology and veterinary sciences. In general, educational subjects like economics, sociology and management, educational received greater attention but not geography or political science. The researchers felt that there was no coordination between various production agencies.

Chaudhary, S. S. (2008) conducted a study, "Teachers' attitude towards school television (STV) and its relationship to mass media behavior and job satisfaction" to know the teachers' attitude towards STV and its relationship with mass media behavior and job satisfaction. He founds that (i) the custodian teachers, on the whole, had a fairly favorable attitude towards STV. They perceived STV as an acceptable medium for teaching students and for presentation of instructional material; (ii) Teachers supported the effect of visuals on students; they perceived STGV as an effective learning medium; (iii) The custodian teachers' attitude towards STV was independent of their personal and academic characteristics; (iv) The teachers who taught the higher classes (Classes IV and V) showed a more favorable attitude toward STV I comparison to those who taught all classes from classes I to V. (v) The custodian teachers were fairly satisfied in their job situation. (vi) Teachers' attitude toward STV and their job satisfaction were positively related. (vii) Job satisfaction were positively related (vii) Job satisfaction was associated with authority-figures responsible for work allocation, work supervision and the role of custodian of STV, (viii) The intensive case study method revealed that the majority of teachers did not operate STV regularly (ix) Most of the sets were out of order, (x) Teachers were not found happy with regard to their training, viewing, arrangement and mode of viewing.

Idayavani, S. (2008) developed two video programmes, one on weathering and another on rivers, and made a study to see how viewing of the video programmes affect their achievements. It was found that students who were exposed to the video method performed better than students taught by the traditional lecture method.

Anuradha, K. (2008) observed that students's television viewing behavior and its impact on personal and educational development. The study also showed that students like watching advertisements and programmes on sports.

Narayanasamy, M. (2008) prepared a video programme for sixth grade students to teach Tamil vocabulary. He found that the experimental group learnt more Tamil words using the programme than the control group.

Kaluuthu, T. (2007) developed a video programme on environmental pollution and compared 'students' performance receiving instruction through video-viewing and through video-viewing and through traditional teaching. The experimental group receiving instruction through the video programme gained more and learnt more concepts as compared instruction through the video programme gained more and learnt more concepts as compared to students of the control group.

Mishra, S. (2007) studied the role of TV in diffusion of Home Making Practices (MHP) among urban housewives of Bhubaneswar. The study revealed that 'IV programmes made little contribution to housewives in their efforts to adopt Home Making Practices.

Sarma, H. N. et al. (2007) conducted a study in Jorhat District and disclosed that a significant correlation existed between the achievement of cohorts of classes III and IV. Regular attendance and academic achievement correlated.

Abrol, U. et al. (2007) conducted a study on Television viewing among students of Delhi schools to know the TV-viewing behaviors of students in terms of duration of viewing and programme preference; to delineate the factors influencing TV-viewing among students, (iii) to determine the relative importance of the factors influencing TV-viewing among students, (iv) to study the impact of TV on the daily life of students, and (v) to study the perceptions of parents regarding the TV-viewing of their students. The major findings of the study were L (i) Viewing was heavier on Saturdays and Sundays than on other others. On week days, on an average students watched TV for one hour and 18 minutes and on Saturdays and Sundays for three hours and six hours respectively (ii) No significant difference was found in the amount of TV-viewing of male and female students. However, the younger students watched TV more that the other ones, (iii) Parental restriction on TV-viewing, home stimulation, parental attitude towards play of students and parents' attitudes towards TV were found to be significantly correlated with the duration of TV-viewing, (vi) The study did not show any significant relationship between the IQ of the child and the duration of TV-viewing. (v) Surprisingly, students programmes produced by Doordarshan were not at all liked by the students: in fact, 94% students were not even aware of such programmes. However, the sponsored students' programmes were quite popular with them (vi) About 81% mothers reported that they restricted their students' TV-viewing.

Ghosh, S. (2007) looked into, the ETV reporting in Tamil Nadu. The survey goes-beyond education and covers programmes on health agriculture and adult, education. It was found that although time-duration of the programmes was generous, the telecast did not come at a convenient hour with the result that the targeted audience had to miss the programmes. A conspicuous neglect was pointed out in the training of teachers, both in writing radio scripts and in utilizing school broadcasts. All teachers agreed that school broadcasts were useful and helpful to students.

Dharunkar, V. L. (2007) looked into the research potentials and priorities of the educational broadcasts. He suggests that comparative studies be taken up to assess the effectiveness of educational broadcasts in South Asian countries. Another point that needs attention is the need to fuse together folk and electronic media.

Jaiswal, K. (2007) took up a study on the effectiveness of TV programmes in science education. The study was conducted on B.Ed. Diploma in Computer Education students. Lecture with demonstration and illustration talk formats were found, quite effective. About 70% of the programmes focused on the lower cognitive skills of knowledge and understanding. About 3/4 of students were satisfied with the quality of the programmes in terms of language used, technical quality, additional information and synchronization and compatibility of sound with visuals.

Kapadia, A. M. (2006) studied the impact of TV on student learning. In contrast to Joshi. V. (1987). The study reported that the TV group gained significantly more than the controlled group. Even retention scores of the experimental group were better. Seventy per cent of the students opined that TV programmes help them in self-learning.

Krishnan, S. S. (2006) conducted a study, "Development of Multimedia Package for Teaching a Course on Audio-Visual Education" with objective to find the effectiveness of the multimedia package in terms of achievement of trainees and change in attitude of the instructor trainees towards the multimedia package and it was find out that the achievement of trainees and their language ability were found to be positively related at 0.01 level of significance. The feasibility of the multimedia package was established in terms of cost involved in reproduction of the various resource materials and the time scheduling in an actual institutional set-up.

Mohrana, S. (2006) conducted a study on "Effectiveness of Educational Television Programme at the High school Level". The main objective of the study was to study the effect of ETV programmes on high school students in terms of academic achievement, attitude towards school and motivation in learning. The study concluded that the academic achievement of students exposed to educational television programmes was higher than those not exposed to educational television programmes. Out of the three comparisons made in three school subjects, two have reached the level of significance. In Mathematics the difference was not significant, though the result was in positive direction and in favor of ETV group.

Seth, I. (2006) conducted a study on "A Study of the Effectiveness of Educational Television on the Educational Development of High School Students". The main objective of the study was to inquire into the effect of educational television (ETV) on the educational development of high school students in terms of language development, acquisition of information related to ETV programmes and scholastic achievement. The study was concluded that language development of students exposed to ETV was higher than those not exposed to ETV. Language development among students exposed to ETV along with intervention programmes was higher than those exposed to ETV alone and those not exposed to ETV. The scholastic achievement of students exposed to ETV programmes along with intervention was higher than the ETV and the non-ETV groups.

Benjamin and Sivakumar (2006) conducted a study, "Multimedia Enhances Effective Self-Learning". They in their study emphasizes the need and importance of learning through multimedia CD-based self-learning and dwells on the quality as well as quantity of teaching and learning bringing forth the need and significance of learning science through self-learning with the help of multimedia CD-based courseware.

Lal, H. (2006) conducted a study on quality educational television programs for students and found out that use of media for educational purposes enriches learning experiences. They also suggested that production on quality educational media programmes relevant to the subject and to different stages of education would facilitate enriched learning experiences.

Ponnusamy, P. and Natesan, M. (2006) attempted to study instructional media and their effect on class room learning and concluded that use of instructional media on high schools and enrich classroom learning experiences of high school students. They also attempted to measure the frequency of use of different media by teachers of primary and upper high schools and concluded that most of the primary teachers were utilizing only models and newspapers in their classroom activities and needed a proper training.

Seth, M. (2003) aimed at studying the learning process or achievement with special reference to Audio-Visual Aids. The audio-visual aids were found to be more beneficial for the girls of the lower I.Q. group than for the girls of high I.Q. but they increased the achievement scores of the girls of higher I.Q. as well. It was concluded that the use of audio visual aids was beneficial and have positive effect on developmental areas, viz., speech learning and language learning.

Sethi, A. S. (2002) conducted a study of a programme in English spelling in relation to Visual and Auditory presentation and attempted to investigate the relative effectiveness of visual and auditory presentation of a programme in English spellings in terms of performance of students. It was found out that auditory and visual presentation has positive effect on students' achievement as well as on their performance.

Roy, P. and Dighe, A. (2001) studied factors affecting comprehension and retention of selected SITE programmes. The emphasis was on hardcore programmes which had never been telecast before-two agricultural programmes, one in the area of health and nutrition and the other in the area of family planning. The study revealed that with regard to interest, utility, attitude and relevance, the comprehension and retention scores showed consistent difference between the groups, which implied that the Indian village TV audience was perceptual.

Ahuja, G. C. and Ahuja, P. (2000) suggested the demonstration of Audio-Visual and reading aids to school students and tested their reading speed in three different languages. Findings of the study indicated that there is an increase in the reading speed and interest of students towards CCTV programmes.

Golani, T. P. (2000) attempted to study the awareness and to present the other measures in the form of concrete proposals and their implications for secondary schools as well as for the professional courses in training teachers and preparing materials for audio-visual aids in education. The findings of the study indicated that according to opinions of the secondary schools under survey, the teaching aids were essential and useful in developing clear concepts and in stimulating learning and use of aids are useful in teaching subjects like social studies, mathematics, sciences and languages.

Paigaonkar, A. (2000) attempted to investigate the use of mass media for second language teaching in India with special reference to Radio and Television and it was found out that the script-writers and subject experts of radio and TV lessons for schools had the knowledge about the principles of linguistics and pedagogy but did not have the training needed to use the media potentials. This was reflected in the actual lessons produced.

Sabharwal, V. K. (2000) attempted to study the comparative effectiveness of Programmed Auto-learning vis-à-vis other methods of teaching English as a Second Language in relation to L-1 and L-2 achievement. The study concluded that the past achievement in L-2 was the best single index of subsequent L-2 learning through the grammar translation and the audio lingual method. Thus use of audio-video material enhances learning.

Biswal, B. (1998) studied the reaction of students and teachers towards effective utilization of school broadcast programmes. The study revealed that the strategies developed for effective utilization of School Broadcast Programmes were significantly effective when compared to the radio broadcast alone. Students and teachers favored the strategies and the strategies were feasible in terms of time, schedule and cost involved.

Singh J. and Shukla, S. (1995) studied the utilization and attitude of teachers towards school broadcasts, the study aimed at the process of programme planning and production and liaison between the directorate of education and akashvani in various stages of programmes planning and production and comprehensibility of radio lessons on the part of students. The study concluded that after listening to the programmes, the experimental group gained on all programmes to the extent of 7 to 17%. Item analysis of the tests showed that the students gained very little on words knowledge and concept formation. Most gain was on acquisition of factual information.

Passi, B. K. et al. (1980) studied the facilities available, reasons and opinions for broadcasting educational programmes for teachers. The main findings was that a majority of the teachers (95%) had facilities for listening to radio broadcasts and they liked to listen to broadcasts related to the ways of motivation and creating interest among students for teaching language and science, maintaining discipline in classrooms as well as in school.

Phutela, R. L. (1980) attempted to investigate the utilization and comprehensibility of School Television Programmes on the part of the students of different classes. The result of four out of five comprehension tests regarding utilization STV programmes showed real difference in the learning of the subject matter, indicating that these lessons were well understood.

Goel (1980) studied the school broadcast in the country covering all the 35 AIR stations engaged in producing school broadcast programmes and it was revealed that there was no coordination between the broadcast divisions and state departments of education. But the study concluded that indeed there is a positive effect of mass media technology in education.

Rao, R. R. and Subrahmanyam, S. (1980) estimated the relative influence of certain factors on reading attainment of students and suggested remedial measures to improve the reading skills. The study found out that among the personal attributes, general mental ability, visual discrimination of words, auditory discrimination of sounds, clarity of speech, reading habits and interest in reading influenced their reading attainment positively.

Krishan, S. S. (1980) conducted a study "Development of Multimedia Package for Teaching a Course on Audiovisual Education." The major objectives of the study were: (i) To develop a multimedia package for teaching a course on audiovisual education for the instructor training programme; (ii) to find the effectiveness of the multimedia package in terms of achievement of trainees and change in attitude of the instructor trainees towards the multimedia package; and (iii) to study the feasibility of the multimedia package in terms of time and cost for the instructor training programme. The major findings of the study were: (i) Ninety-eight percent of the trainees obtained more than 80 percent of the marks on the final post-test; (ii) the mean percentages of the post-test scores varied from 81.41 to 90.46; (iii) the mean gain in the total scores for all the modules was found to be significant; (iv) the mean gain scores of knowledge, comprehension and higher mental abilities were found to be significant; (v) the mean attitude change was found to be significant; (vi) the achievement of trainees and their language ability were found to be positively related; (vii) the feasibility of the multimedia package was established in terms of cost involved in reproduction of the various resource materials and the time scheduling in an actual institutional set-up.

Joshi, V. (1980) worked on the effectiveness of secondary school TV programmes in science. The researcher found that school TV programmes are run of the mill and have not changed over the years. The study also revealed that the programmes were of poor quality, and no significant difference was found in scholastic e achievement and the scientific attitudes of U students exposed to STV programmes.

Rawat, G. S. (1980) reported that eh academic achievement was significantly better when the comparisons were made for the total sample with respect to sex, age and grades.

Education Technology Cell, Meghalaya (1988) conducted a survey of the ETV programmes in the State. The organization interviewed 289 headmasters, 538 teachers, 774 parents and 1,240 students. The survey revealed that students wanted longer duration ETV programmes and with the frequency of one programme a day. Power supply and problems relating to maintenance and repair were blocks to popularizing ETV programmes.

Mohanty, P. C. (1988) took-up a study of the ETV programme for high school students and found that students exposed to ETV programmes had superior scholastic attainment as compared to students of the non-exposed group. The greatest achievement was in respect of "language"

Educational Technology Cell, Shillong (1989) conducted a study on feedback studies of educational broadcasts on continuous enrichment scheme. The objectives of the study were that to enable teachers to improve their teaching skills and to improve the classroom teaching-learning situations and to enrich the experience of both the teachers and the pupils by familiarizing with the latest information on educational innovations. And the findings of the study were that the majority of respondents preferred the afternoons for educational broadcasts, with the present 20 minutes duration, the majority of respondents preferred dramatized programmes. And the academic contents of the programmes was found suitable; the language used was easy to understand; and the method of presentation, suitable.

Educational Technology, Meghalaya (1989) took-up feedback studies on educational broadcasts and found that the broadcast timing was the wrong one, and preference was more for the afternoon. Teachers were of the view that radio programmes were helpful in their teaching and wanted more programmes in service and languages.

Mishra, S. (1989) took up "A Critical Analysis of High school Radio Programmes" and found that radio programmes in "song" and "story" format were liked by the students most. However, students did not like "Quiz" and "talk" programmes. The researcher has also observed that child artists are not invited to narrate stories. He also observed that students did not like long programmes.

Arularam, L. (1990) took up evaluation of the UGC programems popularly known as Country-wide. Classroom Education TV programmes. The study revealed that most of the programmes cater to urban audiences. The needs of the rural students still remain unfulfilled. The study also revealed that programmes in humanities were poor in offering knowledge enrichment.

Behera, S. C. (1990) investigated the impact of ETV on competencies of teachers of elementary schools. The study demonstrated that teachers exposed to ETV programmes achieved significantly more on their knowledge understanding and application in the specified content areas. In actual classroom interaction, ETV teachers significantly differed from Non ETV teachers on Teacher Response Ratio. Teacher Question Ratio, and Pupil Initiation Ratio. Teachers also pointed out power failures, mechanical disorders and unsuitable time slot as some of the vulnerable problems.

Chaudhary, S. (1990) conducted a study on teachers' attitude towards school TV (STV) and its relation with job satisfaction. He found that job satisfaction was associated with the authority responsible. For work allocation, intensive case studies revealed that the majority of teachers did not operate STV regularly and the majority of TV sets were out of order. Teachers perceived STV as a good tool for teaching and were fairly satisfied with their job. Teachers teaching Classes IV and V showed a more positive attitude towards STV than teachers teaching Classes I-IV.

Giri, A. P. (1990), investigated the problems and prospects of school radio broadcast programmes. He found that utilization of radio of broadcasts was more in urban schools than in rural ones. Further, in the rural sector only 1/4th of the schools had the provision of a separate period in the time-table.

Chowdhry, M. (1990) took a development-cum-research project to study the potential of radio programmes for providing enriching experiences to anganwadi and high school students. The findings are quite interesting. Aganwadi students gained significantly more than their counterparts in the control group in' capabilities like listening comprehension, verbal expression. Vocabulary gain and sequential thinking. However, no significant difference was found between the experimental and control groups of high schools.

STUDIES CONDUCTED IN ABROAD

Lee, S. H. (2014) attempts to measure the learning achievement of College students from two intact groups in an art class when a multimedia form of instruction was utilize din place of traditional instruction. Only the experimental group received digital content based instruction and three dimensional visualization modules. A post test and pre test instrument was utilized for both the experimental and control group. A one way ANOVA was used to determine significant difference between groups. The usage of the three dimensional visualization modules (the experimental group) produced a significant difference in student performance as compared to traditional instruction.

Apel, K. and Apel, L. (2011) conducted a study, "Identifying Intra individual Differences in Students' Written Language Abilities" Topics in Language Disorders, Vol. 31, No. 1, pp. 54-72. Students must be able to consciously use their knowledge of phonology, orthography, morphology, semantics, syntax, and pragmatics to successfully read and write. Difficulties in the conscious awareness of 1 or more of these 6 linguistic knowledge components may lead to reading and writing deficits. In this article, we present a componential model of spoken and written language that can guide literacy educators in their assessment of students' written language skills. We then provide some general assessment strategies that measure students' conscious awareness of these different linguistic components to read and write. To demonstrate the use of this model and the assessment strategies, we present 3 student profiles that illustrate how difficulties with written language ability can be the result of different underlying linguistic awareness deficits. On the basis of these individual deficits, we also provide initial suggestions for prescriptive intervention goals. Finally, we discuss some suggestions for ensuring that professionals from varying backgrounds share a common knowledge base and vocabulary so that meaningful clinical and educational services are provided to students who struggle in the area of written language.

Celina, P. (2010) conducted a study on stimulating linguistic, aesthetic and objectified pre-reading skills of pre-scholars and found out that a child has to acquire a lot of skills at the physical, intellectual and emotional levels and these skills can be developed through playful activities. The skills develop not in isolation but as an integral part of the total development of an individual. A multimode programme both in school and non-school environment was implemented for developing basic skills among the pre-scholars. It was found that the programme was very effective in enhancing majority of the pre-reading skills among the pre-scholars.

Arndt, E. J. and Foorman, B. R. (2010) conducted a study, "Second Graders as Spellers: What Types of Errors Are They Making?". In their study beginning second-grade students (N = 60) were administered a researcher-developed, dictated spelling test. Spelling errors of students were analyzed by grade-level spelling patterns and linguistic characteristics: phonological, orthographic, orthographic image, transposition, and morphological. Results revealed that morphological spelling pattern errors occurred most frequently. The frequency of linguistic category errors for this sample, ranging from least to most, was transposition, phonological, orthographic image, orthographic, and morphological. Further analysis of the bottom quarter of students, as determined by their performance on a timed word reading measure, indicated a pattern of spelling errors similar to the rest of the sample, but occurring in significantly greater quantity on average. These findings support previous research suggesting poor spellers display similar error patterns as better spelling peers, but with higher frequency. Initial implications suggest to educators that in spite of the wide range of spelling ability in their classrooms, the pattern of knowledge appears similar. Students rely on multiple sources of linguistic knowledge, and by analyzing their spelling errors based on the information students use to generate their spellings, instruction may be provided to explicitly and systematically target students' weaknesses.

De, S. and Roger, J. (2009) in perspective on the Research and purpose of Reading Comprehension Study Skills and Techniques stated that the primary purpose of reading is to drive the meaning of an author's message, which has been transmitted through print, as it relates to the readers personal need to go from a point of lesser to greater information. The four perspectives cross both basic and applied research needs in comprehension assessment technique, methods and materials.

Hanley, George and Tanksale (2006-07) investigated how the research informed development model affects the pedagogical learning outcomes and design solutions of university students responsible for creating interactive advertising and news content for T.V. An interdisciplinary group of 3 professors and 31 under graduates from advertising, computer science, Journalism graphics and telecommunications employed a research informed development process to create interactive design products and collect feedback from target users about the interactive advertising, news content and interface designs and functionally students used the feedback from user focus groups to revise and improve the design work before each of three rounds of usability tests.

Mayer and Gallini (2007) found that coordinating text with pictures improved learning. They found that students who were present text with a narration by the teacher scored significantly higher on retention, matching and transfer texts.

Koppar, B. (2006) investigated the factors affecting reading comprehension and found out the relationship of reading comprehension with attitude towards academic motivation. The study found out that the reading comprehension was related positively to the reading attitude and academic achievement.

George, E. I., Mathew, V. G. and Nair, K. S. (2005) conducted a pilot study to develop suitable instruments and techniques and determined the relationship of language and play development and academic achievement. The language and play patterns of the three groups were arrived at and compared to obtain the developmental norms.

Antonysamy, L. (2005) found that teaching environmental concepts to school dropouts through video and charts. It was found that learning through viewing of the video films was more effective than learning through charts.

Bates (2005) suggested such parameters as voice, written language, colors, still pictures, animation, dramatic events and full movement where we make the choice between media such as lectures, audio, print, computer and television.

Bodemes, et al. (2005) studied the supporting learning with interactive multimedia through active integration of representation revealed that the active integration of static representations before processing dynamic visualizations resulted in better performance and can provide a basis for a more systematic and goal oriented experimentation behavior during simulation based discovery learning.

Young, (2005) conducted a study "The most exciting thing about multimedia is that is reaches all the senses and that is why, its use in the field of education, is even more justified," Say young, chairman of the Department of Technology, Cognitive at the university of North Texas, Dentan, "Students all given more fodder for their imaginations".

Miller (2005) observed six instructional dimensions affecting successful multi-grade teaching have been identified from research viz. classroom organization, classroom management and discipline, instructional organization and curriculum, instructional delivery and grouping, self-directed learning, and peer tutoring.

Rebecca, O. et al. (2003) conducted a study on learning a language by satellite television: What influences student achievement? A group of 107 students participated in a major study exploring the factors that influence language achievement when instruction is delivered by satellite television. Factors included the students' motivation, learning styles, learning strategy use, gender, previous language learning experience, and course level. Motivation was by far the most significant determiner of achievement, and learning strategy use was also very influential. Gender and learning style (visual, auditory, and hands-on) played potentially important roles, although previous language learning and course level were not especially explanatory. Specific implications are included for satellite language teaching, a delivery system that promises to become more widely used throughout the world as advances in technology continue.

Garnett, H. and Olliver (2003) designed an interactive multimedia package to improve beginning students' understanding of chemical equations. In this three discrete modules that introduce students to chemical equations and develop skills in balancing equations and their interpretation. The materials are designed for use in direct teaching, tutorial or self instructional modes.

Michael, P. (2000) in an article "Comprehension Instruction: What works" opines that without a strong background in basic skills like decoding and vocabulary-building, comprehension is impossible. This article offers research-based strategies for building on these and other skills to increase student understanding of what is read.

Attewell (2000) found out that through the use of text, graphics, audio, video and animation, edutainment steers away from the traditional teaching method. These multimedia appliances help to reinforce learning, and make learning more fun rather than a hassle. Another advantage of edutainment is that it allows the students to control their own learning pace. When students have the ability to control the speed at which they learn the material, it usually requires less time to learn it.

Michel, M. (2000) explained the effects of multimedia on learning in Third world students. The performance scores of two groups of 18 students were recorded before and after using either multimedia or no multimedia to learn mathematics. The students that used multimedia scored significantly higher than those who did not.

CONCLUSION

The review reveals that, so far none of research has been conducted to find out Role of Television Programmes in Understanding Tamil Language for VIIIth Standard Students. The review of related literature has helped the investigator to formulate the relevant hypotheses and suitable methodology, which are discussed in the next chapters to follow.

Chapter - III

Methodology

INTRODUCTION

"The analysis of the principles of methods, rules and postulates employed by a discipline";

"The systematic study of methods that are, can be or have been applied within a discipline".

Research purifies human life. It improves its quality. It is search for knowledge. If shows how to Solve any problem scientifically. It is a careful enquiry through search for any kind of Knowledge. It is a journey from known to unknown. It is a systematic effort to gain new knowledge in any kind of discipline.

When it seeks a solution of any educational problem it leads to educational research. Curiosity, inquisitiveness is natural gifts secured by a man. They inspire to quest, increase thirst for knowledge / truth. Research is the voyage of discovery. It is the quest for answers to unsolved problems. Research is required in any field to come up with new theories or modify, accept or nullify the existing theory. From time immemorial it has been seen so many discoveries and inventions took place through research and world has got so many new theories which help the human being to solve problems.

EDUCATIONAL RESEARCH

Educational Research as nothing but cleansing of educational Research is nothing but cleansing of educational process. Many experts think Educational.

1. Educational Research is the systematic application of scientific method for solving for solving educational problem.
2. Educational Research is the activity for developing science of behavior in educational situations. It allows the educator to achieve his goals effectively.
3. Educational Research aims at finding out solution of educational problems by using scientific philosophical method.

Thus, the Educational Research is to solve educational problem in systematic and scientific manner, it is to understand, explain, predict and control human behavior.

Research methodology involves systematic procedures starting from the initial identification of the problem to its final conclusions. Its role is to carry on the research work in a scientific and valid manner.

Thus, it consists of all general and specific activities of research. Mastery in it enhances understanding of the research activities. Thus, research design and methodology have the identical meaning of mapping strategy of research.

RESEARCH DESIGN

This chapter presents details regarding the following:

1. Selection of Dependent variables and Categorical variables.
2. Construction of tools to measure the Role of Television Programmes in Understanding Tamil Language for VIIIth Standard Students.
3. Methods of establishing the reliability, validity of the tools constructed.
4. Sampling procedure adopted in this study.
5. Scheduling the survey and collecting the data.

RESEARCH PROCEDURE

A research design helps the investigator to obtain answers to research problem and issues involved in the research, since it is the outline of entire research process.

Design also tells us about how to collect data, what observation are to be carry out, how to make them, how to analyze the data. Design also guides investigator about statistical techniques to be used for analysis.

Thus, design guides the investigator to carry out research step by step in an efficient way.

STATEMENT OF THE PROBLEM

The present investigation is entitled as*"A Study on the Role of Television Programmes in Understanding Tamil Language for VIIIth Standard Students".*

OBJECTIVES OF THE STUDY

The objective of this present study will gives the detailed analysis of the research on "Study on the Role of Television Programmes in Understanding Tamil Language". The present study will helpful in understanding ability towards Tamil learning.

The findings of the study will help the people to know various positive aspects of Understanding Tamil Language. This will make the school students effective in understanding through Television programme.

The objectives of the overall studies are

1. To find out the significant difference in the mean scores of Role of Television Programmes in Understanding Tamil Language for VIIIth Standard Students in terms of their Gender as Male and Female.
2. To find out the significant difference in the mean scores of Role of Television Programmes in Understanding Tamil Language for VIIIth Standard Students in terms of their Type of School as Government and Aided.

3. To find out the significant difference in the mean scores of Role of Television Programmes in Understanding Tamil Language for VIIIth Standard Students in terms of their Type of School as Aided and Private.
4. To find out the significant difference in the mean scores of Role of Television Programmes in Understanding Tamil Language for VIIIth Standard Students in terms of their Type of School as Private and Government.
5. To find out the significant difference in the mean scores of Role of Television Programmes in Understanding Tamil Language for VIIIth Standard Students in terms of their Locality as Rural and Urban.
6. To find out the significant difference in the mean scores of Role of Television Programmes in Understanding Tamil Language for VIIIth Standard Students in terms of their Parent Educational Qualification as Educated and Un-educated.
7. To find out the significant difference in the mean scores of Role of Television Programmes in Understanding Tamil Language for VIIIth Standard Students in terms of their Parent Occupation as Self Employment and Government Job.
8. To find out the significant difference in the mean scores of Role of Television Programmes in Understanding Tamil Language for VIIIth Standard Students in terms of their Parent Occupation as Government Job and Private Job.
9. To find out the significant difference in the mean scores of Role of Television Programmes in Understanding Tamil Language for VIIIth Standard Students in terms of their Parent Occupation as Private Job and Government Job.
10. To find out the significant difference in the mean scores of Role of Television Programmes in Understanding Tamil Language for VIIIth Standard Students in terms of their Parent Annual Income as Above 50000 and Below 50000.

HYPOTHESES OF THE STUDY

The Hypotheses should be framed according to the Variables chosen to find the Role of Television Programmes in Understanding Tamil

Language for VIII Standard Students. 'A hypothesis could be defined as an expectation about event based on generalization of the assumed relationship between variable'.

Hypothesis means subject to the verification and statement about solution of the problem.

The Hypothesis of the present study is to find the difference in the mean scores of Role of Television Programmes in Understanding Tamil Language for VIII Standard Students.

1. There is no significant difference in the mean scores of Role of Television Programmes in Understanding Tamil Language for VIIIth Standard Students in terms of their Gender as Male and Female.
2. There is no significant difference in the mean scores of Role of Television Programmes in Understanding Tamil Language for VIIIth Standard Students in terms of their Type of School as Government and Aided.
3. There is no significant difference in the mean scores of Role of Television Programmes in Understanding Tamil Language for VIIIth Standard Students in terms of their Type of School as Aided and Private.
4. There is no significant difference in the mean scores of Role of Television Programmes in Understanding Tamil Language for VIIIth Standard Students in terms of their Type of School as Private and Government.
5. There is no significant difference in the mean scores of Role of Television Programmes in Understanding Tamil Language for VIIIth Standard Students in terms of their Locality as Rural and Urban.
6. There is no significant difference in the mean scores of Role of Television Programmes in Understanding Tamil Language for VIIIth Standard Students in terms of their Parent Educational Qualification as Educated and Un-educated.
7. There is no significant difference in the mean scores of Role of Television Programmes in Understanding Tamil Language for

VIIIth Standard Students in terms of their Parent Occupation as Self Employment and Government Job.

8. There is no significant difference in the mean scores of Role of Television Programmes in Understanding Tamil Language for VIIIth Standard Students in terms of their Parent Occupation as Government Job and Private Job.
9. There is no significant difference in the mean scores of Role of Television Programmes in Understanding Tamil Language for VIIIth Standard Students in terms of their Parent Occupation as Private Job and Government Job.
10. There is no significant difference in the mean scores of Role of Television Programmes in Understanding Tamil Language for VIIIth Standard Students in terms of their Parent Annual Income as Above 50000 and Below 50000.

LIMITATIONS OF THE STUDY

The investigation on the Role of Television Programmes in Understanding Tamil Language for VIIIth Standard Students is limited to 300 data collected in and around Pudukkottai District.

The present educational study survey was conducted to VIIIth standard students only.

The present educational survey was conducted in 2014- 2015 only.

RESEARCH METHOD

The investigator preferred survey method for the present study. In this study, the investigator used survey method to collect data and to identify the Role of Television Programmes in Understanding Tamil Language for VIIIth Standard Students.

RESEARCH TOOLS

The questionnaire is the most tools in collecting both quantitative and qualities information, for the present study questionnaire was prepared with view to gather information in details regarding on Role of Television Programmes in Understanding Tamil Language for VIIIth Standard Students. The word 'tool' is defined "a means to collect evidence".

In the present study the investigation using questionnaire as tool for the most important collecting data because it is used increasingly to enquire the current conditions, opinions and attitude of a groups.

CONSTRUCTION OF RESEARCH TOOLS

The research tool on "Role of Television Programmes in Understanding Tamil Language for VIIIth Standard Students" was standardized by the investigator only and also the personal data sheet was constructed by the investigator in the present study. The responded who respond the correct answers were given scores and these score were considered for data analysis.

SAMPLES OF THE STUDY

After finalizing the variables of present study, consideration was given to whether the entire population is to be made the subject for data collection or a particular group is to be selected as representative of the whole population. The entire population here refers to the VIIIth standard school students studying in Pudukkottai District.

DESCRIPTION OF RESEARCH TOOL AND SCORING PROCEDURE

Before administering the test necessary instruction and directions were given to the students. No time limit is given to the students were asked to complete the inventory as early as possible.

SCORING AND CONSOLIDATION OF DATA

Scoring was done as per the scoring scheme. The scores obtained in all questionnaires along with the personal data are consolidated and tabulated on consolidation sheet for the purpose of analysis.

PILOT STUDY

Based on the pilot study, the main study was conducted by the investigator while administering the research in the pilot study, some doubts were raised by the school students and the investigator clarified all of their doubts and difficulties. The pilot stage is concerned with refining the items collected. The collected items were presented before the expert with a request to offer their considered opinion regarding the suitability objectivity clarity and relevancy of the statement collected from different sources. The opinion of the experts was taken into consideration. The pilot study is an initial study which is conducted by the investigator to know more about the research problem in various aspects. Based on that, the investigator gave the instructions. Further, the investigator obtained some ideas from the experts and modified the irrelevant Item that is coming in the present study. After getting response from the respondents, the investigator gave frequencies for the correct response and these frequencies were converted into scores and those scores were used to Analysis and interpretation of data.

VALIDITY OF THE TOOL

In validation process, the investigator used two measures in order to establish validation of tools. The first measure of validation is called reliability. The second measure of validation process is called validity. The investigator established content validity. To find out the validity of research tool, the investigator discussed each and every item of the questionnaire with the experts in the relevant field of Role of Television Programmes in Understanding Tamil Language for VIIIth Standard Students. Based on the opinion of the experts, the objectivity and worthiness of the items of the questionnaire were arranged.

RELIABILITY OF THE TOOL

The reliability of questionnaire on indentifying Role of Television Programmes in Understanding Tamil Language for VIIIth Standard Students was established by making a rational equivalence method. The reliability of the tool refers to the internal consistency observed in measurement of reliability. And the tool has the sufficient reliability value as **'r'** is equals to **0.78** respectively.

SAMPLING TECHNIQUE USED

Random sampling method was adopted for this purpose. In this method random sampling every individual in the population has an equal and independent chance of being chosen for the samples. After finalizing the variables of present study, consideration was given to whether the entire population is to be made the subject for data collection or a particular group is to be selected as representative of the whole population. The entire population here refers to all the under VIIIth standard school students studying in Pudukkottai District.

In any behavioral research, various methods are utilized for selection and drawing of samples. After a detailed study of all these methods and considering the variables selected for the research work, the Random sampling method was found to be most suitable.

Random sampling method, the entire population will be divided into smaller homogenous groups or strata, and then a sample is selected within each group. Every sampling unit in the population is placed in one of the strata prior to the selection of the sample so that the sum of the strata is identical with the population.

Random sampling method has certain merits as a technique of sampling. 'Random sampling enables the researcher to make a composition of properties of the strata as well as to estimate population characteristics'.

Random sampling method, the investigator has greater control over the selection of the sample when compared with simple random sampling. In simple random sampling, although every group has a chance of being selected and included in the sample, there is every possibility, and sometimes it does not happen, that certain important groups are left unrepresentative. But, in Random sampling methods no important group is likely to be left out. Replacement of units is also possible in the Random sampling method.

Normally, if a particular unit is not accessible for a study, it is difficult to replace it by another, but in this method it is possible. Stephen states that stratification automatically brings about a replacement of persons lost in the sample, by persons of the same stratum, thus partly correcting the bias that would result if there were no replacement of losses.

As the entire population is divided into particular strata it is easy and convenient to replace an in accessible case by an accessible one.

In Random sampling method, much depends on stratification process. The following precaution were taken while stratifying the population: the variables involved in the study were taken note of; care was taken to see that each stratum in the universe was large enough in size so that selection of items could be done on random basis; the strata formed were definite and clear cut; each stratum was free from influence of the other; and there was no overlapping.

COLLECTION OF DATA

The investigator herself met each and every school students who are studying in various high schools located at Pudukkottai District. Before going to administer the research tool, the investigator revealed the purpose of the present study to the school students and then asked them to give their responses for each and every item that are given in the questionnaire. The responses of the school students were recorded.

S.No.	Schools Selected for the Study	Male	Female	Total
1.	Government Higher Secondary School, Lembalakudi.	50	36	086
2.	Government Higher Secondary School, Pilakkudipatti.	-	14	014
3	Ramanathan Chettiyar Higher Secondary School, Nachandhupatti.	50	50	100
4	K.V. Matriculation School, Pudukkottai.	50	50	100
	300			

ANALISIS OF DATA

The term analysis refers to the compilation of certain measures along with searching for pattern and relationship that among groups. For the present study the investigator collected the data from VIIIth standard High school students using the tool developed to find out questionnaire of sample with the Role of Television Programmes in Understanding Tamil Language for VIII th Standard Students with reference to learning atmosphere.

This involves computing measures of central tendency like Mean and the measures of variability like Standard deviation. The computed values are used to describe the property of the particular sample and description of data to manageable size.

STATISTICAL TECHNIQUES USED

Statistical Techniques serves the fundamental purpose of the description and inferential analysis. It is concerned with numerical description of a particular group observed. Any similarity to those outside the group cannot be taken for granted. The data describe one group only. Simple educational research involves descriptive statistics and provides valuable information about the nature of a particular group or class.

Data collected from tests have little meaning or significance until they have been classified or rearranged in a systematic way. The following Statistical Techniques were used in this study.

1. Mean (M)
2. Standard Deviation (S.D.)
3. 't' – test for determine the significance of difference between means of two sub-groups.

ARITHMETIC MEAN

The mean of a distribution is commonly understood as the arithmetic average. It is computed by dividing the sum of all scores by the number of scores.

STANDARD DEVIATION (S.D)

Standard Deviation is the square-root of the mean of the squares of the deviations of all the items from the arithmetic mean. It is represented by the letter 'ó'.

't'- TEST

The t- critical values necessary for rejection of a null hypothesis are higher for the samples of a given level of significances. Each t – critical value for rejection is based upon the appropriate number of degrees of freedom.

The **t – test** would be used upon this formula.

M1= Mean of First Group

M2 = Mean of Second Group

S1 = SD of the first

S2 = SD of the second group

N1 = No. of students in first Group

N2 = No. of Students in Second Group

CONCLUSION

In this chapter the methodology of the study was explained clearly. Each and every step was carefully planned and executed. The research strategies and the collection procedures have been explained. The next chapter deals with the analysis and interpretation of data.

Chapter - IV

Analysis and Interpretation of Data

INTRODUCTION

Analysis and Interpretation of Data is one of the most crucial components of the research project. Only through the analysis of collected data, meaningful result is obtained.

Giels, aptly states that "The very objective of data analysis refers to the process of analysis in which relationships or differences supporting or conflicting with original or new hypothesis should be subjected to statistical test of significance, so as to determine with what validity data can be said to indicate any conclusion". Interpretation, on the other hand, is one of the most important devices in the field of research that translates the statistical result into a legible and understandable narration.

ANALYSIS OF DATA

According to Kaplan, "Analysis attempts to characterize the meaning in a given body to discourse in a systematic and quantitative fashion".

The scores were used to identify the *"A Study on the Role of Television Programmes in Understanding Tamil Language for VIIIth Standard Students".*

HYPOTHESES TESTING

HYPOTHESIS: 1

There is no significant difference in the mean scores of Role of Television Programmes in Understanding Tamil Language for VIIIth Standard Students in terms of their Gender as Male and Female.

TABLE: 1

The table given below shows the mean, standard deviation and "t" values of Role of Television Programmes in Understanding Tamil Language for VIIIth Standard Students in terms of their Gender as Male and Female.

Gender	N	M	SD	df	't' value	Level of Significance at 0.05
Male	159	78.89	8.55			
Female	141	82.70	7.07	298	4.22	Significant

INTERPRETATION:

The computed table value of **t = 4.22**is greater than the critical table value at 0.05 level of significance (i.e.) 1.96, which implies that there is significant difference in the mean scores of Role of Television Programmes in Understanding Tamil Language for VIIIth Standard Students in terms of their Gender as Male and Female.

RESULT:

Hence the null hypothesis is rejected.

HYPOTHESIS: 2

There is no significant difference in the mean scores of Role of Television Programmes in Understanding Tamil Language for VIIIth Standard Students in terms of their Type of School as Government and Aided.

TABLE: 2

The table gave below shows the mean, standard deviation and "t" values of Role of Television Programmes in Understanding Tamil Language for VIIIth Standard Students in terms of their Type of School as Government and Aided.

Type of School	N	M	SD	df	't' value	Level of Significance at 0.05
Government	100	79.97	8.84	198	2.29	Significant
Aided	100	82.60	7.28			

INTERPRETATION:

The computed table value of **t = 2.29** is greater than the critical table value at 0.05 level of significance (i.e.) 1.96, which implies that there is significant difference in the mean scores of Role of Television Programmes in Understanding Tamil Language for VIIIth Standard Students in terms of their Type of School as Government and Aided.

RESULT:

Hence the null hypothesis is rejected.

HYPOTHESIS: 3

There is no significant difference in the mean scores of Role of Television Programmes in Understanding Tamil Language for VIIIth Standard Students in terms of their Type of School as Aided and Private.

TABLE: 3

The table gave below shows the mean, standard deviation and "t" values of Role of Television Programmes in Understanding Tamil Language for VIIIth Standard Students in terms of their Type of School as Aided and Private.

Type of School	N	M	SD	df	't' value	Level of Significance at 0.05
Aided	100	82.6	7.28	198	2.91	Significant
Private	100	79.49	7.84			

INTERPRETATION

The computed table value of **t = 2.91** is greater than the critical table value at 0.05 level of significance (i.e.) 1.96, which implies that there is significant difference in the mean scores of Role of Television Programmes in Understanding Tamil Language for VIIIth Standard Students in terms of their Type of School as Aided and Private.

RESULT:

Hence the null hypothesis is rejected.

HYPOTHESIS: 4

There is no significant difference in the mean scores of Role of Television Programmes in Understanding Tamil Language for VIIIth Standard Students in terms of their Type of School as Private and Government.

TABLE: 4

The table given below shows the mean, standard deviation and "t" values of Role of Television Programmes in Understanding Tamil Language for VIIIth Standard Students in terms of their Type of School as Private and Government.

Type of School	N	M	SD	df	't' value	Level of Significance at 0.05
Private	100	79.49	7.84			
Government	100	79.97	8.84	198	0.40	Not Significant

INTERPRETATION

The computed table value of **t = 0.40** is smaller than the critical table value at 0.05 level of significance (i.e.) 1.96, which implies that there is no significant difference in the mean scores of Role of Television Programmes in Understanding Tamil Language for VIIIth Standard Students in terms of their Type of School as Private and Government.

RESULT:

Hence the null hypothesis is accepted.

HYPOTHESIS: 5

There is no significant difference in the mean scores of Role of Television Programmes in Understanding Tamil Language for VIIIth Standard Students in terms of their Locality as Rural and Urban.

TABLE: 5

The table gave below shows the mean, standard deviation and "t" values of Role of Television Programmes in Understanding Tamil Language for VIIIth Standard Students in terms of their Locality as Rural and Urban.

Locality	N	M	SD	df	't' Value	Level of Significance at 0.05
Rural	189	80.44	8.45			
Urban	111	81.07	7.49	298	0.67	Not Significant

INTERPRETATION

The computed table value of **t = 0.67** is smaller than the critical table value at 0.05 level of significance (i.e.) 1.96, which implies that there is no significant difference in the mean scores of Role of Television Programmes in Understanding Tamil Language for VIIIth Standard Students in terms of their Locality as Rural and Urban.

RESULT:

Hence the null hypothesis is accepted.

HYPOTHESIS: 6

There is no significant difference in the mean scores of Role of Television Programmes in Understanding Tamil Language for VIIIth Standard Students in terms of their Parent Educational Qualification as Educated and Un-educated.

TABLE : 6

The table gave below shows the mean, standard deviation and "t" values of Role of Television Programmes in Understanding Tamil Language for VIIIth Standard Students in terms of their Parent Educational Qualification as Educated and Un-educated.

Parent Educational Qualification	N	M	SD	df	't' Value	Level of Significance at 0.05
Educated	242	80.44	7.91	298	1.01	Not Significant
Un-Educated	58	81.72	8.87			

INTERPRETATION

The computed table value of **t = 1.01** is smaller than the critical table value at 0.05 level of significance (i.e.) 1.96, which implies that there is no significant difference in the mean scores of Role of Television Programmes in Understanding Tamil Language for VIIIth Standard Students in terms of their Parent Educational Qualification as Educated and Un-educated.

RESULT:

Hence the null hypothesis is accepted.

HYPOTHESIS: 7

There is no significant difference in the mean scores of Role of Television Programmes in Understanding Tamil Language for VIIIth Standard Students in terms of their Parent Occupation as Self Employment and Government Job.

TABLE: 7

The table gave below shows the mean, standard deviation and "t" values of Role of Television Programmes in Understanding Tamil Language for VIIIth Standard Students in terms of their Parent Occupation as Self Employment and Government Job.

Parent Occupation And	N	M	SD	df	't' Value	Level of Significance at 0.05
Self Employment	163	81.10	7.64	246	0.41	Not Significant
Government Job	85	80.65	8.51			

INTERPRETATION

The computed table value of **t = 0.41** is smaller than the critical table value at 0.05 level of significance (i.e.) 1.96, which implies that there is no significant difference in the mean scores of Role of Television

Programmes in Understanding Tamil Language for VIIIth Standard Students in terms of their Parent Occupation as Self Employment and Government Job.

RESULT:

Hence the null hypothesis is accepted.

HYPOTHESIS: 8

There is no significant difference in the mean scores of Role of Television Programmes in Understanding Tamil Language for VIIIth Standard Students in terms of their Parent Occupation as Government Job and Private Job.

TABLE: 8

The table gave below shows the mean, standard deviation and "t" values of Role of Television Programmes in Understanding Tamil Language for VIIIth Standard Students in terms of their Parent Occupation as Government Job and Private Job.

Parent Occupation	N	M	SD	df	't' Value	Level of Significance at 0.05
Government Job	85	80.65	8.51			
Private Job	52	79.44	8.84	135	0.79	Not Significant

INTERPRETATION

The computed table value of **t = 0.79** is smaller than the critical table value at 0.05 level of significance (i.e.) 1.96, which implies that there is no significant difference in the mean scores of Role of Television Programmes in Understanding Tamil Language for VIIIth Standard Students in terms of their Parent Occupation as Government Job and Private Job.

RESULT:

Hence the null hypothesis is accepted.

HYPOTHESIS: 9

There is no significant difference in the mean scores of Role of

Television Programmes in Understanding Tamil Language for VIIIth Standard Students in terms of their Parent Occupation as Private Job and Government Job.

TABLE: 9

The table gave below shows the mean, standard deviation and "t" values of Role of Television Programmes in Understanding Tamil Language for VIIIth Standard Students in terms of their Parent Occupation as Private Job and Government Job.

Parent Occupation	N	M	SD	df	't' Value	Level of Significance at 0.05
Private Job	52	79.44	8.84			
Government Job	163	81.10	7.64	213	1.22	Not Significant

INTERPRETATION

The computed table value of **t = 1.22** is smaller than the critical table value at 0.05 level of significance (i.e.) 1.96, which implies that there is no significant difference in the mean scores of Role of Television Programmes in Understanding Tamil Language for VIIIth Standard Students in terms of their Parent Occupation as Private Job and Government Job.

RESULT:

Hence the null hypothesis is accepted.

HYPOTHESIS: 10

There is no significant difference in the mean scores of Role of Television Programmes in Understanding Tamil Language for VIIIth Standard Students in terms of their Parents Annual Income as Above 50000 and Below 50000.

TABLE: 10

The table gave below shows the mean, standard deviation and "t" values of Role of Television Programmes in Understanding Tamil Language for VIIIth Standard Students in terms of their Parents Annual Income as Above 50000 and Below 50000.

Parent Annual Income	N	M	SD	df	't' Value	Level of Significance at 0.05
Above 50000	53	82.26	7.24	298	1.69	Not Significant
Below 50000	247	80.35	8.25			

INTERPRETATION

The computed table value of **t = 1.63** is smaller than the critical table value at 0.05 level of significance (i.e.) 1.96, which implies that there is no significant difference in the mean scores of Role of Television Programmes in Understanding Tamil Language for VIIIth Standard Students in terms of their Parents Annual Income as Above 50000 and Below 50000.

RESULT:

Hence the null hypothesis is accepted.

CONCLUSION

In this chapter data collected from the respondents through questionnaire has been tabulated, analyzed, interpreted and inferred. The next chapter deals with the summary findings and conclusion of the investigation.

Chapter - V

Findings and Conclusion

INTRODUCTION

The nature of the resource and the facility of access to it suggest that television can be a rich source of data for language learning, beyond as well as within the classroom. Where learning goals are related to communication skills, the authenticity of such data is an important consideration. Television affords authenticity to language learning in three ways:

1. It presents language in cultural contexts.
2. Language learners tend to be able to 'read' such cultural contexts, in terms of participants' social and economic status, and purposes and motivations in interactions.
3. Television viewing is an activity which language learners are familiar with, and engage in for information, education and recreation.

Principles need to be observed to ensure that the use of television in the classroom provides rich opportunities for language learning.

1. Select data on the basis of language learning objectives and activities;

2. Select short pieces (1-5 minutes);
3. Provide a transcript and integrate use of the transcript in the activity;
4. Mine the activity in ways appropriate to the learners language level and age for example, for elementary classes, focus on comprehension and word identification; for language courses develop the analysis dimension of tasks; for adult or workplace classes explore personal responses to television programme characteristics;
5. Link television viewing outside the classroom to language analysis and communication within the classroom;
6. Link television viewing to work on other media such as websites, discussion boards, newspapers and magazines;
7. Develop student involvement by structuring and facilitating inclusion of student selected television material.

STATEMENT OF THE PROBLEM

The present investigation is entitled as *"A Study on the Role of Television Programmes in Understanding Tamil Language for VIIIth Standard Students".*

OBJECTIVES OF THE STUDY

The objectives of the overall studies are

1. To find out the significant difference in the mean scores of Role of Television Programmes in Understanding Tamil Language for VIIIth Standard Students in terms of their Gender as Male and Female.
2. To find out the significant difference in the mean scores of Role of Television Programmes in Understanding Tamil Language for VIIIth Standard Students in terms of their Type of School as Government and Aided.
3. To find out the significant difference in the mean scores of Role of Television Programmes in Understanding Tamil Language for VIIIth Standard Students in terms of their Type of School as Aided and Private.

4. To find out the significant difference in the mean scores of Role of Television Programmes in Understanding Tamil Language for VIIIth Standard Students in terms of their Type of School as Private and Government.
5. To find out the significant difference in the mean scores of Role of Television Programmes in Understanding Tamil Language for VIIIth Standard Students in terms of their Locality as Rural and Urban.
6. To find out the significant difference in the mean scores of Role of Television Programmes in Understanding Tamil Language for VIIIth Standard Students in terms of their Parents Educational Qualification as Educated and Un-educated.
7. To find out the significant difference in the mean scores of Role of Television Programmes in Understanding Tamil Language for VIIIth Standard Students in terms of their Parents Occupation as Self Employment and Government Job.
8. To find out the significant difference in the mean scores of Role of Television Programmes in Understanding Tamil Language for VIIIth Standard Students in terms of their Parents Occupation as Government Job and Private Job.
9. To find out the significant difference in the mean scores of Role of Television Programmes in Understanding Tamil Language for VIIIth Standard Students in terms of their Parents Occupation as Private Job and Government Job.
10. To find out the significant difference in the mean scores of Role of Television Programmes in Understanding Tamil Language for VIIIth Standard Students in terms of their Parents Annual Income as Above 50000 and Below 50000.

HYPOTHESES OF THE STUDY

The Hypothesis of the present study is to find the difference in the mean scores of Role of Television Programmes in Understanding Tamil Language for VIIIth Standard Students.

1. There is no significant difference in the mean scores of Role of

Television Programmes in Understanding Tamil Language for VIIIth Standard Students in terms of their Gender as male and female.

2. There is no significant difference in the mean scores of Role of Television Programmes in Understanding Tamil Language for VIIIth Standard Students in terms of their Type of School as Government and Aided.
3. There is no significant difference in the mean scores of Role of Television Programmes in Understanding Tamil Language for VIIIth Standard Students in terms of their Type of School as Aided and Private.
4. There is no significant difference in the mean scores of Role of Television Programmes in Understanding Tamil Language for VIIIth Standard Students in terms of their Type of School as Private and Government.
5. There is no significant difference in the mean scores of Role of Television Programmes in Understanding Tamil Language for VIIIth Standard Students in terms of their Locality as Rural and Urban.
6. There is no significant difference in the mean scores of Role of Television Programmes in Understanding Tamil Language for VIIIth Standard Students in terms of their Parents Educational Qualification as educated and Un-educated.
7. There is no significant difference in the mean scores of Role of Television Programmes in Understanding Tamil Language for VIIIth Standard Students in terms of their Parents Occupation as Self Employment and Government Job.
8. There is no significant difference in the mean scores of Role of Television Programmes in Understanding Tamil Language for VIIIth Standard Students in terms of their Parents Occupation as Government Job and Private Job.
9. There is no significant difference in the mean scores of Role of Television Programmes in Understanding Tamil Language for VIIIth Standard Students in terms of their Parents Occupation as Private Job and Government Job.

10. There is no significant difference in the mean scores of Role of Television Programmes in Understanding Tamil Language for VIIIth Standard Students in terms of their Parents Annual Income as Above 50000 and Below 50000.

FINDINGS OF THE RESEARCH

1. There is significant difference in the mean scores of Role of Television Programmes in Understanding Tamil Language for VIIIth Standard Students in terms of their Gender as male and female.
2. There is significant difference in the mean scores of Role of Television Programmes in Understanding Tamil Language for VIIIth Standard Students in terms of their Type of School as Government and Aided.
3. There is significant difference in the mean scores of Role of Television Programmes in Understanding Tamil Language for VIIIth Standard Students in terms of their Type of School as Aided and Private.
4. There is no significant difference in the mean scores of Role of Television Programmes in Understanding Tamil Language for VIIIth Standard Students in terms of their Type of School as Private and Government.
5. There is no significant difference in the mean scores of Role of Television Programmes in Understanding Tamil Language for VIIIth Standard Students in terms of their Locality as Rural and Urban.
6. There is no significant difference in the mean scores of Role of Television Programmes in Understanding Tamil Language for VIIIth Standard Students in terms of their Parents Educational Qualification as educated and Un-educated.
7. There is no significant difference in the mean scores of Role of Television Programmes in Understanding Tamil Language for VIIIth Standard Students in terms of their Parents Occupation as Self Employment and Government Job.

8. There is no significant difference in the mean scores of Role of Television Programmes in Understanding Tamil Language for VIIIth Standard Students in terms of their Parents Occupation as Government Job and Private Job.
9. There is no significant difference in the mean scores of Role of Television Programmes in Understanding Tamil Language for VIIIth Standard Students in terms of their Parents Occupation as Private Job and Government Job.
10. There is no significant difference in the mean scores of Role of Television Programmes in Understanding Tamil Language for VIIIth Standard Students in terms of their Parents Annual Income as Above 50000 and Below 50000.

SUGGESTIONS FOR THE FURTHER RESEARCH

1. The present study is conducted in high school students in various districts.
2. It may be extended to some other educational district in that same state or other states in the nation.
3. It may be conduct to other level of students such as primary, secondary, higher secondary and also in the Arts and Science College.
4. A study may be conducted to find relationship between learning and teaching among students using Television.
5. A study of general problems of Matriculation higher secondary school students.
6. A comparative study may be conducted between primary school teachers and secondary school teachers in utilizing Television..

RECOMMENDATIONS OF THE STUDY

From the findings of the present study the investigator gives the following recommendations

1. Dynamic method such as seminar, symposia and workshop should be given through TV programmes to the students.
2. Teachers should create awareness on innovative Visual Aids among the students.

3. Developing positive attitude to life towards utilizing the concept of TV among the students.
4. Teacher participation should be needed more.

The following recommendations, if implemented will go a long way in the development minds of students.

1. Academic freedom for students learning
2. Re-construction of curriculum through innovation.
3. Proper climate for learning and teaching through Tele programmes.
4. Facilities for introduction of new technology in classroom.
5. Sound teachers organization.

CONCLUSION

Television material represents an embarrassment of riches for the language teacher. It provides an extensive range of material, which always involves language in a social context.

Comprehension activities can be based narrowly on the language used, or more broadly, engage understanding of the social and cultural issues which our shared television visual literacy increasingly facilitates. Television material can be a mainstay of a course, especially where the learning goals relate to intercultural learning and communication skills, or an occasional activity, supplementing a course book-based programme. Either way, it is likely to ne most successful where some consensus to work with television data is forged in the learning context; the technological demands in terms of recording and playback for both teacher and students are met and there is an interest in culture learning as an integrated part of a language programme.

Thus the research concluded there is significant difference in the mean scores of Role of Television Programmes in Understanding Tamil Language for VIIIth Standard Students in terms of their Gender as Male and Female, Type of School as Government and Aided, Type of School as Aided and Private due to the gender difference and different school climate.

BIBLIOGRAPHY

1. Alex, N.K. (1988). Using film, video, and TV in the classroom. ERIC Digest, No 11. Bloomington, IN: ERIC Clearinghouse on Reading and Communication Skills.
2. Anderson, D.R.; Huston, A.C.; Schmitt, K.L (2001). Early childhood television viewing and adolescent behavior: The recon tact study. *Monographs of the Society for Research in Child Development*, vol.66, no.1, p. 1-147.
3. Anderson, D. R. & Lorch, E. P. (1983) looking at television: action or reaction? In J. Bryant and D.R. Anderson, (Eds.) (1983). *Children's Understanding of Television: Research on attention and comprehension.* New York: Academic Press.
4. Anderson, D.R., and Bryant, J. (1983) Research on children's television viewing: the state of the art. In J. Bryant and D.R. Anderson, (Eds.) (1983). *Children's Understanding of Television: Research on attention and comprehension.* New York: Academic Press.
5. Anderson, J. A. (1983). Television literacy and the critical viewer. In J. Bryant and D.R. Anderson, (Eds.) (1983). *Children's Understanding of Television: Research on attention and comprehension.* New York: Academic Press.
6. Aspen Institute (1993). National leadership conference on media literacy. Conference report. Aspen Institute: Washington, D.C.
7. Barss, K. (2002). Putting public television to work for you. *Science Scope.* Vol. 25, No. 6, pg. 58.
8. Boser, F.J., Meyer, G.S., Roberto, A.J., & Inge, C.G. (2003). A report on the effect of the Unitedstreaming™ application on educational performance. United Learning, August 2003.
9. BrandonBarnes, B. ed. (1997.) The power of classroom TV: a marketing and advocacy document for the use of classroom television professionals. Columbia, SC: Center for Instructional Communication, National Educational Telecommunications Association.

10. British Film Institute. (2000). *Moving images in the classroom: A secondary teachers' guide to using film & television.* London: British Film Institute.

11. Bryant, J., and Anderson, D. R. (Eds.) (1983). *Children's Understanding of Television: Research on Attention and Comprehension.* New York: Academic Press.

12. Bryant, J.; Alexander, A.F.; & Braun, D. (1983) Learning from educational television programs. In Howe, M.J.A.(Ed.) (1983). *Learning from Television: Psychological and Educational Research.* London: Academic Press.

13. Bryant, J., Dolf, Z., and Brown, D. (1983) Entertainment features in children's educational television: Effects on attention and information acquisition. In J. Bryant and D.R. Anderson, (Eds.) (1983). *Children's Understanding of Television: Research on attention and comprehension.* New York: Academic Press.

14. Bryce, J. W. & Leichter, H. J. (1983). The family and television: forms of mediation. Journal of Family Issues, Vol. 4, No. 2 (June 1983) pp. 309-328.

15. Calvert, S.; Kotler, J.; Kuhl, A.; Riboli, M. (2001). Impact of the children's television act on children's learning. Greensboro, NC, Smith Richardson Foundation. 2001.

16. Carnegie Commission on Educational Television. (1967). *Public Television: A Program for Action.* New York: Bantam Books.

17. Chu, G.C., & Schramm, W. (1975). Learning from television: What the research says. (ERIC Document Reproduction Service No ED 109 985).

18. Clovis, D.L. (1997). Lights, television, action! *Educational Leadership*, Vol. 55, pp 38-40, November 1997.

19. Dhingra, K. (2003). Thinking about television science: How students understand the nature of science from different program genres. *Journal of Research in Language Teaching,* Vol. 40, No. 2, pp 234-256.

20. Durbin, C. (2000). Moving images in geography, in *Moving images in the classroom: A secondary teachers' guide to using film and*

television. London: British Film Institute. *Education Digest.* Watch Mr. Wizard: Still crazy (for science) after all these years.

21. Fisch, S.M. (2004). *Children's learning from educational television: Sesame Street and beyond.* Mahwah, NJ: Lawrence Erlbaum Associates.
22. Fisch, S.M. & Truglio, R.T., eds. (2001). "G" is for growing: Thirty years of research on children and Sesame Street. Mahwah, NJ: Lawrence Erlbaum Associates.
23. Fisherkeller, J. (2000). *"The writers are getting kind of desperate": Young adolescents, television, and literacy.* Journal of Adolescent & Adult Literacy. Vol 43, Iss. 7,pp. 596-607.
24. Flood, J. & Lapp, D. (1995). "Television and reading: Refocusing the debate. *The Reading Teacher,* Vol. 49, Iss. 2, pp. 160-164. Gardner, H. (1999.) *Intelligence reframed: Multiple intelligences for the 21st century.* New York: Basic Books.
25. Grunwald Associates (2002). *Video and television use among K-12 teachers.* Survey results in Powerpoint format prepared for CPB. November 2002.
26. Healy, Jane M. (1990). *Endangered Minds: Why Our Children Don't Think.* New York: Simon and Schuster. Herberman, E. (2000). Sci-fi high school. *Current Science,* Vol. 85, Issu., 13, p. 4.
27. Hobbs, R. (1998). The seven great debates in the media literacy movement. *Journal of Communication,* Vol. 48, Iss. 1, pp. 16-32.
28. Howe, M.J.A.(Ed.) (1983). *Learning from Television: Psychological and Educational Research.* London: Academic Press.
29. Stipp, H. (2003). How children can learn from television. *Journal of Applied Developmental Psychology,* Vol. 24, Iss.3, August 2003, pp. 363-365.
30. Thompson, F.T. & Austin, W.P. (2003). Television viewing and academic achievement revisited. *Education.* Chula Vista, CA. Vol. 124, No. 1, pp. 194-202. Fall 2003.

31. Tiene, D. (1996). Educational television in the nineties: A global survey. *Journal of Educational Media,* Oct 1996. Vol. 22, Iss. 3, page 151-160.

32. Winn, M. (1985). The Plug-In Drug (rev. ed.). New York: Viking. Wolfe, Pat. (2000). Brain-compatible teaching: What educators need to know about brain research and teaching, and why. *Cable in the Classroom,* March 2003.

33. Wright, J. C. & Huston, A. C. (1995). *Effects of educational TV viewing of lower income preschoolers on academic skills, school readiness, and school adjustment one to three years later.* (A report to children's television workshop, Center for Research on the Influences of Television on Children, University of Kansas).

34 Zigerell, J. (1991). *The Uses of Television in American Higher Education.* New York: Praeger.